DIE HARD

THE ULTIMATE VISUAL HISTORY

DIE HARD

THE ULTIMATE VISUAL HISTORY

BY **JAMES MOTTRAM** AND **DAVID S. COHEN**

FOREWORD BY **JOHN McTIERNAN**

TITAN BOOKS

London

An Insight Editions Book

CONTENTS

FORE**WORD**
BY **JOHN McTIERNAN**

I'm going to do something no one ever does in things like this: I'm going to tell you the truth. (I doubt you'll ever get to read it, so it doesn't matter.)

Die Hard . . .

Frankly, we've really got to thank Joel Silver for this one.

He showed a whole lot more courage than one would expect from a studio movie producer.

We had just done *Predator*, which had worked out well, so we had some credibility. Joel kept sending over this script called *Nothing Lasts Forever* about a cop fighting terrorists. I kept sending it back, saying, *There's simply no fun in this.* I mean, why would an audience want to see a mythical cop beat up a bunch of even more mythical terrorists? I didn't want to spend a year of my life immersed in a story like that, so why would an audience want to actually spend money on it?

But what I think—or for that matter, what just about anybody thinks—doesn't matter. Predatory capitalism, remember . . . ? Movie studios are effectively a couple of fifty-five-year-old men surrounded by a crowd of sycophants who'll say absolutely anything they think the boss wants to hear. (Not kidding; it is the only job requisite.) So the fifty-five-year-olds, given their hormones or, let's face it, pretty narrow circle of acquaintances, were certain that a cop fighting terrorists was what the audience really wanted to see.

And if I wanted to work in the movie business, this was a problem I was going to have to solve.

So the next time Joel sent the script over, I said, "Look, if you'll let me figure out how to make this fun . . . I'll do it."

He said, "What do you mean?"

I said, "Like in the first scene. They send a limo to the airport."

(Probably to show how big and important the guy is. Boy!) "If it's Bruce Willis, he's a working-class guy. He's never ridden in a limo before. So he sits in the front with the driver. And they talk. Like regular human beings."

He said, "Can the limo driver's name be Argyle?"

I said, "Argyle?"

He said, "Argyle."

I said, "Why the hell not?"

Done.

Now, sorry, but to explain this next step, I've got to take you into the weeds. . . .

History is short. Really short. There's only been industrial civilization for 250 years. And people have only been entertaining audiences with plays—which are essentially the same as movies—for about four hundred years. Study the work of twenty-five to fifty playwrights, and you'll pretty much know every solution anybody has ever come up with for telling a story to an audience.

In this case, it was easy. It was right in Shakespeare. He wrote a bunch of plays he called comedies. They weren't funny ha-ha the way we mean it. They were fun. Basically, fun adventures. And I was pretty sure that one of them fit.

It was about a festival night on which something crazy happens—and for everybody involved, the world is turned upside down. The princes become asses, and the asses become princes, and in the morning the world is put back right and the lovers are reunited.

Now the plot of *A Midsummer Night's Dream* is way more complicated than that, but don't look at that. Look at the totality. It was right there: Tell the story not of the cop and the terrorists but of the people who are part of the event. Let the audience sit back and watch the craziness as a whole. Let them enjoy it.

Put the joy in it. It sounds easy. But this was the big step. And this was where Joel showed a lot of courage.

He'd always made a big pretense of being a philistine. (To reassure his bosses, I suspect.) He was always saying things like, "I buy art, I don't make it." In reality, he was way smarter and more sensitive than that. He knew a lot about movies. And he actually cared about them. Which was lucky . . .

Because I had to go to Joel and say, "Terrorists are not entertaining. They only make people feel sad. There's no upside. You can only feel miserable that there are such desperate people in the world. Why would somebody hire a babysitter and spend twenty-five bucks to go see something that makes them feel like shit?

"Robbers, on the other hand, are fun. Good guys or bad, they're fun to watch. Could we make these guys robbers?"

Joel said, "Robbers?"

"Yeah," I said. "Like they used to be terrorists. They look like terrorists. Sound like terrorists. Everybody thinks they're terrorists . . . but it turns out they're actually trying to steal a bunch of money from the corporate vault."

Joel walked in a circle. Really didn't take long. And he just said, "Okay."

He went around for a while after that making noises like Curly from the Three Stooges about our plot. He was entitled to, it's true. But the piece did have joy in it.

The rest was easy. Compress the story down from two days to one night. For a festival, use Christmas. Make it part and parcel of the story.

The sidekick character on the radio had to be a failure, a disparaged man. Someone the important people paid no attention to.

The various princes—the cops, the FBI, and the media—they all had to be self-important . . . and foolish (which took no great leap of the imagination).

All the rest? It just followed: McClane was on his own case, so of course he should talk to himself. The dirty undershirt just went with the package. So did Powell wrecking his car. Johnson and Johnson in the helicopter. The SWAT cop in the pricker bushes. The terrorist thinking twice before stealing candy.

The Beethoven piece, which Stanley Kubrick had used in *A Clockwork Orange*, had always seemed to me to be the anthem of joyous, guilt-free violence. So it would be our anthem. A month later, I was humiliated to learn that the actual name of the choral finale at the end of the Ninth Symphony was "Ode to Joy." (Weird the stuff your brain comes up with when you think you're looking the other way.)

We started shooting with only thirty-five pages of the new script finished. But it didn't matter. By then, Joel and I, plus Steven de Souza, the writer, and maybe a dozen of the guys, we all knew how the piece went.

Where we didn't know the words, we knew at least how to hum it.

McT.

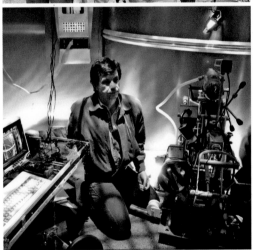

PAGE 2 *Bruce Willis as John McClane.*

PAGES 4–5 *John McClane (Willis) catches a ride with chauffeur Argyle (De'voreaux White) to Nakatomi Plaza.*

OPPOSITE TOP *John McTiernan directs the aftermath of the iconic fire hose scene in* Die Hard.

TOP *McTiernan,* Die Hard *visual effects producer Richard Edlund, pyrotechnics expert Thaine Morris, and model shop supervisor Mark Stetson.*

ABOVE *McTiernan on the Nakatomi Plaza vault set.*

INTRODUCTION

"Welcome to the party, pal!" –JOHN MCCLANE

In 1988, moviegoers received an invite they'd never forget. The film was *Die Hard*. The star was Bruce Willis. And the character was John McClane. He arrived in cinemas like a modern-day cowboy. He had no horse. He had no hat. But the urban gunslinger came armed with an all-American attitude. If *Die Hard* was *High Noon* in a high-rise, Willis was Gary Cooper and McClane was Marshal Will Kane. The action movie—and its heroes—would never be the same again.

A New York cop unwittingly caught up in an elaborate heist in a Los Angeles skyscraper, McClane was instantly refreshing. He wasn't like the muscular and monosyllabic heroes made famous by Arnold Schwarzenegger and Sylvester Stallone in the 1980s. In *Die Hard*, McClane bleeds almost as much as he cracks wise. When he takes a punch in the mouth from a thug, when he plucks shards of glass from his bare feet, you feel his pain.

If McClane was instantly relatable, Willis made him more so. The former New Jersey bartender brought his own rough-hewn appeal to the part. *"Die Hard* is probably the closest I've ever come to showing what is in my head on-screen," he says. "I really wanted to play a vulnerable guy. I didn't want to be a superhero. I didn't want to be one of these larger-than-life kind of guys that nobody really knows. [It's] about an ordinary guy thrown into extraordinary circumstances."[1]

McClane is the ultimate underdog. Engaged in a one-man war of attrition against a group of criminals, he lives from moment to moment, existing on his wits and adapting to his surroundings. He doesn't have gadgets like James Bond; hell, he doesn't even have shoes for most of the film. He makes do with makeshift bombs and duct tape, and even uses a fire hose to pull off one of the greatest escapes in cinema history.

Yet McClane's biggest weapon, aside from his bravura ballsiness, is his sense of humor. Even in the most desperate situation, he can't help himself. "Come out to the coast, we'll get together, have a few laughs," he mutters, impersonating his wife Holly's invitation to spend Christmas in California, as chaos breaks out in Nakatomi Plaza. His frame of reference is strictly blue-collar: While Alan Rickman's villain Hans Gruber recites Plutarch, McClane quotes the game show *Jeopardy*. Audiences immediately embraced him.

John McClane became Willis's most iconic role, every bit as memorable as Clint Eastwood's Dirty Harry or Stallone's John Rambo. "I think that part defined him and he defined the movie," says *Die Hard*'s cowriter Steven E. de Souza. Channeling the charm he'd displayed on his TV hit *Moonlighting* into a more physical role, Willis became the everyman hero, oft imitated in other movies but never bettered.

Die Hard, meanwhile, shoved a stick of dynamite down the action genre's throat. It inspired a rash of similar films that emulated its winning formula: the claustrophobic setting, the lone wolf facing impossible odds, and the ruthless, sociopathic villain with a plan to cause maximum mayhem. Years later, movies continue to successfully borrow from the *Die Hard* recipe.

Die Hard also returned to its own blueprint—to paraphrase John McClane in *Die Hard 2*, it turned out audiences really did want to see the same shit happen to the same guy twice. Smartly, *Die Hard*'s four sequels each retuned the formula with precision engineering. The settings became increasingly expansive: an airport (*Die Hard 2*), New York City (*Die Hard with a Vengeance*), Washington, DC, and Baltimore (*Live Free or Die Hard*), and finally, Russia (*A Good Day to Die Hard*). But the directors behind each installment never forgot what made the original *Die Hard* so special: a world-weary, vulnerable John McClane.

McClane may have got older, but he never lost his sense of the spectacular, jumping from a helicopter to the wing of a 747 jet as it speeds down the runway in *Die Hard 2*, bursting through the ground on a geyser of water in *Die Hard with a Vengeance*, using a car as a missile to take down a helicopter in *Live Free or Die Hard*, or driving over gridlocked Moscow traffic in *A Good Day to Die Hard*. The franchise isn't called Die Hard for nothing.

Over time, the Die Hard mythology has expanded far beyond the films to include video games, graphic novels, an adult coloring book, and even *A Die Hard Christmas*, a Yuletide-themed storybook. *Die Hard* itself has become a holiday perennial—some insist it's the greatest Christmas movie ever—even if it is peppered with gore and profanities.

Thirty years on from the moment he stepped out of LAX and took a limo toward a whole heap of trouble, John McClane has become as much a part of the American imagination as Roy Rogers and John Wayne. But his journey there took decades of grit, determination, and resilience. This is the story of how one man defied the odds to become a legend.

Yippee-ki-yay, motherfuckers . . .

ABOVE *Bruce Willis's John McClane takes travel tips from Robert Lesser's businessman in* Die Hard.

9

PART 1 DIE HARD

"Just a fly in the ointment, Hans. The monkey in the wrench. The pain in the ass." —JOHN MCCLANE

ROAD RAGE

Jeb Stuart needed a paycheck.

Things shouldn't have been this tight. He was a writer on the rise. After five years of graduate school, he'd written a hot spec script that had landed at Columbia Pictures with Robert Duvall attached to star, and he had a new four-script deal at Disney. He should have been the envy of young screenwriters and flush with cash.

But in that first half of 1987, Columbia had dropped his "hot" script just before it was to go into production. He was broke. With a young kid and a pregnant wife at home, the pressure was on. Stuart remembers telling his agent, Jeremy Zimmer, "I can't get paid at Disney, I gotta do something." There was one thing going in his favor: He was about to deliver his first Disney script, and that opened a six-week window where he could work for another studio. So Stuart's agent put in a call to Lloyd Levin, the head of development for Lawrence "Larry" Gordon over at Twentieth Century Fox.

Gordon was already a seasoned producer, who had cut his teeth working with director Walter Hill on a series of films, including *The Warriors* (1979), *The Driver* (1978), and *48 Hrs.* (1982). After a two-year stint as president of Twentieth Century Fox Entertainment Group, he resigned in 1986, though he remained a producer there with Lawrence Gordon Productions and the Gordon Company, formed with his brother Charles.

A New Jersey native, Lloyd Levin was Gordon's eyes and ears, seeking out potential projects. "Larry trusted Lloyd implicitly," says Stuart. Among the projects Levin was trying to get off the ground was a novel adaptation that had been languishing at Fox. Written by Roderick Thorp, *Nothing Lasts Forever* was a sequel to Thorp's book *The Detective*, which Fox had made into a 1968 film starring Frank Sinatra. Stuart jumped at the chance to write the script. "If it had been the Dead Sea Scrolls," he admits, "I would have taken the deal and written it."

The Detective, which features Sinatra as the titular lawman, Joe Leland, was considered somewhat groundbreaking at the time. It took a more adult view of the life of a policeman than most Hollywood films, touching on infidelity and homosexuality, the latter of which had been mostly taboo in studio films. Fox had acquired the rights to the still unwritten sequel long ago. (Thorp, undoubtedly embellishing the story, later suggested that when Levin showed Larry Gordon a copy of the finished novel, with a helicopter and burning building on the cover, Gordon instantly demanded: "I don't need to read it. Buy it.")

The author hadn't actually written *Nothing Lasts Forever* until 1979, although the idea had been on his mind for some time before that. The basic concept was the result of a dream Thorp had in which a man was being chased through a building by gun-wielding assailants. Tellingly, he experienced the dream on the very night he saw the 1974 disaster film *The Towering Inferno*.

In *Nothing Lasts Forever*, Joe Leland, now in his sixties, is divorced from the unfaithful wife who plagued him in *The Detective* and has retired from the NYPD to become a security consultant. He flies to Los Angeles to visit his daughter Stephanie Gennaro, an executive at foreign-owned Klaxon Oil. He has some chemistry with a flight attendant on the plane, Kathi, and gets her phone number, but parts ways with her at the airport to go meet his daughter. Once he arrives at the Klaxon Oil Christmas party, held at the company's skyscraper, he realizes Stephanie is involved in shady business deals. Another disappointment for the world-weary Leland.

Tired from his flight, he takes a stranger's advice to remove his shoes, wash his feet, and walk around barefoot to fight jet lag. Then, terrorists burst in and take over the office. Peeking out into the hall, Leland recognizes the German-born Anton Gruber, aka Antonino Rojas, "Little Tony the Red," a dangerous international terrorist leader he'd recently been briefed on. He sees Anton kill the top Klaxon executive in cold blood. Barefoot, armed with

RIGHT *Roderick Thorp's novel* Nothing Lasts Forever, *the source material for* Die Hard, *published in 1979 by W. W. Norton & Company.*

Thorp

DETECTIVE

NOTHING LASTS FOREVER

only a pistol, Leland slips away. Alone and exhausted, he takes out the terrorists one by one during the night, battling them across the building's unoccupied upper floors. At times he escapes by crawling through ventilation tunnels or climbing up and down elevator shafts. Though the fight is grueling and he accrues a series of injuries, he has hours alone with his thoughts during the night—time to daydream about Kathi, to think back to his unfaithful wife, to ponder that his own daughter, too, has been tainted by the world's corruption.

Joe tries to get help using a radio, eventually connecting with a citizens band (CB) radio enthusiast in the Hollywood Hills who lends a little support, and with a young cop on the ground, Al Powell, who becomes his confidante. When Joe finally confronts the terrorist leader, the criminal grabs Stephanie. For a moment, Anton and Stephanie dangle out the window, with Anton holding on to her watchband. Leland is unable to save her, and both the terrorist and Stephanie fall to their deaths. Just when everything seems to be over, a surviving terrorist, Karl, bursts through a staircase door with a Kalashnikov to try to kill Leland. Al Powell shoots Karl dead, saving Joe's life, although the officious police captain Dwayne Robinson takes a fatal bullet during the shootout.

The action in *Nothing Lasts Forever* takes place over just one day, and the story is steeped in noir overtones, thanks to Thorp's sparse but punchy, hard-boiled prose. Describing the moment Klaxon's CEO, Mr. Rivers, is shot dead, Thorp writes, "Gruber put the muzzle of the Walther on Rivers's lapel and pulled the trigger. Rivers had a split-second of incredulous horror as the shot was fired, and then he was dead, sitting down and sprawling back with a little bounce, like a load of wash."

Thorp's high-rise setting is compellingly drawn. "With the elevators disabled, it was better than a medieval castle," the author writes. "Not even assault troops could retake the place." He casts it as a claustrophobic prison in the clouds, a hissing, creaking, humming building with grimy elevator shafts, labyrinthine stairwells, and dimly lit corridors.

This atmospheric backdrop feeds into the sour, grim tone of Thorp's novel. Leland is cynical and a little bitter about, well, pretty much everything. "It seemed too sad for me," says Stuart, who also felt that having an action hero in his sixties didn't make much sense. Whilst suggesting that the book had the makings of a big action movie, Levin gave Stuart creative freedom. There was one suggestion though: "Lloyd always wanted it to snow," Stuart recalls. "He said, 'I've always wanted to do a movie where it snows in LA.'" While Los Angeles is not exactly prone to such conditions, it left Stuart determined to keep the Christmas setting.

Stuart struggled with Thorp's book. "I was living in Pasadena, my office was down at the Disney lot in Burbank, and I would come home at night, tuck my two little children in to bed, have dinner with my wife, and then go back to the studio and work all night." Looking back, he says, the eighteen-hour days and financial pressure aren't unusual for young people trying to break into the business. But the long hours and the stress put him on edge. "I got into a huge, knock-down, drag-out fight with my wife over probably something completely incidental," he remembers. "She was completely right, I was completely wrong. And, instead of apologizing on the spot, I got back into the car angry, got on the freeway, and took off from Pasadena back down to Burbank at about seven o'clock in the evening."

He sped through the usual obstacle course of aggressive Los Angeles drivers, trying to figure out a way to apologize to his wife. Cars wove in and out of lanes around him. Then, just ahead, he saw a huge refrigerator box in his lane. "I couldn't go right or left, and I went right through it at about sixty-five miles an hour." Luckily for Stuart, the box was empty. "I pulled over to the side of the freeway, and my heart was pounding and I thought: I know what *Nothing Lasts Forever* is. It's not about a sixty-year-old man who drops his daughter off of a building, it's about a thirty-year-old who should have said he's sorry to his wife and something really bad happens." His fight with his wife and the collision with a piece of freeway debris had helped him crack the biggest problem with the story.

"Up to that point I didn't have a character," says Stuart. There was no John McClane, the hero of *Die Hard*, just Joe Leland. "But to have a guy who is stubborn enough that he would come all the way out to LA to apologize and then not do it when he had that wonderful opportunity—that was sort of where I was at that particular moment."

He wrote thirty-five script pages that night, a prodigious evening's work. "Unfortunately, I still had to go back in the morning and apologize to my wife," he says, "but that was very instructive for the start of *Die Hard*."

Cracking McClane's character gave Stuart a starting point, but there was no clear road-map before him. Having abandoned the name Joe Leland, Stuart was going to call his hero John Ford, but Levin told him that film director John Ford was too important a name in the history of Fox to use for an action-movie character. "I promptly ran through fifty last names," Stuart says. He eventually hit on the right one, swayed by his own Celtic roots. "McClane I always heard was a good strong Scottish name, and that's what I wanted to put in there."

Although Levin was initially unsure how Stuart should approach the adaptation, the producer's input would be invaluable throughout the process of writing the script. "Lloyd was my connection to the book," says Stuart, who believes Levin to be the unsung hero of *Die Hard*. "As Harrison Ford always says, the secret to success is working with people smarter than you," says Stuart, "and Lloyd was really terrific."

Stuart had no experience writing action films, but he had written thrillers. So he decided to follow the old saying "write what you know"—in more ways than one. First, he knew what sells a thriller. "Thrillers don't work unless you really love the character," he says. "I really want to be invested in this guy, and I really want him to get together with his wife. And I really want the family to kind of work."

By making his hero younger, Stuart had made him one of his own peers, at least in age, and that too provided some guidance. Many of the writer's friends were going through marital struggles. Some were divorcing. Some would vent to him about how their wives had changed back to their maiden names before their divorce was final. Stuart drew on their resentments in ways large and small, from McClane's conflicted attitude toward his wife, Holly, to the anger he feels when he sees her maiden name, Gennaro, in the office-building directory.

Stuart wrote McClane as a man who knows he has made mistakes in his family life but is determined to make his wife understand, somehow, that he loves her and needs her back. But at the same time, he also wrote his hero as a man who can be exasperating, especially to his wife. In one of the key scenes Stuart wrote, the terrorist Karl throws things around in a rage after failing to kill McClane. "Everybody's terrified except Holly," says Stuart. "[She] smiles and says, 'He's still alive.'" When another captive asks how she knows, Holly simply replies: "Only John can drive somebody that crazy."

McClane is a flawed, angry hero, a man learning a life lesson in the hardest way possible. "And he does," says Stuart. "He manages to become a better person through the movie"—but not an entirely different person. "At the end of the movie, he's still who he is."

Despite support from Levin, Stuart still had to take his unfinished first draft and pitch it to Lawrence Gordon and assorted Fox executives in a boardroom on the Fox lot. "I'd never pitched before," he remembers, believing at the time that he was expected to perform a detailed description of the entire story. "About fifteen minutes into this excruciating pitch," he recounts, "Larry, who was sitting at the end of the table, said, 'Where are you from?'

"And I said, 'I'm from North Carolina.'

"And he said, 'Well, I'm from Mississippi.' And we did a little southern geography, because my father was from Mississippi, and he said, 'Look, you're supposed to be pretty good. Just go write it.' I remember Larry walking out of the door, and all of these Fox executives and Gordon Company executives just kind of staring at me like, 'That doesn't happen.' I got up and ran for the hills." Stuart finished his first draft in just five and a half weeks.

During his research period, Stuart realized he needed to intimately get to know the inner workings of a tall building. Coincidentally, Twentieth Century Fox had a new office tower of its own, Fox Plaza, in the Century City office development adjacent to its lot. Stuart went over and made friends with the construction superintendent, who took him for a ride in the high-speed elevator and allowed him to stand on the wire grate over the ventilation system. As his knees buckled with vertigo, he began to think. "How can you take a building and integrate it into a story so it becomes another character in the movie?"

In the evolution from Thorp's book to Stuart's first draft, Stuart made several smart changes for the screen, notably in the way he used the supporting characters. "There's more importance to them in the screenplay than in the novel," he says. Much of the novel was internalized, in Leland's head, but Stuart decided to use Thorp's characters to give McClane more people to interact with. Thus, McClane's relationship with Al Powell became more prominent; Powell's film character was written older, with an expectant wife back home, giving father-of-two McClane someone to relate to.

"DIE HARD"

FADE IN

1   405 FREEWAY - LOS ANGELES - EARLY EVENING   1

Christmas tinsel on the light poles. We ARE LOOKING east
past Inglewood INTO the orange grid of L.A. at night when
suddenly we TILT UP TO CATCH the huge belly of a landing
747 -- the noise is deafening.

2   INT. 747 - PASSENGERS - SAME   2

The usual moment just after landing when you let out that
sigh of relief that you've made it in one piece.

3   ON JOHN MCCLANE   3

mid-thirties, good-looking, athletic and tired from his trip.
He sits by the window. His relief on landing is subtle but
we notice. Suddenly, he hears a voice next to him.

> MAN'S VOICE
> (o.s.)
> Don't fly much do you?

McClane looks over at a grinning middle-aged BUSINESSMAN
sitting next to him.

> MCCLANE
> No.

> BUSINESSMAN
> Want to know the secret of
> surviving air travel?...Take off
> your shoes and socks when you get
> where you're going and walk
> around ten minutes barefoot.
> Better than a shower and a cup
> of coffee...

> MCCLANE
> (warily)
> Thanks...I'll remember that.

The Businessman picks up on McClane's scepticism and takes
it as a challenge. His salesman's smile broadens.

> BUSINESSMAN
> You think I'm crazy don't you?
> Trust me. I've been a salesman
> for twenty years. I know what
> I'm talking about.

(CONTINUED)

A98

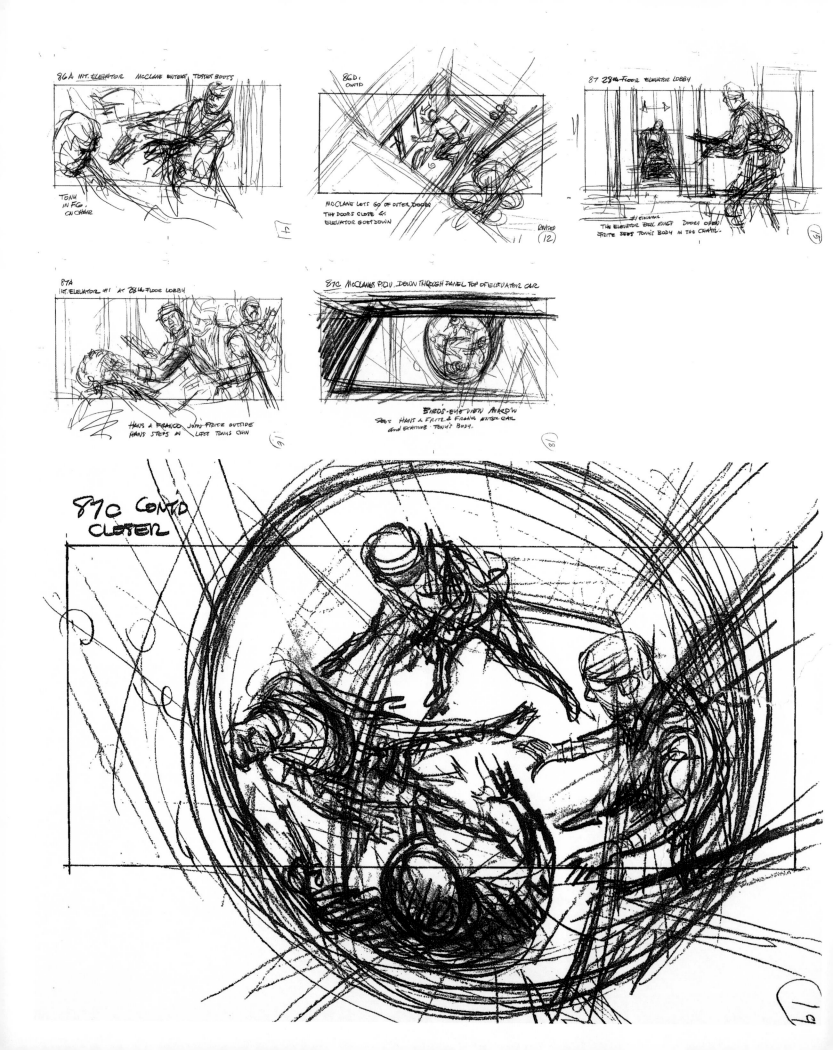

86A INT. ELEVATOR   McCLANE ENTERS. TOSSES BOOTS

TONY
IN FG.
ON CHAIR

[7]

86D.
CONTD

McCLANE LETS GO OF OUTER DOORS
THE DOORS CLOSE &
ELEVATOR GOES DOWN

REVISED
(12)

87 28th FLOOR ELEVATOR LOBBY

#1 ELEVATOR
THE ELEVATOR BELL RINGS DOORS OPEN
FRITZ SEES TONY'S BODY IN THE CHAIR.

[15]

87A
INT. ELEVATOR #1 AT 28th FLOOR LOBBY

HANS & FRANCO JOIN FRITZ OUTSIDE
HANS STEPS IN LIFT TONY'S CHIN

[16]

87C McCLANE'S P.O.V. DOWN THROUGH PANEL TOP OF ELEVATOR CAR

BIRDS-EYE VIEW ARROW
SEES HANS & FRITZ & FRANZ ENTER CAR
and EXAMINE TONY'S BODY.

[18]

87C CONTD
CLOSER

Other characters morphed. Thorp's Klaxon employee Harry Ellis is Stephanie's sleazy boyfriend, whose cocaine habit disgusts Leland. Stuart retained Ellis and his drug use, although Holly—Stuart's replacement for Stephanie—has no romantic links with him. Also kept was Dwayne Robinson, the LAPD police captain, who is on the ground during the hostage crisis. Stuart dropped the CB enthusiast, Taco Bill, but created Richard Thornburg, the unscrupulous newshound who discovers the identity of McClane when he's holed up in the building fighting the terrorists and tracks down Holly and John's children.

The unnamed chauffeur who picks McClane up from the airport in Thorp's book was also given an expanded role and a name: William. Stuart even had McClane nickname him Taco Bill, in a nod to Thorp's character. In Stuart's draft, William uses his own CB radio to warn McClane about an imminent ambush and then jams Gruber's communication by blasting rap music on the terrorists' chosen radio channel.

Many scenes were taken straight from the book and tweaked as needed. McClane still removes his shoes and socks to fight jet lag, although Stuart changed the advice to curling up your feet into little balls. He got the idea from his days working as a quality-assurance spy for Pacific Southwest Airlines, when a fellow traveler informed him of this very trick.

In Stuart's script, once the film's terrorists arrive to take hostages, McClane hides and starts to cause havoc, picking them off one by one. Just like Leland, he throws one foe off the building to attract police attention. But the result is different; shot by McClane during a shootout in a boardroom, terrorist Marco's corpse lands on the hood of Sgt. Powell's cop car, causing him to manically hit reverse in fright. McClane also puts the body of another fallen terrorist, Tony, in an elevator with a note saying, NOW I HAVE A MACHINE GUN (in the book it's NOW WE HAVE A MACHINE GUN, a possible attempt by Leland to fool the gang into believing they have multiple opponents). As in Thorp's book, in Stuart's story the terrorists are armed with explosives and detonators, which McClane steals. Just like Leland, McClane also drops a C-4 bomb strapped to a chair down an elevator shaft, causing a huge explosion on a lower floor. Thorp's book also features helicopters blown from the skies by the terrorists. Stuart further developed this idea, having Karl take out the choppers with stinger missiles.

He didn't follow the pattern of Thorp's bleak ending, however. In Stuart's draft, Holly (Stephanie's replacement) survives, and so does Dwayne Robinson. Recalls Stuart, "I remember in a conversation with Larry's team, someone saying, 'It doesn't sound as dark as the book,' and I said it can't be as dark as the book. If I'm going to put you through two hours of suspense, you have to know that it's not going to end darkly. It was never intended to be a noirish story."

A fan of John Wayne, Stuart also began to develop a Western theme that would run through the story, suggesting McClane as a latter-day cowboy. In the original draft, Al Powell calls McClane "partner," and McClane has lines like, "I ain't the cavalry, fella," and, "I should have taken scalps." Stuart also invented two new characters, FBI agents Johnson and Johnson, and came up with a scene where the barefoot McClane accidentally steps on discarded fluorescent lightbulbs. Injured, he has a rather novel way of stopping the blood spilling from his feet, using maxi pads he finds in a drawer.

Stuart was happy with his script but nervous nevertheless. After all, the screenplay that was supposed to launch his career had stalled at Columbia. So he delivered his *Nothing Lasts Forever* script on a Friday in June and decided to get away from it all, packing his family into the car and driving up the coast to Carmel for a weekend getaway. He returned home Sunday to find his voicemail full. "They had read it and green-lit it on Saturday and we were going forward with the movie," he recalls. As it turned out, the timing couldn't have been better for the project. It was a "one in a million situation," says Stuart: Fox needed a big-event movie for summer 1988 but had nothing lined up at the time.

There was just enough time to rush the project through, although it would be tight. "That was really exciting for me," says Stuart. "Every writer should have one of those wonderful moments where it just gets done that quickly."

OPPOSITE *Storyboards by John L. Jensen depict the moment when Tony's body is discovered by the terrorists.*

```
                    MCCLANE
Don't know but I've killed three
including the one who fell out
of Santa's sleigh.

                    POWELL
        (dryly)
Yeah, let's not forget him.

                    MCCLANE
The leader goes by the name, Hans.
He's locked down the elevators.
Also, I haven't found one of them
yet who didn't carry a radio so you
can bet they're monitoring this
call.  Channel twenty-six seems to
be their inter-office number but
they move it around and it's in
German, so get someone who speaks
it to give you a play by play.

                    POWELL
Sounds like you know this
bunch pretty well.

                    MCCLANE
We've gotten pretty intimate
waiting on you guys to get here.

                    POWELL
I hear you...Well, we're here
now, partner...What do I call you?

                    MCCLANE
'Partner' suits me fine.

                    POWELL
You got it.  Now, listen to me,
if you think of anything else you
let me know.  In the meantime I want
you to find a safe place and hole-up
and let us do our job.  Understand?

                    MCCLANE
        (to CB)
They're all yours, Al.  Good luck.
```

A FORCE OF NATURE

Following the green light, another producer came on board the Gordon Company's estimated $28 million project: Joel Silver. An established hit-maker in his own right, Silver was Gordon's protégé, having worked on several Gordon productions including *The Warriors* and *48 Hrs.* before establishing his own wildly successful Silver Pictures, producing *Commando* (1985), *Lethal Weapon*, (1987), and the action sci-fi *Predator* (1987), a coproduction for Fox with Lawrence Gordon Productions. Veterans of Silver films often use the same phrase to describe him: "a force of nature."

In the summer of 1987, Silver was on a European publicity tour for both *Lethal Weapon* and *Predator* when he took a call from Gordon. Still keen on bringing *Nothing Lasts Forever* to the big screen, and buoyed by his time with Silver on *Predator*, Gordon wanted to recruit Silver as a producer. When Silver read Stuart's script, he agreed there was potentially a good movie in there.

When Silver came on board, Gordon let Stuart know exactly where the writer stood: "This is Joel's gig. He's the guy who's going to be in the trenches with this." That became clear on the very first day they met. "Within five minutes," recounts Stuart, "[Silver] said, 'It's nothing personal, but you're going to get fired. You are fired. This has nothing to do with the script. I love the script, but I don't know you. I gotta make a movie and I gotta make a movie fast. This is how it's gonna be.'"[1]

But fortunately for Stuart, Gordon protected him and kept him on for further drafts before Silver brought on Steven E. de Souza to handle the film's anticipated production rewrites. A hot screenwriter at the time, de Souza had penned *Commando* and cowritten the script for *48 Hrs.* For the moment though, the gig was still Stuart's. Silver's first note was that he'd always wanted to do a movie called *Die Hard*. No argument, the title was changed. "From that moment on it was *Die Hard*," says Stuart.

Although, at the time, Stuart thought it was Silver's idea, the title actually came from Shane Black, who'd acted in Silver's *Predator* and written *Lethal Weapon*. *Die Hard* was Black's original title for the script that became 1991's *The Last Boy Scout*. He'd mentioned the name to Silver, who asked if he could use it. Black agreed, and Silver gave it to Stuart. "I'm just glad [the title] wasn't *Nothing Lasts Forever*," says Stuart. It left the author, however, apoplectic—Silver got a letter from Thorp bitterly complaining that the movie adaptation had been titled after a well-known make of battery. Stuart remembers a subsequent meeting with the author, who complained about the title change. "[Silver] said, 'The best thing that ever happened to your book is . . . this movie.'"

Stuart calls Silver a great facilitator of every phase of *Die Hard*, although the producer's hard-driving style often presented a challenge. Early on, he gave Stuart the kind of major note that can send a writer's head spinning: "The one thing that isn't working is that the top of the building doesn't blow up." Stuart argued that if the top of the building blew up, that would be a failure for McClane, and the hero couldn't fail that way. Silver told him, "That's not my problem. My problem is, I'm not gonna make somebody pay twelve dollars for a movie ticket, and stand in the rain in Westwood for two hours outside the theater, and then the top of the fucking building doesn't blow up. That's *your* problem."

Chastened, Stuart went back to his keyboard to figure out how to do it without making McClane seem a fool. He adapted a scene from Thorp's book, in which Leland jumps off the roof to flee terrorist fire. Leland wraps a fire hose around himself, swings downward, and wrenches a window frame loose. In Stuart's draft, McClane, having saved the hostages, is trapped on the roof knowing it's about to blow up. McClane improvises the same escape as Leland before shooting his way through a window below.

The experience taught Stuart an important lesson: His job, first and foremost, was to create a blueprint for a piece of entertainment. "There's a little bit of tongue-in-cheek in [the scene]," says Stuart. "There's a little bit of, 'OK, just give me a little bit of slack here and we'll have fun going through it.'"

Silver and Gordon needed a director. "It went to Paul Verhoeven first," says Stuart. "Verhoeven had just done *RoboCop*—he was so hot—but he passed." Then it was sent to John McTiernan. The New York–born director had two feature films under his belt: the well-reviewed but little-seen *Nomads* (1986) and the Silver-Gordon produced *Predator*, which was on the verge of becoming one of the big summer hits of '87 with a $98 million worldwide gross.

OPPOSITE *Joel Silver and Lawrence Gordon stand outside the Fox Plaza building.*

ABOVE *Silver tries on some Japanese-inspired headgear on the set of* Die Hard.

McTiernan did not immediately jump at the chance to direct *Die Hard*. After the grueling shoot of *Predator*, filmed in the extreme humidity of the jungles of Palenque, Mexico, he wanted to take some time off to recuperate. He also wasn't keen on Stuart's script, and in particular the McClane persona as originally written. "The hero was, I don't know, a super-cool, suave, asinine gentleman," he says. "[It] was standard TV movie superhero fare."

There were bigger issues bothering McTiernan, however. "It was about terrorists, originally," he says. "Terrorism is not entertaining. Terrorism is a sad thing in the world no matter where your politics are." As a result of these major qualms with the material, McTiernan said no, more than once. "I turned it down over and over," he explains. "Joel kept sending it and calling me, and Larry Gordon did." Together, they wore him down. "Eventually, I sat down with them and said, 'OK, I think I can see a way to do this.'"

He began to imagine McClane as more grounded. "I said, 'I've got a weird idea.'" He pointed to the limousine scene near the beginning, when William picks up McClane. "Could we make it that he gets in the front seat of the limo because he's never ridden in a limo before?" The way McTiernan sees it, riding shotgun is a sign of McClane's salt-of-the-earth decency. "And Joel said, 'OK. And I'd like the limo driver's name to be Argyle.' I said, 'I don't know why that is, but it sounds just fine.'"

In the original book, *Nothing Lasts Forever*, the Anton Gruber–led terrorists are politically motivated and plan to steal documents to expose the Klaxon corporation's dealings with Chile's junta. They even dump the $6 million cash proceeds from the corrupt dealings out of the tower window.

McTiernan considered what might happen if these politically motivated terrorists decided to give up the ideological fight and go into business for themselves. Making the bad guys thieves instead of ideologues turned the story into a caper film, albeit one where the hero was working to stop the caper. In McTiernan's mind, this was a date movie.

"Everybody likes a robber," he says. "Everybody has fun with cool robberies. I know there have been a million caper movies since, but at the time there hadn't been that many. So I said, 'OK, they seem to be terrorists and we can use all that stuff, but ultimately what they're doing is they're in it for the money.' And that's what's important . . . so that implacable right-wing hate quality that goes into all terrorist movies doesn't have to be there."

Silver went with the idea. "I have to bless Joel for saying, 'Alright, that sounds crazy but let's do it,'" says McTiernan. "He had the nerve to say, 'Yes, I see the entertainment value here.'" It was late summer, just a couple of months before production was due to begin in November. "We started madly rewriting," adds McTiernan, whose work impressed Stuart. "He came in and he got the flaws in the script right away," says the writer. "He was very complimentary about the script, but he said, 'Here are the things that I think are really, really important.'"

In Stuart's second revised draft, dated October 2, 1987, Anton Gruber became Hans Gruber, a far less idealistic leader. "He had to drive the story," says Stuart of his villain. The script's Gruber uses a terrorist hijack as a smokescreen while he and his gang raid the building's super-secure vault to steal $100,000 in treasury bonds. The loot was later changed to a more rewarding $640 million in bearer bonds, unregistered debt securities that show no record of ownership, typically issued by banks, governments, and corporations. "The bearer bonds had always been mentioned in my conversations," says Stuart, although he credits Silver and McTiernan for developing the idea.

One of the most intriguing choices in the revisions made McClane's wife, Holly, the employee of Nakatomi Trading, a Japanese finance company based in Los Angeles. The film came at a time when flourishing Japanese corporations were purchasing significant (and sometimes iconic) American buildings and businesses, including the Tiffany and Exxon buildings in New York and the Los Angeles–based Union Bank of California. While the choice to put a Japanese company at the heart of *Die Hard* was a reflection of the times, McTiernan says it wasn't a barbed piece of social commentary. "There was no notion of really trying to take potshots at the Japanese," he says.

OPPOSITE *Gruber's gang hunts down McClane in these storyboards by John L. Jensen.*

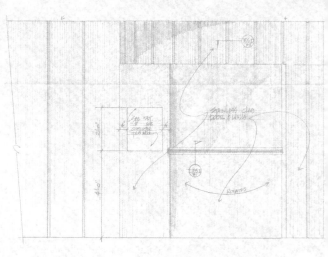

CONTINUED:

                    MCCLANE
          Yeah...Merry Christmas...

The Businessman moves down the ramp and is lovingly gre
by his family. McClane watches, moved by the sight, the
looks around the waiting area, just on the chance his fa
might be waiting. Instead he spots a thin, gangling, b
id, WILLIAM, in an ill-fitting chaufeur's uniform. As
waits he beats out a rhythm on a card with J. MCCLANE p
on it. McClane pauses in front of him.

                    MCCLANE
          I'm John McClane.

                    WILLIAM
          William, Sir...I'm your limo
          driver. Nice bag.

He turns and starts walking.

                    MCCLANE
          Don't you take this?

                    WILLIAM
              (stops)
          Do I?

116C
INT NARROW PASSAGE. AT HATCH DOOR TO ELEVATOR SHAFT (CLOSED)

KARL & FRANCO
GET SET TO
BURST IN-HATCH

SCENE 112
MOVED to 2
116C CONT'D

HANS VOICE ON RADIO: "KARL? FRANCO? WHERE IS HE?"

FRANCO: "IN THE ELEVATOR SHAFT.   HANS VOICE: THE ELEVATORS
                                   ARE DOWN HERE - LOCK HIM
FRANCO LOCKS?   KARL DOESN'T ANSWER   IN."
DOOR, LEAVES   HANS VOICE MORE FIRMLY   LOCK HIM IN THAT'S AN OR...
                KARL TURNS OFF THE RADIO   FRANCO IS STUNNED

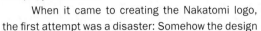

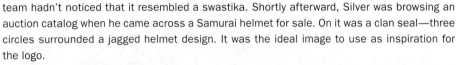

Mr. Rivers, the CEO of Klaxon, became Joseph Takagi, president of Nakatomi Trading. The name Nakatomi was found, remembers Silver, after he came onto the project. "[Someone] told us that the battleships in the Second World War were all named for famous Japanese clans," says Silver. "We got a list of all these Japanese battleships, and we liked the sound of Nakatomi the best, so we called the company Nakatomi."[2]

When it came to creating the Nakatomi logo, the first attempt was a disaster: Somehow the design team hadn't noticed that it resembled a swastika. Shortly afterward, Silver was browsing an auction catalog when he came across a Samurai helmet for sale. On it was a clan seal—three circles surrounded a jagged helmet design. It was the ideal image to use as inspiration for the logo.

During the process of finessing the script, the producers mandated that McClane should never get a chance to take a rest (unlike the original book's Joe Leland, who even sinks into sleep at one point in *Nothing Lasts Forever*). Adding to this sense of urgency, McTiernan told Stuart that he wanted to cut in and out of McClane's travails and highlighted some scenes that could be moved around. Stuart remembers the opening act in particular. "He really liked to tighten the tension on that so we could get more [swiftly] into that first part [where the action begins], so he definitely had some of that moved around."

McTiernan also encouraged him to trim some lines. The director knew he could convey ideas with imagery instead of words, so dialogue that had been necessary to sell the script to studio executives could now be cut.

The soft-spoken, even-keeled McTiernan also knew how to work with the demanding Silver. "He knew what he wanted to get across and he knew where the big moments were going to be," says Stuart. "He was a great shield for me from the forces of Joel. . . . John would say, 'No, no, no, that's working. Don't screw that up. Here's how we're gonna do it,' and he could visually take what was on the page and put it into a place where Joel would immediately say, 'Oh, I got it now, okay, very good, let's move on.' He was a terrific visualist."

McTiernan also conjured up what he calls his "secret melody" for the film. *Die Hard*, he felt, was like Shakespeare's *A Midsummer Night's Dream*, although he "didn't have the nerve" to tell Silver or Gordon for fear of seeming too pretentious. Along with the fact that Stuart's story took place across one "festival night"—in this case, Christmas—where the world is inverted, in McTiernan's eyes there were numerous other parallels: "All of the princes become asses, and all the asses become princes, and in the morning the two lovers are reunited, and everyone goes back to their regular lives but the world is better for the crazy thing that happened on that midsummer night."

The metaphor was perfect for *Die Hard*: The thieves pretend to be terrorists; McClane hides the fact he's a cop and Holly's husband; the FBI agents and police chiefs are made to look stupid; the beat cop—Sgt. Al Powell, whom McClane confides in over the airwaves—and even limo driver Argyle become princes. And, yes, after a single night of mayhem, the lovers are reunited. *Die Hard* was definitely going to be an action movie, but McTiernan was determined it would have a light touch.

LEFT *A sign for Nakatomi Plaza featuring the fictional company's samurai-inspired logo.*

TOP *The front entrance to Fox Plaza (aka Nakatomi Plaza).*

INSERT *Set designer Roland Hill's construction plans for the Nakatomi Plaza sign used on the Avenue of the Stars side of the building.*

PICKING THE PLAZA

As summer turned to fall, the prep for *Die Hard* continued at a breakneck pace. Preproduction would only be a few weeks long. "This was broken-field running," says McTiernan. "We started shooting five weeks from the day they said go. It wasn't a six-month prep time. We were going like crazy."

One key element threatened to derail the production's rapid progress: finding the location for the Nakatomi offices. The very idea for Roderick Thorp's original story had started with a high-rise and, in Stuart's script, the Nakatomi building had become a central character. Having considered the options, the production team decided it was essential to use a real skyscraper for a large portion of the action. Moreover, says McTiernan, using studio sets "would never be the same" when it came to shooting some of the more complex sequences—not least the rooftop scene, which would feature not only McClane and the hostages, but also an FBI helicopter. "This was before there were computer effects. . . . It would've been very hard to do," says the director.

Houston was initially scouted for potential Nakatomi Plaza stand-ins. The Texan city had a number of skyscrapers under construction that were still vacant and available to rent—perfect conditions for a large production involving stunts and pyrotechnics. McTiernan balked at the idea. With just eight months between the start of principal photography and a proposed release in July, moving the shoot to another state would mean extra time setting up the production logistics. "I said, guys, don't hobble us by making us work halfway across the country. If we can work right here, we can get this done in time."

TOP *The first three floors of the Fox Plaza building.*

ABOVE *The exterior facade, so precious that the production was forced to fly in extra Spanish marble in case it was damaged.*

OPPOSITE *The Fox Plaza skyscraper standing 150 meters and 35 floors tall.*

FOX PLAZA

The solution was right in their backyard: the Fox Plaza building Stuart had visited when researching his script. "It was in my very first meeting with Joel Silver and John McTiernan; they were talking about [needing a] building," says the writer. "I just literally pointed out of the window of Joel's office and said, 'That's the building I did all the research in.' It was looming over us."

The tower, designed by noted architect William Pereira, had been commissioned to become Fox's corporate headquarters and had only just opened that year. Its upper floors were not yet entirely rented out, so it had open spaces that could be used for shooting. It was an enticing opportunity for the *Die Hard* production. Having the Nakatomi building in Los Angeles, within walking distance of the soundstage, would simplify logistics enormously and save on travel costs.

"We had a meeting with the studio," remembers Beau Marks, *Die Hard*'s associate producer and unit production manager, who had worked with McTiernan and Silver on *Predator*. "They wanted to start shooting within six, seven weeks. And we looked out the window and I said, 'As long as I can have that building and these stages, we can get going.'"

Yet Fox Plaza wasn't at the studio's disposal. It was a working office building, run by a separate management company, and many of its tenants were outside firms that expected their landlord to provide a safe, reliable environment for their office workers. The script, however, called for gunfire, explosions, action in the elevator shafts, an armored tank attack on the lobby level, and helicopters flying around the building—not to mention Joel Silver's exploding roof.

A difficult negotiation ensued. McTiernan called it a "guerrilla war" between the two sides, with the real estate division forcing unreasonable expenses on the production, including exorbitant rent rates for the unused floors. Fortunately, in time, a deal was struck. "Fox wanted to make the thing and they owned the building!" exclaims the director. "It was edict from on high—we *are* shooting in this building."

The stewards of Fox Plaza were especially concerned about damage to their brand-new, architecturally significant design and exterior. To assuage building management, the production was forced to fly in tons of Spanish marble matching the exterior of the building, in case any damage was sustained during the filming. Although such damage was successfully avoided, McTiernan notes that relations between the production and Fox Plaza remained cool throughout the shoot. "The manager of the building didn't really like us," he says.

THESE PAGES *Rooftop views from the Fox Plaza building, including the helipad that would be used for a key scene in the film's final act.*

A SCANDALOUS DEAL

While finding Nakatomi Plaza proved problematic, it was nothing compared to the search for John McClane. Silver brought on casting director Jackie Burch, a veteran of *Weird Science* (1985), *Commando*, and *Predator*. "I had worked with Joel," she says, "so it was just assumed I was going to do it."

The first "no" to the part of John McClane was not only expected, but also something of a relief. Frank Sinatra's contract for *The Detective* stated that he had first refusal on the sequel, and any adaptation of *Nothing Lasts Forever*, even if the hero had been reimagined with a different name, was technically a sequel. According to Steven de Souza, the screenwriter waiting in the wings to replace Stuart, Sinatra was candid in his response. "He said, 'I'm too old and too rich.'"

ABOVE *Bruce Willis as a bloodied and battered John McClane.*

OPPOSITE *Willis poses for promotional photography in his iconic John McClane outfit.*

Jeb Stuart claims Clint Eastwood was the next choice. "I think he wrote something on the cover of the script saying he didn't get the humor," says Stuart. "Which was ironic because his type of aside-like humor, that 'make my day' thing, was the jumping-off point for John McClane."

"It went to Paul Newman next," says Stuart. It was another no, the star of *Butch Cassidy and the Sundance Kid* (1969) having decided he no longer wanted to carry a gun in his films. Other actors who were offered the role and passed were rumored to include Arnold Schwarzenegger, Sylvester Stallone, Harrison Ford, Don Johnson, Burt Reynolds, James Caan, and Richard Dean Anderson, although McTiernan questions these rumors. "I don't think it was offered to many people." Burch agrees, "I never heard most of those names [in connection to *Die Hard*]."

While Burch remembers Al Pacino was in the frame, McTiernan recalls another star under consideration. "It was offered to Richard Gere; in fact it had been written for Richard Gere," he says. Certainly Stuart's original incarnation of McClane was tailor-made for the *American Gigolo* star. "The hero was suave, he wore a sports jacket, he was elegant, all sorts of stuff," says McTiernan. Silver wanted Gere; they were friends and he figured the actor could play an action role, something he hadn't done. The producer wouldn't let up, pushing him hard to agree to the movie, but Gere wouldn't budge.

During the summer, Silver was on a flight with the agent Arnold Rifkin, with whom he happened to be friendly. The conversation turned to one of Rifkin's clients, Bruce Willis. The combination of Willis and *Die Hard* was an intriguing possibility for both sides. Willis had come to the attention of the entertainment industry in off-Broadway theater, then burst into the public eye as the colead in the hit ABC romantic dramedy series *Moonlighting*, alongside Cybill Shepherd. After watching him on the show, Silver was convinced, believing Willis had the same swagger as Mel Gibson or even Golden Age of Hollywood star James Cagney.

Despite his obvious potential, Willis's movie career had gotten off to a shaky start. He'd starred in the romantic comedy *Blind Date* (1987), directed by Blake Edwards, but the film had not been as successful as expected; Willis was in danger of becoming perceived as a small-screen star who couldn't quite make the leap to feature films.

Willis needed a film like *Die Hard* as much as *Die Hard* needed an actor like Willis, although he was initially forced to pass because of his *Moonlighting* schedule. "I wasn't able to do it," he explains. "[Then] a miracle happens. Cybill Shepherd gets pregnant with twins. [Showrunner] Glenn Caron shuts down the show and I get to go do *Die Hard*. If I had got Cybill Shepherd pregnant myself, I couldn't have planned it better. So I always thank Cybill Shepherd!"

A six-week block opened up in Willis's schedule, and Rifkin negotiated a remarkable $5 million payday for his client. Industry insiders were shocked that a studio would take such a gamble on a TV star with just one underachieving film under his belt. "This throws the business out of whack," grumbled Alan Ladd Jr., then MGM chairman and former head of production at Fox. "Like everybody else in town, I was stunned."[3] Fox president at the time, Leonard Goldberg, countered that Willis's fee was a sound investment, as *Die Hard* would hinge on the charisma of its lead: "We reached out for Bruce Willis because we thought we had the potential of a major film that is a star vehicle." The news broke on September 17, 1987. Three days later, Willis won his Emmy for *Moonlighting*. The timing could not have been better.

"In retrospect, it did change my career," reflects Willis. "I had no awareness of that happening then. I just thought, wow! In Hollywood, everyone else had an awareness because they said, 'They're paying a television actor $5 million to be in an action picture?' The next day, every male actor's salary rose up to $5 million. I didn't get a Christmas card or anything!"

It helped that Willis immediately understood the character. "John McClane loves his family, he loves his country," says the actor. "He has a healthy disrespect for all authority. He's got a very dark, gallows sense of humor—and he has zero tolerance for allowing anyone to hurt an innocent person. He will always step in between that threat and the innocent person." Jeb Stuart met with Willis before the actor had even read the script, and Stuart was floored. Willis, he saw right away, *was* McClane.

AN ENGLISHMAN IN NEW YORK

The casting of Willis, with his regular-guy persona, changed the way Hans Gruber would be portrayed, too. Hans had originally been depicted as more downscale, just as the original McClane was suave and sophisticated. With Willis on board, the paradigm shifted. "Because I had a working-class hero," says McTiernan. "I now wanted an upper-class villain."

Jackie Burch had just the man in mind. Earlier in the year, Burch had been in Hungary casting the Arnold Schwarzenegger–Jim Belushi buddy-action film *Red Heat*. She'd received a submission for an English stage actor who had appeared in some television shows but had never been seen in a theatrical film: Alan Rickman.

Rickman was something of a late bloomer as an actor. His breakout performance on the London stage had come in 1985 as the seducer Valmont in the Royal Shakespeare Company's production of *Les liaisons dangereuses*.

He was thirty-nine at the time, old for a leading man first making his mark, but his age didn't seem to limit his sex appeal. His costar, Lindsay Duncan, claimed that audiences would leave the show wanting to have sex, "and preferably with Alan Rickman." When the show transferred to Broadway in 1987, he earned a Tony Award nomination.

Burch was familiar with Rickman from his Broadway run, but she didn't feel he was right for the Russian heavy role she was trying to fill in *Red Heat*. When she read the *Die Hard* script, though, she says, "I knew [Hans Gruber] was Alan Rickman. Luckily, Joel had seen him in a play. I said, 'We need to fly him out here,' and we got him out to Los Angeles almost immediately."

When Rickman arrived, Burch recorded a taped audition with him to show to the studio and producers. "I had to teach him how to hold a gun," she remembers, "and I don't even know how to hold a gun, but he was limping his wrist down, and I knew that wasn't going to look good. So we worked on that." The tape was good enough to convince the powers that be. "I thought he was fabulous," says McTiernan. Two days later, he was offered the role of Hans Gruber.

Although the *Die Hard* filmmakers were enthusiastic, privately Rickman had his doubts about taking the role: "I read it, and I said, 'What the hell is this? I'm not doing an action movie.' Agents and people said, 'Alan, you don't understand, this doesn't happen. You've only been in LA two days, and you've been asked to do this film.'"[4] In early October, he accepted the part. "I'd done some television in England, but to do a movie in Hollywood with a capital *H* . . . it was like a great big adventure for me."

Rickman never saw Hans as the traditional antagonist; he wasn't playing the villain but rather somebody who simply identifies what he wants and goes after it. "Hans Gruber had only really one goal and that was money," he said. With that in mind, Rickman made Hans everything McClane wasn't: cosmopolitan, elitist, arrogant. Yet for all their differences, "there's a mutual respect," said Rickman. "I always thought that was key. I think they're cut in a weird way from the same cloth."

THESE PAGES *British actor Alan Rickman as* Die Hard's *German villain, Hans Gruber.*

INSERT *Rickman plays Gruber in a series of security footage prop photos created for use in the film.*

SUPPORT NETWORK

For the role of Sgt. Al Powell, McClane's cop confidante, John McTiernan wanted Robert Duvall. "The studio was not going to do that," says Burch, "and I kept pushing Reginald VelJohnson, because I knew how great he would complement Bruce, because he's a wonderful theater actor, warm, funny, loving. I wanted to make sure that every actor around Bruce gave depth, and warmth, and credibility."

When VelJohnson got the call to audition for *Die Hard*, he remembers, "I was living in my mother's basement, with a dream and two dollars in my pocket." He'd had a few small roles in TV shows and movies that had shot in New York—*The Equalizer* and *Kojak* for CBS, and the films *Wolfen* (1981) and *Ghostbusters* (1984)—but he hadn't "made it." It had been a long time since he'd been cast in a TV show or movie; he was desperate and was considering giving up acting in favor of a career in advertising.

When VelJohnson went in to audition on videotape for *Die Hard*, his mood was a world away from that of the jovial character he desperately wanted to portray. He looked into the camera and said, "I'm not sure you're going to give me this role, but if you do, I'll give the best performance you could ever hope for." The audition got him a callback to meet the producers and the studio executives in Los Angeles. He was flown in from New York and found himself in an LAPD uniform, auditioning in front of Silver and others. Even then, McTiernan wanted a big-name actor and was still focused on Duvall. "We even had a huge meeting," recalls Burch, "and I kept saying, 'I'm going to go on the line, Reginald is the way to go for this movie.' I had cast him in some of my other movies before, and I've always loved him. When I read the script, I knew what he would bring to it." They hired him soon after.

Having been cast without much enthusiasm from the director, VelJohnson had to make good on his promise. But he knew little about the life of a police officer. To get some perspective, he went on police ride-alongs. "I got a sense of what they go through," he says. Having gained at least some firsthand knowledge of how difficult the life of a policeman could be, he was better able to reflect that angst in the character of Al, the cop haunted by a fatal shooting in his past.

Burch's strategy of surrounding Willis with warm actors with depth led her to Bonnie Bedelia for the role of Willis's on-screen wife, Holly. Like Willis, Bedelia was a New York stage actor. Willis had seen her Golden Globe–winning performance as drag racer Shirley Muldowney in *Heart Like a Wheel* (1983) and liked the idea. "Bruce thought that Bonnie would be wonderful; he had enormous respect for her as an actor, and he was so right!" says McTiernan. "She was again completely a working-class lady, but solid and honest as the day is long—and that is who he [McClane] would have as a wife." Successful and self-assured, Holly is a dynamic character who is able to keep her head when Hans takes over. "She's the leader of the hostages through most of the movie," says Bedelia. "When you have fifty people, and you're the one they're looking to . . . that might force you to become a little stronger, and a little bit less a bundle of raw nerve tissue."[5]

Cast alongside Bedelia and VelJohnson was De'voreaux White, who plays Argyle, the slick-but-sweet limo driver who collects McClane from the airport. The chauffeur character, named William in Stuart's original script, had been fleshed out considerably, and Argyle would become a key element of the story. Not only would he promise to wait for McClane if he "strikes out" with Holly at the Nakatomi party, he would later help foil the terrorists' plot by smashing his limousine into their escape vehicle. White had just come off the Silver-produced *Action Jackson* (1988), but Burch remembered him from his role as a boy lynched by a racist gang in Robert Benton's Depression-era drama *Places in the Heart* (1984). He was called in to read for *Die Hard* in front of Willis and Silver. "Before I got home, they called and I was on board," says White.

White immediately plugged into the character of Argyle, who reveals to McClane that it's his first day on the job (and is so inexperienced, he doesn't even offer to carry McClane's bag at the airport). "He's this young guy and he's just happy-go-lucky," says White. "He's not confrontational. He just wants to be cool with everybody without trying to be cool. . . . I took that and I ran with that." The actor adds that he "put in a little bit of me" into the part. "I always liked to be upbeat."

OPPOSITE *Bonnie Bedelia as Holly McClane.*

TOP *Reginald VelJohnson as Sgt. Al Powell.*

ABOVE *De'voreaux White as limo driver Argyle.*

The character worked perfectly. "He was hugely sincere," says McTiernan. "Underneath all of his hipness, he was a genuinely sweet kid and it shows up. The audience genuinely likes him. He isn't a smart-ass asshole. They actually think, 'He's a nice kid!' When he becomes a minor hero, and he's wildly proud of himself for having done it, the audience is on his side for that."

It was all part of McTiernan's plan. "All those people had a similar quality of straight-ahead, lower-middle-class decency and honesty," he says. "They were absolutely the opposite of the terrorists—which is why the terrorists had cool clothes and all that other shit—and the official [law enforcement] bozos who were jackasses. There was this spine of good people threaded through the piece, who were all, in a way, very similar to Bruce."

While this is true, the script was not so black-and-white that it tarred all those in positions of authority with either villainy or stupidity. Take the Nakatomi president Takagi who, underneath the John Phillips suit, is a man of honor. "Takagi had dignity and decency about him," says McTiernan. "He's a very genuine man." McTiernan evolved this idea, creating a moment where Hans reads out Takagi's biography in front of his employees as he searches for him in the crowd of scared hostages. "I made up that business—Mr. Takagi was from a Japanese American family that had been interned during the war, and he'd gone to Manzanar [concentration camp]," says McTiernan. "[It was] just to say, this is a good guy, he's a nice man. He doesn't deserve all this shit that's happening to him." McTiernan cast veteran actor James

Shigeta, who began his career singing in nightclubs and made his first film appearance in Samuel Fuller's *The Crimson Kimono* (1959).

Burch also needed actors able to play "princes who become asses." She found Hart Bochner for Harry Ellis, Holly's coked-up, lecherous, and ultimately doomed coworker. "[He could project] this kind of arrogance, or something about him that made me think, 'Oh my God, this will be so fun,' and he did an amazing job. He was great in it," she remembers. Coincidentally, Bochner's father, Lloyd Bochner, had been in *The Detective* with Frank Sinatra.

Equally repellent is the ambitious newsman Richard Thornburg, who reports live from the Nakatomi Plaza and later doorsteps Holly's maid Paulina, threatening her with deportation unless she allows him inside to interview the McClane children. William Atherton, who had played the vile Environmental Protection Agency official Walter Peck in *Ghostbusters*, was cast. "William Atherton is such a great guy and can play such a fantastic villain," says Burch. Prior to filming, Atherton spent time at the Columbia School of Broadcasting to prepare, learning how to read news bulletins from a teleprompter. "I wanted to get it so that it was second nature to me, and that I knew what I was doing so that there wouldn't be a shift that was awkward," he says.

Another master of playing the "great asshole" was Paul Gleason. Burch had previously cast him in John Hughes's *The Breakfast Club* (1985) as the bullish teacher overseeing Saturday detention in a Chicago high school. He was a perfect fit to play LAPD Deputy Chief Dwayne T. Robinson, relishing the profanities in his dialogue much like his private detective in the John Landis comedy *Trading Places* (1983). Playing the dumbass cop, "Paul Gleason was just so perfect," says McTiernan, "so fucking perfect!"

When FBI agents Johnson and Johnson ("no relation," as they quip) arrive, Robinson's authority is immediately undercut. Landing the roles of Big Johnson and Little Johnson, respectively, were Robert Davi and Grand Bush, both veterans of Joel Silver films. Davi had been in *Action Jackson*, while Bush had been in both *Lethal Weapon* and *Streets of Fire* (1984). Bush remembers the casting for *Die Hard* as a somewhat unusual process: "All my agent could tell me was that Joel Silver had offered me a part in a Twentieth Century Fox project and wanted to meet him at this newly constructed skyscraper in Century City." Silver was the only person who met with him during casting, and for the first time he was cast without having to audition, a prestigious step for an actor. "He had hired me for previous projects, so he was familiar with my talent and work ethic," says Bush.

THIS PAGE *(clockwise from center left) Hart Bochner's Harry Ellis talks with Bonnie Bedelia's Holly McClane; William Atherton as news reporter Richard Thornburg; Grand Bush as Special Agent Little Johnson; Robert Davi as Special Agent Big Johnson.*

OPPOSITE *Dancer Alexander Godunov as henchman Karl.*

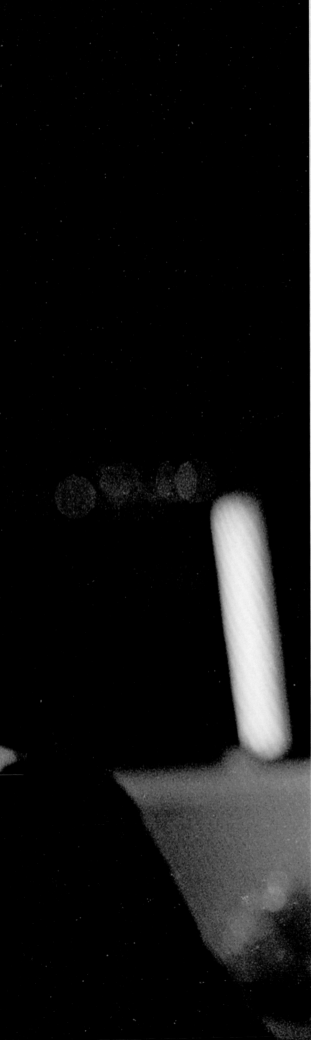

The actor never saw a script. "Joel said he wanted me to play the role of an FBI agent," Bush recalls. "He did not reveal the name of the movie, nor did he tell me what the project was all about. He did say, however, that I was about to become part of the most amazing movie ever made." And from there, Bush was whisked off to be fitted for his FBI agent suit.

For Hans's crew of terrorists, Burch had a scheme in mind. "I decided to make them all good-looking international guys," she says. One of the most prominent roles in the group was Karl, Hans's chief henchman. Burch had her eye on Alexander Godunov, a former principal dancer for the Bolshoi Ballet who had appeared in a couple of feature films, notably playing Kelly McGillis's taciturn Amish suitor in *Witness* (1985). "I thought he would be amazing in it," says Burch. "[But we had to] convince him to do the movie."

The actor's reluctance to take the role of Karl arose from a very practical concern: he wasn't confident speaking English. During the pursuit of Godunov (known to his friends as "Sasha"), Jeb Stuart was at work on the Fox lot when he got a call from Silver. "[Silver] said, 'Look, there's an actor walking over to your office. He wants to talk to you about the script. I want him desperately. Don't say anything to screw it up.'" Stuart asked who it was, and for what part, and Silver replied, "You'll know him." Stepping out of his office onto the porch of Fox's new writers' building, Stuart watched as the tall, lithe, flaxen-locked Godunov appeared. "People came to their windows and the doors, and walked out to see this guy. He just was a physical specimen."

Stuart assumed that Godunov wanted more dialogue. But when he addressed the issue with the actor, "He said, 'No, no, no! I want to take some of the lines away!' I said oh! I'd never had an actor say that to me before. So we sat there and went through the script and he really had gotten this character into his head, and he said, 'I think I can get away with a lot more with my look.'" Stuart obliged by trimming down Karl's dialogue, most notably for an early scene where a silent Karl cuts the building's communications using a chainsaw to slice through four tubes containing telephone wires, much to the annoyance of his meticulous brother, Tony. Godunov agreed to take the part.

Andreas Wisniewski, a German actor and former dancer, was cast to play Tony, the first terrorist McClane kills when they cross paths on the under-construction thirty-second floor. Wisniewski had just appeared in the James Bond film *The Living Daylights* (1987). "I was kind of hoping to capitalize on that," he says, "and ride the wave and come over to LA."

Wisniewski credits his casting essentially to luck: "They already had Sasha Godunov, and I just happened to look like him, and since we were playing brothers, it was obvious. They couldn't cast anybody else." Coincidentally, Wisniewski and Godunov already knew each other: They had both danced for the Berlin ballet a few years earlier.

LEFT *Karl (Godunov) and Hans Gruber (Rickman) find their carefully laid plans derailed when John McClane starts fighting back.*

TOP *Andreas Wisniewski, cast as Karl's brother, Tony.*

Wilhelm von Homburg, a German-born former wrestler and boxer, was cast as James, the rocket-loading muscle who meets his fate when McClane's homemade C-4 "chair bomb" falls down the lift shaft. Playing the coiffured Fritz would be Hans Buhringer, whose acting career began and ended with *Die Hard*. And future Italian soap star Lorenzo Caccialanza was cast as Marco, the thug McClane shoots in the Nakatomi boardroom before throwing his body out of the window to get Al Powell's attention. Also joining the cast was Clarence Gilyard Jr. as Theo, the tech specialist in Hans's crew who is responsible for cracking the vault that contains the bearer bonds. Born in Moses Lake, Washington, Gilyard had come to prominence through a regular role on the TV cop show *CHiPs*, and brought a darkly comic sensibility to his portrayal of Theo.

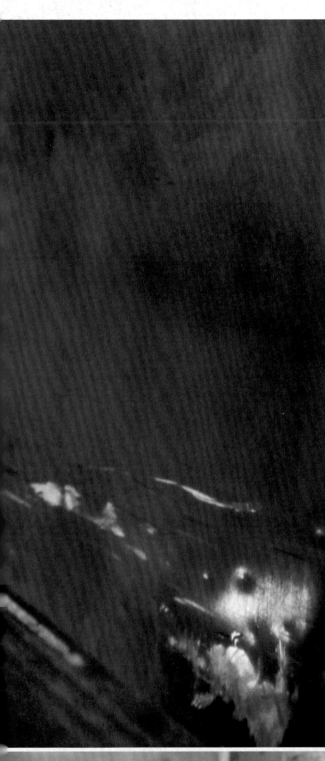

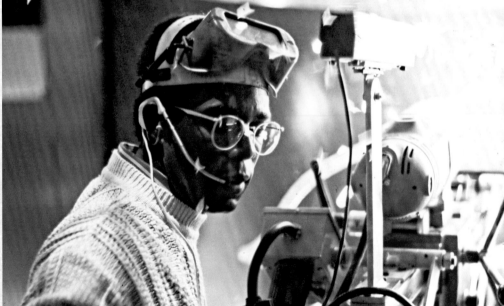

THESE PAGES (clockwise from opposite top left) *Hans's gang:*
Wilhelm von Homburg as James; Gary Roberts as Heinrich;
Lorenzo Caccialanza as Marco; Clarence Gilyard Jr. as Theo;
Bruno Doyon as Franco; Gérard Bonn as Kristoff.

THOUSAND-YARD STARES

Joel Silver was keen to elevate *Die Hard*'s visual aesthetic to the highest level possible, so he brought in production designer Jackson De Govia to create the film's sets. Prior to *Die Hard*, De Govia had worked on the miniseries *The Winds of War* (1983) and the feature film *Red Dawn* (1984), both of which included military-themed action. For the latter, De Govia had overseen the construction of faux military hardware so convincing that CIA aerial photos of the props alarmed intelligence officials. "That must have been why Joel Silver called me," says De Govia.

De Govia came with a strong staff, including art director John Jensen. "John was a graduate of the apprentice program at Universal Pictures," says De Govia. "He was an incredible art director." The assistant art director was Craig Edgar, whom De Govia credits for the beautiful drafting of many of the film's sets, with E. C. Chen filling the role of set designer.

Hired in September, De Govia had just eight weeks before the shoot was due to begin in early November. "Our time scale was so compressed," he says. "We started off in emergency mode." Construction crews worked in three shifts, around the clock. Some supervisors were working double shifts. "You would go and talk to people who were running the construction, and they had that thousand-yard stare," says De Govia. "And we had every good prop maker in Hollywood that we could hire." The pressure was particularly intense because much of the construction involved complex machinery, and the sets needed to be robustly built to cope with the stunts and explosions. "You could not make a mistake," he says.

A few scenes would be shot on location, including the opening sequence, filmed at the Tom Bradley International Terminal within Los Angeles International Airport, and McClane's subsequent limo ride through Century City to Nakatomi Plaza. Holly's house was also real. "I remember John [McTiernan] and I scouted that house, and it had to be a house that gave you a view of the [Fox Plaza] building as the TV truck comes up the hill," says De Govia, referring to a scene where Thornburg thunders up the road in a news van to browbeat Holly's maid into letting him interview the McClane children. A twenty-four-hour convenience store was also selected because of its proximity to Fox Plaza for the scene that introduces Sgt. Al Powell. After buying some Twinkies, Powell gets the dispatch call to investigate Nakatomi Plaza before walking out onto West Olympic Boulevard and seeing suspicious flashes from the top of the building.

The rest of the production would be split between a stage on the Fox lot and the adjacent Fox Plaza. The biggest set built was the Nakatomi atrium on the thirtieth floor, the luxurious area where Hans's gang holds the employees hostage. Built on Fox's spacious Stage 15, the atrium set was by far the production design department's largest single expense, costing $1.5 million. "It was the size of an aircraft carrier," says De Govia. "It was about as big as a set can be and still be indoors."

Joel Silver was a fan of Frank Lloyd Wright. He owned two homes designed by the legendary architect and even had Wright design touches added to his bungalow on the Fox lot. Silver wanted the atrium set to echo Wright's work, so De Govia and his team styled it after the architect's famous house design Fallingwater, a structure built over a waterfall with a stream running through it.

"That's what the atrium was," says De Govia. "That big rock with the water coming from the top, that's a match for the site of the house. The house is above the rock. Its thrusting platforms are the Frank Lloyd Wright house. It was very, very close to the original from the points of view that we had." More subtly, the inclusion of Wright's work "echoed concerns at the time that a resurgent Japan was buying America out from under us," De Govia adds.

Another Frank Lloyd Wright creation can be seen in the museum adjacent to the boardroom, situated on the thirty-fourth floor, where Hans demands Takagi open the Nakatomi vault. The white tabletop model of a bridge that Takagi calls "our project in Indonesia" is actually the Butterfly Bridge, designed by Wright in 1953 as a planned construction linking San Francisco and Oakland. De Govia discovered the project, which had never come to fruition, in a book on Wright. When Silver realized the model still existed, he had it shipped out from Wright's Taliesin West residence in Scottsdale, Arizona, to use in the film.

LEFT *Preparations are made for filming the Nakatomi Christmas party scenes.*

ABOVE *Hans Gruber addresses the Nakatomi CEO, Mr. Takagi (James Shigeta), by the model of Frank Lloyd Wright's Butterfly Bridge.*

PAGES 40–41 *Concept art for the Nakatomi atrium by Jackson De Govia.*

INSERT *Assistant art director Craig Edgar's construction drawing for the thirtieth-floor garden area plan.*

De Govia also ensured Asian creative influences ran through the Nakatomi Plaza design scheme. For example, the wall of the lobby's front desk, made of stone cladding, "slopes outward exactly like the outer wall of a medieval Japanese fort," says De Govia. In front of the building, there is a giant bonsai tree for cars to circle around. And on the balcony outside the boardroom, De Govia placed statues of Chinese warriors. The inspiration was the real-life Terracotta Army unearthed from the tomb of Emperor Qin Shi Huang in 1974. "They seemed appropriate even though Chinese," says De Govia, who had three statues made.

Behind the Nakatomi office interior set, a 350-foot-long, 30-foot-tall backdrop, or cyclorama, that vividly simulated the Los Angeles skyline was installed. Created by scene artist Ed Strang and his son, Ron, assisted by a crew of fourteen, the backing was augmented with a combination of careful lighting, shallow depth-of-field photography, and some clever use of embedded light. Some parts were even out of focus, just as they would be to the human eye. "What these people did," says De Govia, "you cannot do anywhere else in the world."[6]

De Govia also put his touch on the thirty-third-floor computer room where McClane would come under heavy fire from Hans's men. The room was constructed in the Fox Plaza building, with state-of-the-art computer hardware borrowed for the production. In his research, De Govia noticed that industrial-sized computers tended to be placed on raised tiles, necessary to help circulate air and keep the machines cool. He ran black tape over the seams of the white tiles, creating a contrasting look that he compares to the design of a Rubik's Cube.

De Govia saw the Nakatomi building as a "steel jungle" and the story as "a survival drama in the context of architecture that's under construction. This is a guy lost in the jungle and he doesn't know where he is. This is a new environment for him and he adapts. He sets traps. He figures out where and how to hide. He improvises."

De Govia was reminded of J. G. Ballard's novel *High-Rise*, in which a modern building becomes a battleground for the residents. He was also inspired by the 1966 film *The Naked Prey*, which stars Cornel Wilde as an elephant hunter pursued through the jungle by violent natives. The building-as-jungle metaphor extends to other details, like the serpentine shape of the conference table that McClane crawls under while a terrorist shoots at him. "[We] wanted something that moves like a river," says De Govia, "and that gives you places to dodge and hide.

"To me, we [were] not designing sets," he says. "We [were] revealing the story, the secret thing that's underneath the words on the paper, the ideas people have, the soul of the building, the characters, and everything. That's the absolute blood and bones of the movie." De Govia even describes Nakatomi Plaza as a living thing, with a skeleton and a circulatory system: a giant creature with McClane and Hans and his gang inside it. The building itself isn't trying to kill McClane, he says, but "it may be rejecting Hans and the terrorists."

Even amid all the pressure faced by the design team, there was time for adding flourishes and details. De Govia decorated the truck that the terrorists use when they first approach Nakatomi Plaza with a design that incorporated a fictional company named Pacific Courier. He later reused the same logo in *Speed* (1994) and in 1995's *Die Hard with a Vengeance* (where an "Atlantic Courier" truck blows up early in the film).

OPPOSITE TOP AND LEFT *Asian influences run through Jackson De Govia's designs for the Nakatomi boardroom.*

TOP RIGHT *Mr. Takagi addresses the Nakatomi employees in the ornately decorated atrium.*

ABOVE *Hans Gruber passes by one of the models for a Nakatomi project in the Nakatomi boardroom.*

LIGHTS, CAMERA . . .

When it came time to choose a cinematographer, Beau Marks introduced John McTiernan and Joel Silver to the work of Jan de Bont. When the Dutch director of photography first came to America, he'd worked with Marks on a couple of movies, including the 1981 comedy *Private Lessons*. "I think the world of him," adds Marks. "He's a brilliant cinematographer."

The Eindhoven-born de Bont had made an impact working on a series of Paul Verhoeven projects, including *Turkish Delight* (1973), *Flesh + Blood* (1985), and erotic thriller *The Fourth Man* (1983), which had impressed McTiernan. "I think the work in it was really revolutionary," comments McTiernan, who planned to move the camera on *Die Hard* in a way that captured emotion and didn't just follow the action.

During preproduction, McTiernan and de Bont hatched a plan to give *Die Hard* a fresh, modern look, one that was more realistic than that of most 1980s action movies. The photography, they decided, should almost be documentary style, so the action felt like it was

ABOVE *McTiernan with Bruce Willis on the set of* Die Hard.

RIGHT *Joel Silver and Jan de Bont during a Fox Plaza exterior shoot.*

44

real life and the camera just happened to be there. "The camera had to be like a floating bystander," explains de Bont. "Every time you saw something, the camera could basically almost intuitively move left or right, up or down." Nothing about the camera moves or lighting should look formal or overly complicated. "The lighting had to look like it was really happening, and if it was dark at times, then it was dark at times," adds de Bont. "We didn't want to just light everything and make it look phony."

"Bruce's character drives the movie," adds de Bont, "and the camera has to get that same sense of drive." The camera would not only bring energy, it would also evoke tension. "What's going to happen next? What's around that corner? Where is he now? That was a really important facet of what John and I talked about." Such edgy filming would only be possible if the entire set or location was always lit so it could be shot from any angle, or from multiple angles.

All the lamps and lighting that appeared on-screen would look like regular office lights, but in fact they were designed specifically for movies, so de Bont could control the illumination of the set. De Govia and de Bont worked together to install similar lights in both the sound-stage sets and in Fox Plaza, so the lighting would match. They also had fluorescent lighting installed on some floors of Fox Plaza that could be easily manipulated to create specific lighting setups for certain rooms and hallways. Giving each location its own look through lighting would help the audience keep track of where the action was taking place in the rapidly moving story.

De Bont, like De Govia, saw the Nakatomi building as another character in the movie. "You're looking at the building for eighty percent of the movie. It had better be interesting," he laughs. "The key thing was how to treat a building so it looks real, looks alive, when at the same time it's not finished yet and a lot of the floors are empty."

To illuminate the Century City exteriors, de Bont planned to surround the base of Fox Plaza with sixty large xenon spotlights, pointed straight up like landscape lighting. "They basically gave an outline of the building," he says. "It never hits inside the building because that would make it look artificial."

McTiernan and de Bont also made another bold choice for the time: They would deliberately incorporate a lot of lens flare. "In the eighties, people hated that," says de Bont. "I even used specific old Panavision lenses that would give a double reflection in the camera. And that was so effective because it made it look real. Everybody's doing it now, but at the time it was very unusual and very daring."

McTiernan also planned to cut from one moving shot to another, a technique that defied the conventional wisdom of breaking a scene into master, medium, and close-up shots. "A moving camera is really like a musical composition," the director explains. "At this time, they still had rules—you're not allowed to make a cut while the camera is moving. You have to wait until the camera stops and then you can make it. All sorts of rules. Primitive stuff like that. We had to fight all of that and we had to learn the techniques: Well, how do you cut while the camera is moving? And the answer is a musical one. You conceive of it almost the way you would as a musical composition. You can cut between moving cameras if the two shots are, in effect, in the same key. There is such a thing as shots being in the same visual key, which has to do with speed and lens length and lighting."

When it came to cutting the film, McTiernan found a key ally in Frank J. Urioste, an editor who came from a family of musicians and had exactly the sensibility the director required.

"He brought along his family's closeness to music in the way he would cut, literally," McTiernan says, noting that Urioste came from the predigital era where editors cut and spliced physical reels of film. "He used to be able to tell if a scene was the way he wanted it by simply the rhythm of the tape splices hitting his fingers. So his whole concept of cutting was a musical one; rather than some buttoned-down literary theory of how filmmaking works, he had a musical concept of it. His approach to cutting was sensual."

Urioste was a hot commodity at the time, having just cut Paul Verhoeven's 1987 action hit *RoboCop*. He'd never worked with McTiernan or Silver, but he knew Larry Gordon. "I had an interview with John [McTiernan]," Urioste remembers. "I almost blew the job because I said I don't work with another editor!" He later compromised on that condition, with the addition of a second editor, John Link.

In Urioste's own view, one of his strengths was that he got along with people, even *Die Hard*'s demanding producer. "People told me, 'Oh boy, when you meet Joel Silver he's gonna be this, he's gonna be that.' But Joel and I became best pals. Because he knew I had my rules, and if he got a little out of line, I'd either leave or hang up the phone."

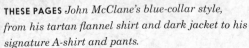

SHOPPING BEYOND BORDERS

Heading up the costume department was Marilyn Vance. The designer was a veteran of the Gordon-Silver team, having worked on several of their films, including *48 Hrs.* and *Predator.* A New Yorker who had owned a thriving fashion business before transitioning into movies, Vance pioneered the incorporation of Italian couture into Hollywood costumes. On *48 Hrs.*, the script had called for Eddie Murphy's ex-con to spend the film in a red silk suit. Vance insisted that was wrong for the character and dressed Murphy instead in a bespoke Armani suit with a conservative Prince of Wales check. Such style sense surely endeared her to Silver, a man who appreciated beautiful clothes. The two have now collaborated on twenty-two films together.

Once she got the call for *Die Hard*, Vance began developing her own take on McClane. She'd grown up in a white working-class neighborhood in Brooklyn, around people who reminded her of the fictional cop.

"His wife has a career and he can't understand it," she says. "He's coming to LA at Christmastime to see his children and win his wife back. He's that loyal kind of guy, but he's a chauvinist." Most of all, though, Vance saw him as an unassuming, accidental hero. "He's so exposed," she says. "If he were a lesser character, he wouldn't be able to rise to the occasion. But he's so devoted to his feelings about family, his wife, he just rises to it."

For the early scenes, as McClane arrives at the airport in Los Angeles, Vance put the character in wintry East Coast colors: a dark jacket, dark corduroy pants, and a black-and-white tartan flannel shirt. Nothing smooth, no tie, lots of texture. The look evokes "cement, the sidewalk, the dark street," she says, and it sets him apart from the Angelenos around him, establishing a strong first impression.

Rather like Indiana Jones with his fedora or James Bond with his tuxedo, one item of clothing symbolizes McClane above all others: the white undershirt. First revealed as McClane freshens up in a Nakatomi executive washroom, and soon to be soiled with blood, sweat, and grime, the undershirt would become indelibly linked with the character. When choosing the garment, Vance rejected the idea of using a T-shirt, choosing instead an off-the-rack A-shirt, also known colloquially as a wifebeater. "He wasn't a guy who would put on that kind of T-shirt,

then put a shirt over that, then put a sweater over the shirt, then have a coat," explains Vance. McTiernan felt it was an entirely apt choice of apparel. "He's a working-class hero. How [else] should he look?"

Since McClane would sport just pants and the undershirt for most of the film, both garments required meticulous attention. Before shooting started, Vance not only had to make the multiple undershirts she'd acquired look used, she also had to work out how many degrees of dirt and distressing each would need for specific scenes within the chronology of the story. She knew the film's scenes wouldn't be shot in chronological order, and that in some scenes McClane would be sweatier or bloodier than others. In all, she created seventeen different versions of the shirt, in various states of distress.

Around a dozen pairs of pants were made in the costume shop at Fox, tailored one way for Willis and another way for the stunt performers, so they'd look identical on-screen regardless of whether it was the star or a stuntman in the shot. "I had to use the same fabric," says Vance, "and that was difficult, to keep getting the right fabric for the pants, because the corduroy was a little thin."

Vance conceived Holly's look to convey professionalism and power, with browns and pinks that complemented Bonnie Bedelia's hair color and skin tone. A business suit was never an option. "She was a softer character," says Vance. "But at the same time, she had a very important position, so her clothing, to me, had to be suede and leather and something more sumptuous. And it was the right time of year for that because it was Christmastime." Vance shopped for Holly's clothes at department store Saks Fifth Avenue, then had the studio's costume shop use them for inspiration when creating the character's wardrobe. "The whole idea was for her to be strong but not tailored," says Vance. "She's soft as a person but she still means business."

When it came to Hans and his gang, the original concept was to dress them in overalls and protective clothing. "I went in for the fitting and they had all this terrorist gear lined up, all this padded stuff," noted Alan Rickman. "I'd seen all the people who were being interviewed to play my gang, and I said, why would I be wearing this stuff when I've got these human mountains who are working for me? I never actually get my hands dirty."

Rickman suggested that Hans wear a suit. "For a while I think people looked at me a bit quizzically, and then I went back to England, and then I came back to LA to start shooting and I was handed a bunch of pages of the new script. Joel said, 'Read that,' and they'd put [the suit] in."

With the decision made to dress Hans in a suit, Vance had a bold proposal for getting the right style. She wanted to fly to Europe to shop for him and his gang. McClane could look like he got his clothes at a mall or from a catalog, but the terrorists had to have a convincingly foreign style. "Otherwise they would have looked like J. Crew, they would have looked like the Gap, anywhere that you could get everyday clothing," she says. "[Their clothes would have had] no flair compared to a European look." But the studio wasn't initially sold on flying Vance across the world, believing it was an extravagance given that the terrorist group would be essentially background players in the film. The costume designer held her ground, firmly believing that the details were important to selling the idea that these were foreign terrorists: "You'll see enough [of them for the details to be significant]," she argued. "We hear their accents, they have long hair, they have a different look." Fortunately Lawrence Gordon and the sharply dressed Silver, who appreciated European style, backed Vance, and she won the argument. She jetted to Italy and Paris to shop.

Vance felt that Hans had to be impeccable, and so she bought his suit in Italy, from Cerruti, the fashion house known for its meticulously crafted, luxurious fabrics, especially woolens. The cut of Hans's suit is unusual—double-breasted, with notch lapels instead of the typical peak. The look suggests bespoke tailoring, something Hans appreciates when he casts admiring glances at Takagi's John Phillips suit and notes he has two of his own.

For both Hans's suit and his coat, Vance selected smooth fabrics like gabardine. "That helps the slickness of his character," she says, "which also makes him so scary, because he's so entitled, and fashion-y, and perfectly tailored." The dark cloth of Hans's outfit was in stark contrast to Takagi's "light-colored suit," chosen purposefully, says Vance, "to stand out" against the terrorists.

Of Hans's overcoat, she says, "It's a washed silk trench coat, double-breasted, belted, with wider lapels." A couple of years later, she reused the pattern to create a coat for Richard Gere's character in the hit movie *Pretty Woman*. "On Hans it looked like a completely different coat," she says.

JERSEY SHORE

His costume aside, Alan Rickman noticed some other changes to the script during preproduction. The dynamic between Hans and John McClane was evolving as rewrites continued. "When I met Willis, my immediate comment was that they're such cartoon-like characters that it would be much more interesting if they could make each other laugh," said Rickman. "There was no emotional development to chart with my character, so it needed something extra, and that came as the script was rewritten. In fact, the script was rewritten so much I could hardly say we filmed the script I agreed to do."[7]

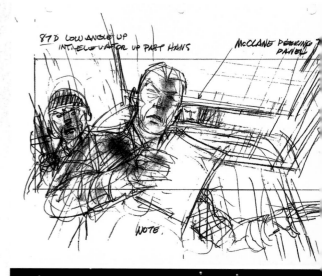

With the shoot fast approaching, Steven de Souza had come on board to revise Stuart's script. With a background in television, de Souza had a reputation as a problem-solver, able to work within strict budget parameters and deliver to deadline. Silver hadn't made a film with Stuart before, but he knew de Souza and was sure he could handle whatever urgent situations arose in production. Stuart returned to his other projects, though McTiernan kept him looped in on the rewrites as a courtesy. Although he enjoyed the thrill of observing the shoot, Stuart had little to do with the script after de Souza arrived.

De Souza admired Stuart's script and the work he'd done to adapt it from the Roderick Thorp book. In particular, he was impressed that *Die Hard* and its hero took a big swerve away from the action-movie tropes of the era. "In all the [1980s] action movies, the hero is like this formidable physical specimen," says de Souza. "Remember, in *Rambo: First Blood Part II*, they torture Stallone, they beat him, they strap him to a metal mattress, they put electrodes on his genitals. Then he breaks loose, beats them, grabs the radio, and says, 'I'm coming to get you myself.'" De Souza saw *Die Hard* as an antidote to that kind of over-the-top action: "In the whole first act of the movie, the hero's trying to get help. All he's trying to do is call 911, trying *not* to be a hero. In the second act he's being hunted. And in the third act he takes the hunter down."

Once de Souza was brought on, a meeting was quickly arranged between him and Bruce Willis. De Souza says he was warned that Willis was sick of constant revisions to the *Moonlighting* scripts and wanted the *Die Hard* script locked. As a result, the writer approached the meeting with some trepidation. But when they met, they formed an instant rapport upon discovering they had grown up near each other in the Atlantic City area. "We knew all the same stuff, the same shops," says de Souza. "We talked about playing army under the boardwalk. We were bonding on our childhood stuff." Willis asked if de Souza could put some of these reminiscences into the script. When de Souza mentioned he'd heard Willis wanted the script locked, the actor put him straight. "He said, 'I don't know who the hell told you that, but anything you can do to put some fun in this picture, do it!' And we shook on that. I took that as gospel."

Willis wanted Stuart's script to lighten up, echoing McTiernan's instinct to turn *Die Hard* into a caper movie, and Rickman's assessment that the hero and villain needed to "make each other laugh." Thorp's *Nothing Lasts Forever* was a grim book where the hero's doomed daughter is a drug addict, involved in a deal with Chilean fascists; Stuart's script, while not that bleak, "had a lot of that . . . 'there are evil men in the world and we must do battle against them' kinda stuff," notes McTiernan.

McTiernan gave de Souza wide latitude to change the script within certain limits. He was given floor plans of the building where the film would be shot and told he could write whatever he wanted, as long as he didn't introduce new floors or new sets. He could add jokes, create new scenes, change dialogue—he just couldn't invent anything that would involve the crew having to build anything new.

Several scenes from Stuart's revised draft, dated October 2, 1987, were either dropped or modified. In a scene from Stuart's draft, set at a police station, Powell is on the phone with his pregnant wife (who is having food cravings) just as two cops arrive and make a joke about him being "very deadly with a handgun"—a cruel reference to the incident in his past in which he "shot a kid." The police station scene was excised by de Souza, who also embellished a scene from Stuart's draft in which Sgt. Powell confesses to McClane over the airwaves that he accidentally killed a thirteen-year-old boy who was brandishing a toy gun.

Additionally, the exchange in the convenience store where Powell buys his Twinkies, claiming they're for his expectant spouse, was shortened. In Stuart's script, two teenage employees in the store seem to find his purchase amusing. When he gets the code-two call, one comments to the other: "Wonder what a 'code two' is . . . cupcake alert?"

The writer also added some memorably pithy lines. In the scene where McClane scrawls "now I have a machine gun" on the late Tony's sweatshirt, de Souza capped the sinister message off with the ironic "ho-ho-ho" at the end. He also punched up the dialogue in McClane's

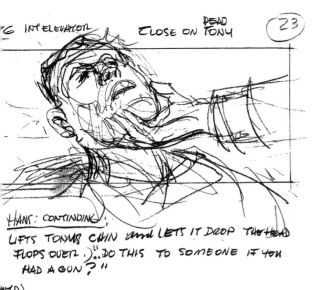

HANS: CONTINUING
LIFTS TONY'S CHIN and LETS IT DROP THE HEAD
FLOPS OVER). "DO THIS TO SOMEONE IF YOU
HAD A GUN ? "

(MD)

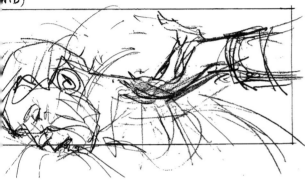

conversation with the LAPD dispatcher, when he is desperately trying to alert the authorities to the hostage situation. "Do I sound like I'm ordering a pizza?" he shouts in de Souza's script (in Stuart's version it was: "What the hell you people want?—a fucking engraved invitation?").

De Souza also invented the notion that Hans's crew must crack seven barriers to break into the vault: a code, five locks, and an electromagnetic seal. "Otherwise," he says, "it would be preposterous to have them trying to break into one lock for ten hours."

He also worked on the walkie-talkie conversation between Hans and McClane. "Just another American who saw too many movies as a child," taunts Hans. "Another orphan of a bankrupt culture who thinks he's John Wayne. Rambo. Marshal Dillon." McClane then tells him he's partial to Roy Rogers before cutting the conversation short saying, "Yippee-ki-yay, motherfucker"—the character's first use of what would become an iconic line.

The precise origin of the line is disputed, although it stemmed from Willis and de Souza bonding over TV shows and actors they watched as kids, notably "the king of cowboys," Roy Rogers. De Souza says he wrote the line, although another account says Willis made the line up on the spot to crack up the crew, and never thought it would get into the movie. "That's the one [line] that everybody claims," smiles Stuart. "You could ask the grip on *Die Hard* and he's going to claim he wrote that line!"

Whoever thought it up, the line is almost certainly a contraction of the lyric "yippee yi yo kayay" from the song "I'm an Old Cowhand," a 1936 Bing Crosby hit that was covered by Roy Rogers in his 1943 film *King of the Cowboys*. The movie features singing cowboy Rogers fighting German saboteurs during World War II and is just the sort of fare Willis and de Souza—and therefore McClane—might have seen on TV as kids. Willis remembers there was even debate about the pronunciation. "We had a really adult conversation about what was the proper way to say it: Was it yippee-*ki*-yay or yippee-*ti*-yay? I'm glad that I held on to yippee-ki-yay."[8]

For all the additions de Souza made, there's one thing he wants to make very clear: "The thing that's all over the internet that's completely wrong is that *Die Hard* was originally the sequel to *Commando*. That is not true. I wrote the sequel to *Commando*, it is not it."

OPPOSITE CENTER AND RIGHT
Andreas Wisniewski poses for a photo prior to being made up to look like Tony's corpse, complete with Christmas-themed touches to his outfit applied by John McClane.

ABOVE, OPPOSITE TOP, AND OPPOSITE BOTTOM
Storyboards by John L. Jensen show the late Tony.

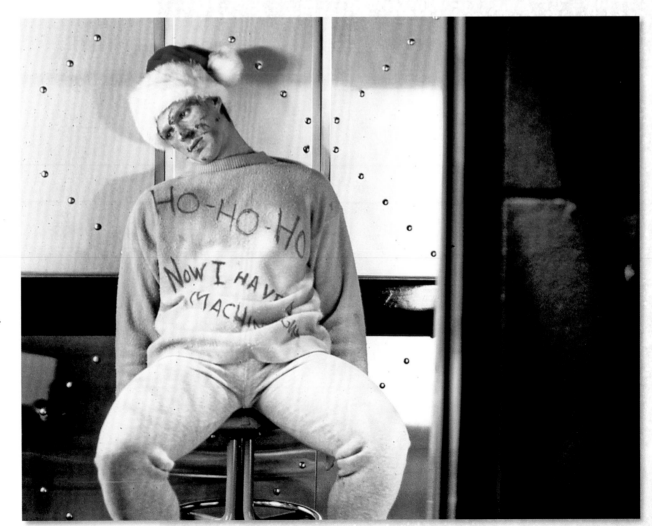

ACTION UNDERWAY

Shooting began on *Die Hard* on November 2, 1987. With just eight months and counting until it was due in cinemas, the schedule was insane for a movie of this scale. "It was a stunt from the beginning," says McTiernan. "Here we sit early in November: Can you get this movie delivered to us, the studio, so we can open it [in] July?"

The screenplay revisions were only a third complete at this point. "I write a script the same way you shoot one, out of order," explains de Souza. "And John quickly realized that he could work this way. He'd say, 'Here's what I need right away.' A lot of what he wanted right away were the things that would affect the logistics of making the movie." In particular, the third act needed work: Nobody had quite figured out what the bad guys' getaway plan was. "When we started shooting, we only had thirty-five pages [ready to shoot]," adds McTiernan.

During shooting, the production would regularly switch between the Fox Plaza building and the Fox soundstages. "We were going back and forth all the time," says McTiernan. "We would shoot in the building while they were preparing a set on a stage. The official scenery

very often would come in late, and it would take a while for that stuff to get done. So we shot a lot in the building at first, which was fine."

The sets constructed on the Fox stages included the lobby elevator, Harry Ellis's office, the KFLW TV studio that airs Thornburg's reports (Silver changed the initials from the original script's "KCBS" as a nod to Frank Lloyd Wright), Holly's office (with her surname spelled *Gennero* on the door, not *Gennaro* as it is in the computer directory), and the executive bathroom where Holly and McClane argue just before the terrorists arrive.

At Fox Plaza, a wide range of interior locations were found, including the computer room, the elevator shaft, the basement, the garage where Argyle waits for McClane, the Nakatomi boardroom, and the rotating ventilation fan that McClane wedges his gun into so he can crawl through it. Exteriors used included the building's roof and the driveway in front of the lobby. De Govia's team even erected a sign for the Nakatomi Convention Center, glimpsed as Sgt. Powell's cop car reverses past it, that humorously credits set designer E. C. Chen as the building's "architect."

ABOVE *Bruce Willis takes a break.*

OPPOSITE BOTTOM *John McClane climbing into the bowels of the Nakatomi building.*

TOP RIGHT *Joel Silver and Willis on set.*

INSERT *Art director John R. Jensen's construction plans for the KFLW TV studio set.*

Since the story unfolds between dusk and dawn, the film was shot largely at night during a chilly winter by Los Angeles standards (above freezing but plenty cold enough for the crew on exterior locations to become uncomfortable). The upper floors of Fox Plaza, where nighttime shooting took place, were cramped, so only a small crew, the actors, and the director were permitted on set. The support crew stayed downstairs, in trucks and trailers. If de Bont needed a lens, film, or anything else, he'd have to call down. Often there'd be no answer, his team sleeping, exhausted from the unsociable hours that played havoc with their body clocks. "Someone would have to go downstairs and find them, and bring them back up to the top," the cinematographer recalls.

McTiernan and de Bont also clashed at times. "Janny is very opinionated and very certain," says the director. "We used to scrap like cats and dogs, and terrorized the crew."[9] Creative sparks flew. "Jan and John were brilliant together, but sometimes brilliance has friction," says Marks. "They would clash but never [over] personal shit. It was just professional, trying to figure out how to get the best film that they could get."

Urioste recalls that McTiernan would annoy de Bont by doing extra takes that the cinematographer believed were unnecessary: "He'd do a close-up here, then he'd move in three inches, then another three inches. It was driving Jan crazy." Those multiple takes didn't reflect indecisiveness on McTiernan's part; he was thinking about what would be needed to cut the film together in the editing room. He wasn't entirely sure how much he could move the camera and still be able to cut from one moving shot to another. Even with Urioste willing to embrace the technique, there were limits—and McTiernan wasn't quite sure where they were. "For quite a while I was shooting alternate takes of most shots," says McTiernan. "I would shoot the move at a different speed so Frank [Urioste] could match the movement speed."

The methodical approach to shooting, though, was anathema to de Bont, who felt strongly that long breaks sap energy from the crew, and that lack of energy bleeds into the visuals. "Quite often I just got the camera and shot handheld," he says. "I just ran like Bruce through the building, and if things weren't quite ready, I'd just avoid those areas or make them darker. It creates more energy, and I thought this movie was going to be so dependent on that continuous energy."

De Bont's athletic method was no mean feat given that he was using Panavision cameras much heavier than the lightweight machines of today. "My elbows were killing me with lifting a seventy-five-pound camera all day long," says de Bont. When he wasn't dashing off with a camera on his shoulder, de Bont often opted to operate the camera using a mini jib arm, a device on wheels that made the camera almost weightless and let him quickly tilt it, pan it, or raise it smoothly up to nine feet in the air. "I like to connect actors with action in the same shot, not cutting," he explains. "When I see an actor do something and react, I immediately pan the moving camera over to where the action has had an effect."

OPPOSITE AND TOP LEFT *John McClane takes control on the Nakatomi rooftop.*

TOP RIGHT *Harry Ellis looks on as the McClanes embrace.*

ABOVE *Bruce Willis takes a moment between shots.*

WORKING WITH WILLIS

In the early days of the shoot, McTiernan was also facing issues with his leading man. "We had a sort of difficulty early, first week or two," he says. The star was overriding the director's carefully planned blocking—the actors' positions in relation to the camera in any given scene. "Bruce kept reblocking, which drove me up the wall. I had a whole visual concerto [that I'd worked out] . . . and he'd say, 'No, I don't think he'd stand there, I think he'd stand over here.' And he kept doing this stuff to us. I couldn't figure out what the fuck was going on."

Thankfully, Joel Silver—"who can say anything to anyone," says McTiernan—solved the problem by addressing Willis directly. "Finally, he got it out of him. Bruce was having thinning hair problems and he didn't ever want to stand where there was some light coming through behind his head that might reveal his thinning hair. . . . Once we realized it, we said, 'Don't you know it's our business to take care of that! By the time we'd got this lit, there isn't going to be any light coming through your hair. It's our job to make you look good.'" Willis soon relented. "That was a major accomplishment on Joel's part," adds McTiernan.

In truth, Willis had other worries. From an acting standpoint, *Die Hard* was a major challenge for him, as it would've been for any actor. With multiple scenes featuring McClane alone, with no other actors for Willis to bounce off, the role required the sort of internal acting that he'd rarely been asked to do on-screen. "It's a different way of working, it really is," he says. "This part was a lot harder than just about anything [I'd] done, for a lot of reasons. That was one of them. It's a different way of working. You have to bring it all inside yourself."[10]

ABOVE *Bruce Willis gets ready for a close-up.*

OPPOSITE *John McTiernan directs Willis as John McClane loots his latest casualty.*

He needed help, particularly during the scene when McClane is talking to Al Powell over a walkie-talkie while painfully picking glass out of his feet (the result of treading on shards following a shootout in the computer room). Willis asked for VelJohnson to be flown out early to Los Angeles before he was due on set, so he could have his costar there to read his lines. "Whenever he was talking to Al Powell, he wanted me there," says VelJohnson. "So I was right there in the room with him."

The shooting schedule was very much built around Willis, who initially had a hiatus from *Moonlighting* before the show restarted in the New Year. "We had a very small window," remembers Marks. The plan was to shoot Willis first, then focus on the scenes that didn't require him. "He only had these six weeks, through Christmas and New Year's, and then he was gone," says Silver. "So we had all of his stuff inside the building, which we could shoot during the six weeks. Then all the stuff outside the building, another six weeks."[11]

After Christmas, the plan was to shoot without Willis, capturing the exterior scenes with the cops and FBI on the ground and moments involving the terrorists and hostages. Willis would then have to return for the sequences at the end of the film, after the Nakatomi atrium is destroyed. De Govia's team would have to completely redress the atrium set to look decimated, so those scenes could only be shot later on, once all the other atrium scenes were completed.

The film's night shoots were so physically demanding on Willis that the role began to take its toll. De Souza remembers, "John [McTiernan] came to me and said, 'Look, we're killing this guy, he's coming to me and he's more and more exhausted.'" To give Willis some nights off to recuperate, McTiernan asked de Souza to expand the roles of some of the peripheral characters and add new scenes.

De Souza's rewrites also led to some additional terrorists being added to Hans's gang. "It made the film much richer as a result," he says. Playing new addition Uli is Al Leong, primarily a stuntman who'd been in the Silver-produced *Action Jackson* and *Lethal Weapon*. "We actually shot one week out of the twelve," Leong remembers, "because they were rewriting the whole script." He even helped out, suggesting to McTiernan that Uli filch a candy bar in one memorable moment.

The terrorist Eddie was also added to the script. Played by Dennis Hayden, another *Action Jackson* star, Eddie was originally set to be killed off early on, until Hayden had a chance meeting with de Souza's sister-in-law, publicist Bobbi Marcus. "I said, if you can get Steven to make me the last person Bruce Willis kills instead of the first, I'll hire you as my publicist," recalls Hayden. A week later it was done. "I just made Eddie the last man standing," shrugs De Souza.

Since he was now required on set for the duration of the shoot, the Kansas-born Hayden got to hang out with Willis, who spent his downtime trying to crack up the guys on set. "[Willis] had this smile on his face," Hayden says. "I call it a shit-eating grin. He's thinking something funny all the time. So he gets up and he's doing a whole comedy act, and we'd all be playing around, and he'd go, 'C'mon! Tough crowd!'"

ABOVE *Dennis Hayden is gun-ready as Gruber gang member Eddie.*

BELOW *The McClane family portraits stored inside John McClane's wallet.*

OPPOSITE *McClane under attack from Gruber's men.*

INSERT *A series of prop photos of the McClane family minus John, created by the production.*

le the henchmen were hanging out, Sylvester Stallone visited Joel Silver
es me from the [*Action Jackson*] trailers," says Hayden, "but he acts like
st walks up, he looks straight at me, and he goes, 'Hey.' And I looked up
t, 'Hey.' Bruce was still a young actor and Stallone was this major star, so
me after he walks by and says, 'You know *Stallone*?'" Hayden just looked
olly went, "Hey."

Willis continued to work well together throughout the shoot. The argument
d Holly when McClane first arrives at Nakatomi Plaza resulted from Willis
sing in front of the writer. "I took notes and then rewrote [the scene] and
nprovements," he reveals.

recalls coming home from a full day on the set, only to get a call at 2:00
e said, 'You gotta come right back!'" For the scene where McClane crawls
the production team had purchased a real vent, rather than building a
to fit Willis's frame. Unfortunately, it was so tight the actor took an age to
needed more lines to pad out the scene. De Souza rushed back to the
iven a walkie-talkie. Willis, in turn, was given a receiver with an earpiece
-camera, and the two of them improvised dialogue. De Souza fed Willis
waves, while Willis came up with a few zingers of his own, including the
I know what a TV dinner feels like."

HERE'S HANS

When Alan Rickman arrived on set, he wasn't thinking of anything but his character. "I was just fighting for the story," he said. "I was doing all I knew how to do." In other words, he was doing basic character work on Gruber in order to fully flesh out the role. In the script, there was little information about Hans other than that he was a former revolutionary expelled from the West German Volksfrei Movement. Rickman wanted to know more. "Where was he born? How did he grow up? What was the backstory?"

OPPOSITE *Hans Gruber stands by the office directory from which he borrows the "Bill Clay" name.*

ABOVE *Alan Rickman and Bruce Willis in the Bill Clay scene.*

Rickman instinctively grew into the role, adding elements that weren't in the script. During the scene where Hans informs the Nakatomi employees that the murdered Takagi won't be joining them "for the rest of his life," Rickman perched himself on a buffet table and improvised a moment where Hans helps himself to some Christmas party food. "Why don't I eat a sandwich? There's some food. He's hungry," he reasoned. McTiernan laughed. "But he let me do it," said Rickman.

One of the actor's most significant contributions was a result of his own versatility. When he arrived on set, Rickman was asked if he could do an American accent. "He said, 'Well I don't know if I actually do an American accent, but I sort of do a California accent,'" recalls de Souza. Rickman tried it out and got a laugh from the filmmakers. Along with being entertaining, his impersonation immediately fired de Souza's imagination about a script problem he'd been wrestling with. One of the issues in Stuart's draft was that Hans and McClane never met face-to-face until the very end of the film. "Steve just said, 'There's something you've got to do in a movie like this: The hero and the villain have got to meet each other somewhere,'" remembers McTiernan. "And we scratched our heads and said, 'Yeah, Steve, I think you're right!'" The problem was, in terms of story logic, if they met face-to-face, surely Hans would kill McClane or McClane would kill or arrest Hans. Game over.

In Thorp's book, Joe Leland sees Anton Gruber kill the Klaxon Oil executive, while Stuart's script had John McClane secretly witness Hans shoot Takagi dead, which made any

subsequent encounter impossible, as McClane would instantly recognize Hans. The solution lay partly in Stuart's drafts, which saw McClane encounter Hans's terrorist cohort Theo, who pretends to be one of the hostages, "Bill Clay," to keep his real identity secret. McClane even lends him a gun, which he soon turns on McClane. But McClane is playing him; the gun is empty and McClane takes Theo out with a submachine gun burst.

When Rickman performed his California accent, de Souza realized that he could substitute Hans for Theo in that scene. Hans could pretend to be the American Bill Clay and fool McClane long enough for them to have a scene together. The screenwriter pulled Rickman, Silver, and McTiernan aside and asked Rickman to do his American voice. "See! Now Bruce can meet him," de Souza said excitedly.

McTiernan was intrigued. Fortunately, the killing of Takagi hadn't yet been shot and was planned for the next day. De Souza asked if there was a way to shoot it so McClane wouldn't see Hans's face. The producers, McTiernan, and de Souza looked at the boardroom set and saw that if they rearranged the table, McClane's view of Hans would be blocked.

McTiernan told de Souza to go write the new Hans-McClane scene and bring it back at the end of the day. "I threw somebody out of the closest office," says de Souza. "It was the first time I had used a typewriter in three or four years. But I wrote the scene."

Again, there was a ripple effect on the script. In de Souza's version, the scene moved later in the film. It also meant that Theo could be used as Hans's computer expert, helping him crack the vault. Theo's comeuppance was also moved much later, when he suffers a humiliating knockout blow from Argyle in the building's basement car park.

The last-minute addition of the McClane-Hans encounter was a particular challenge for Jan de Bont. "This is really about [Hans and McClane], and it shouldn't be about anything else," says the cinematographer. "How can you make the audience feel the tension they both have?" As the scene was set on the Fox building's thirty-fifth floor, with the actors surrounded by machinery belching steam, de Bont didn't have much choice but to shoot in close-up, because there was no space to position the camera farther away. Nevertheless, the camera blocking worked out well. "The narrowness of the space, the almost claustrophobic space, made it even more suspenseful and exciting in a way," says de Bont.

The scene also includes an in-joke. Along with the name Clay, which Hans borrows as his alias, the directory on the wall behind him features several crewmembers' surnames, including de Souza, De Govia, and de Bont, among others. "Everybody who worked on that movie is on that list," says de Souza.

When it came to shooting the scene, McTiernan actually filmed several takes because he wasn't entirely convinced by Rickman's American dialect and felt he could hear his English accent come through. Rickman, though, felt it "was a great acting opportunity," playing a German character who is faking an American accent.

Apart from the challenges of nailing the accent, the scene featured a piece of physical action that nearly knocked Rickman out of *Die Hard* altogether. Prior to meeting McClane, Hans has to scale up a wall to check the explosives that his crew has planted. But while performing a moment where he jumps down from a ledge, landing at Willis's bare feet, Rickman felt something crack in his knee. The actor went to see a doctor straight away. "They said, 'We won't know until tomorrow whether you've torn a ligament'—in which case I would be out of the movie—'or a cartilage,' in which case it'll sort itself out. 'In the meantime, don't put any weight on that leg.'" On crutches and with his leg in plaster, Rickman went back up to the thirty-third floor to continue shooting the scene where McClane and "Bill Clay" take a cigarette break. When the elevator door opened, Joel Silver was standing there. "I remember him looking at me and he just said, 'Can we lose the crutches for the next shot?' True story," said Rickman. For the moment when Hans turns the gun on McClane, Rickman actually had to stand on one leg so as not to put any weight on his damaged limb. Thankfully, the next morning, the doctors determined it was torn cartilage and told him he'd make a quick recovery.

OPPOSITE TOP *John McTiernan and Bruce Willis on the computer room set.*

OPPOSITE BOTTOM *Hans Gruber spies an opportunity.*

TOP AND ABOVE *Filming the Bill Clay sequence in the steamy confines of the thirty-fifth floor.*

BELOW *Willis films the Takagi murder sequence, augmented so his character is unable to get a good look at Gruber.*

Rickman was convinced early on that he was going to be replaced. "Stories came to my ears that there were concerns in the early days of rushes. . . . I think they [the studio executives] weren't sure what I was doing." While Silver thought Rickman was "magnetic" when he saw him on stage, the studio was less than impressed when the footage of the Bill Clay scene came in. "That's the first stuff the studio saw," says Silver. "There was a casting girl . . . and she said, 'We can't have this guy be the bad guy, he's just too weak. Look how weak he is!' I said, 'But that's the scene.' So we had this battle about keeping him in the movie. She was on a campaign to fire this guy. But these things happen."[12] Another who stuck up for Rickman was Jan de Bont, the actor recalled. "It was Jan who said, when he's looking down the lens of the camera, 'No, no, leave him alone. There's something interesting going on here.'"

Rickman survived these early scares to stamp his authority on the role. Hans's speech to the Nakatomi staff in which he seeks out Joe Takagi among the hostages was shot early in the schedule, and marked the first time many of the cast had seen Rickman acting. Leong, who plays Uli but considers himself first and foremost a stuntman, was taken aback by Rickman's languid, methodical delivery.

"It was so strange," says Leong, "but it seemed like he was talking so slow. I'm not an actor but still I watch a lot of actors act, and I'm watching him on the set and I'm saying, 'Why is this guy talking so slow? They can't use this.'" But Andreas Wisniewski, playing Tony, understood at once that Rickman was creating "a great civilized villain." He adds, "He was so skillful, and he was so unusual. There'd always be stuff that was unexpected and fresh." Coming in the wake of the terrifying office invasion, replete with gunfire, Rickman's icy, almost diffident delivery added stomach-churning tension to the scene.

"He was a masterful actor," reflects Hart Bochner, who got his chance to go mano a mano with Rickman in a scene where Ellis foolishly tries to negotiate with Hans before inevitably meeting his demise. "He was so charming and affable, but you know, there's an edge to that performance. Behind that charm are the eyes of a killer."

Both actors were encouraged to improvise during that scene. "Bouncing things back and forth with somebody like that was absolutely joyous, " says Bochner, who added the word *bubbe* to a line in the script where Ellis tries to ingratiate himself with the terrorist leader, saying, "Hans, bubbe, I'm your white knight." The actor pitched the idea to Silver, suggesting that having Ellis throw around a little Yiddish would be funny. "Joel said, 'Do it, do it!'" says Bochner. "I said, 'Do you like *bubbe* or do you like *boychik*? He said, 'Do the bubbe one.'"

Rickman was popular with others in the cast too. Dennis Hayden (Eddie) had performed in a lot of live theater in Los Angeles, and the two bonded over their stage experience. Hayden remembers that after Rickman read one of Silver's upcoming scripts, *Road House*, he suggested to Hayden that he might be right for one of the supporting roles. Rickman even pushed the idea with Silver. But when Hayden eventually got in a room with Patrick Swayze, who was set to play the lead, it fell apart. "They put us in this little bitty room together," says Hayden, "and I was just so much bigger than Swayze, he just went, 'Nah, it ain't gonna work.'"

Wisniewski also struck up a lifelong friendship with Rickman, who taught him some valuable lessons about acting, including what to do when a director demands an action that doesn't seem true to the character. "Alan was great at how to wrangle his way through this, keep his authenticity, and still satisfy what was asked," says Wisniewski.

Willis, too, was greatly impressed with his costar, feeling Rickman delivered one of the greatest villains of all time and lamenting the lack of acclaim for exceptional performances in big-budget action movies. "Somehow action films seem to have this taint," he says. "There's this misconception that they require less work and that they don't really match up to a dramatic film. I think Alan Rickman should have been nominated for an Academy Award. He did a great acting job in that film."[13]

LEFT AND FAR LEFT *Hysteria hits the office as the Gruber gang rounds up the Nakatomi personnel.*

BELOW *Hans Gruber and Karl show their authority.*

FIGHT NIGHT

Die Hard's stunt team was led by stunt coordinator Charles Picerni, who began his career working on television perennials such as *The Untouchables*, *Kojak*, and *Starsky & Hutch*. It was his job to choreograph the film's fight sequences. "I try [to] put myself in that situation," he says. "Not just a Hollywood fight. What would I do if I was locked up in that building, how would I get out? That's what I envisioned."

Picerni's immersion in the project gave a real, visceral quality to the fights, notably during McClane's brutal encounter with Tony in which the two men tumble down the stairs, leaving Tony with a snapped neck. Keii Johnston doubled for Willis during the scene, while Andy Epper took the place of Wisniewski. "I think it took two, maybe even three stuntmen, because this was a very, very dangerous stunt," says Wisniewski. "I mean the first one threw his shoulder out and had to be replaced. It's that sort of thing. You do one take and you're out for a month or something. I mean, what a job."

The climactic scrap between McClane and Tony's brother Karl was another Picerni-driven fight. Again, the violence seems raw and real, with McClane head-butting and punching Karl, smashing his face into pipes and finally strangling him to (apparent) death with a chain. "I choreographed the whole thing," Picerni says. Johnston and Don McGovern, who doubled for Alexander Godunov, rehearsed the moves, although it was Picerni who demonstrated it to McTiernan, Willis, and Silver. Recalls Picerni, "Joel says, 'That's it! You double Bruce! You double Bruce!' I said, 'No, Joel. It'll work out fine. Keii will do it. And that's how we did it. Bruce, he saw what I was doing, he got right into it and it was terrific. That fight was one of the best fights I choreographed . . . and Bruce did a lot himself."

OPPOSITE TOP AND OPPOSITE BOTTOM LEFT *Bruce Willis and Andreas Wisniewski fight it out.*

LEFT AND OPPOSITE BOTTOM RIGHT *Stuntmen Keii Johnston and Andy Epper do battle before taking a tumble down the stairs.*

ABOVE *John McClane takes a swing at Karl.*

For numerous scenes, the actors were fitted with squibs—controlled miniature explosions rigged with blood pouches that simulate the gory impact of bullets into flesh. Picerni tutored all the actors on how to work with squibs, "[to] prepare them and make sure that when the squib goes off, they don't have their hands in front of them. Little things that you can get hurt with, and thank God, nobody got hurt on the movie." At least, not seriously hurt, that is.

Picerni's stuntman son, Steve Picerni, proved crucial during the shootout in the computer room scene that follows the Bill Clay sequence. The elevator door opens, revealing Karl, Fritz, and Franco. McClane kills Fritz and then shoots Franco in both knees, sending him tumbling through a glass door. "John wanted him to go headfirst through this breakaway door. And my son did it . . . and it worked out terrific. Got a little cut on his eye but everything was pretty well planned," says Picerni. That "little cut" needed eleven stitches.

Jeb Stuart's original draft had the barefoot McClane accidentally step on fluorescent tubes, but during de Souza's rewrites, it changed so that Hans cannily directs Karl to shoot out the glass in the computer room, knowing McClane will have to run barefoot over the shards. Silver wanted this part of the sequence to be as spectacular as possible. He turned to Al Di Sarro, *Die Hard*'s special effects coordinator, who like so many on the film had worked with the producer on *Action Jackson* and *Predator*. As Di Sarro recalled, Silver said to him, "Aldo, this whole room is about glass. I want to see it all gone! Flying in the air!"[14]

ABOVE *Alexander Godunov's Karl takes cover in the Nakatomi Plaza computer room.*

OPPOSITE TOP *John McClane lets rip with his Heckler & Koch MP5.*

BELOW *All hell breaks loose during the filming of the computer room shootout.*

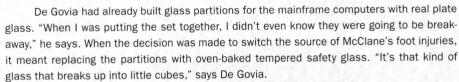

De Govia had already built glass partitions for the mainframe computers with real plate glass. "When I was putting the set together, I didn't even know they were going to be break-away," he says. When the decision was made to switch the source of McClane's foot injuries, it meant replacing the partitions with oven-baked tempered safety glass. "It's that kind of glass that breaks up into little cubes," says De Govia.

Di Sarro, who ran different tests to determine how the glass would blow and where it would fall, estimated the production went through around $130,000 of glass. He even arranged for a specialist glass company to stay open after hours. "He woke up somebody," says De Govia. "Los Angeles is the best place in the world to do stuff like this." Within a matter of hours, a team came to carefully install the special glass.

Fortunately, because the plan had always been that Willis would walk over broken glass in some form, protection for the actor's feet had already been created. Silicone booties were made from a life cast of Willis's feet, and between six and eight pairs were fabricated. Made of latex with an impervious hard-rubber sole, "they were like slippers, but they would completely fit his feet," says makeup supervisor Scott Eddo, another veteran from the Silver stable. Eddo's makeup team would blend them with Willis's skin on the set. "They were rubberized, he could stretch them over. They only went above the ankles, so when he put them on he was standing right in front of you barefoot. You would swear [he was barefoot]." Of course, Willis's uncovered feet were shot during close-ups, but for any medium shots, out came the booties.

The skills of Eddo's artists were also required in the gorier moments, often at a moment's notice. For the scene in which McClane picks broken glass from his soles after running over shattered plate glass, "we created the gash in the bottom of his foot," Eddo says.

Normally on a film featuring numerous bloody lacerations, prosthetics are prebuilt, fitted, and tested, and the shooting schedule includes time to apply them. "On *Die Hard* we were running more like a 'conversation' feature film, where people sit and talk and they just keep rolling the cameras," Eddo explains. "We didn't take a lot of time out to shift the camera somewhere else and go shoot something else while we prepared a gag. It just wasn't built in that way." McTiernan and de Bont wanted that kind of fluid shooting, but it meant there wasn't prep time for makeup effects. "You just grab it out of your box and you make it work. You take your makeup kit, you open it up at the feet of the actors, and you build something real quick, and you shoot it."

The guns were also a crucial part of *Die Hard*. Silver sent property master Tommy Tomlinson and weapons specialist Michael Papac to research the most up-to-date weaponry used by terrorists. Hans is seen using a Heckler & Koch P7 MI3, Karl brandishes a Steyr AUG assault rifle, and the others use Heckler & Koch MP5 9mm submachine guns. McClane was outfitted with a Beretta 92. Papac, who used blank loads on the noisier end of the scale, even fitted plugs inside the gun barrels to restrict the airflow, making the muzzle flashes more dramatic.

When it came to training the actors, the production turned to Bobby Bass, credited with special weapons training. "You'll never find another gun master like Bobby Bass. He was an unbelievable guy," says Picerni. "This guy instructed people in the army. . . . When [the actors] first started firing, they jumped, but then they got used to it. And that's what I wanted them to do, get used to having that machine gun like it was part of their body."

Some of the actors took to it. "We'd go through these drills, like you'd go through a house and they have pop-up targets and things like that," says Hayden. "I'm just somersaulting, coming up, throwing clips out, loading the gun, and take out every target. Just having fun, you know, to me, I'm just being a kid. I'm like thirty-five years old at the time."

ABOVE AND TOP RIGHT *Bruce Willis between takes as the barefoot and bloodied John McClane.*

OPPOSITE *Scott Eddo applies bloody makeup to the soles of Willis's feet.*

PAGES 72–73 *Willis and the crew prepare to shoot the bathroom sequence.*

Godunov said that he couldn't get the sense of power out of his mind: "It was strange because I was comfortable with the gun, and it made me uncomfortable knowing that."[15] Silver even told him, "You look like a professional now." Others were less at ease. Rickman found the computer room shootout especially difficult. "The most challenging thing was not to blink or flinch at the noise and the power of it," he said, "because you'd have looked like a wimp and you're supposed to know what you're doing."

The residents of Fox Plaza were also not thrilled by the sound of gunshots. "One particular big law firm . . . it was about four floors down from where we were," says McTiernan. "They were hugely annoyed that we were making noise. Being lawyers, their annoyance was accompanied with all sorts of threats, so we had to dance around a lot about when we could do gunfire and not do gunfire."

The production team was forced to compromise. "Because there was a lot of gun firing and explosions and whatnot, we could only do that after hours in the building," says Marks. "So we worked out a way of shooting half days, half nights." As McTiernan explains, "We'd go to work at noon, or maybe two in the afternoon, and we'd work to midnight or two in the morning, so you never have that situation of workers going home in the morning and seeing the sunlight. Their world was completely upside down."

The production also created black frames from plexiglass to block the windows, allowing them to film night scenes when it was daylight outside. "It was these sorts of tricks we did all the way through," says Marks.

Even fake guns were causing problems on the set. One day, during a sequence being shot in the building's basement, Marks got a call from the Secret Service. The outgoing President Ronald Reagan, who had an office in the Fox Plaza building, was paying a visit. "They said, 'You cannot have any weapons, anything that could possibly be a threat to the president.'" Marks complied, and all the prop guns were stowed away. Later, he received a second call: The Secret Service had spotted someone stealing an assault weapon from one of the prop trucks and arrested him. A crewmember had decided to take a replica weapon. "This dumb guy picked the wrong day to steal!" says Marks.

DRIVE-BYS

Although the stunt team took on the film's most dangerous moments, there were some scenes where the actors performed their own action. Most notably, in the sequence where McClane drops Marco onto the hood of Sgt. Powell's police cruiser, causing Al to reverse at top speed, VelJohnson actually drove the car. "He's not a superhero," says McTiernan of the character. "He was just a guy doing the best he can. So I deliberately . . . made it goofy, [as he] drives out backward and crashes over the wall."

The camera department had made a meticulous plan to film Powell's frantic escape. In addition to the wide shots that would capture the car speeding backward, they rigged cameras so they could also get coverage of VelJohnson's reactions inside the car. One camera was set up outside the car looking in, another in the back seat, shooting over VelJohnson's shoulder. To ensure the actor's face would be properly lit, lights were fitted where the sun visor would normally be. The only issue was that VelJohnson was no stunt driver and wasn't even aware that he was going to be required to drive the car during the scene.

VelJohnson remembers being in the makeup trailer when McTiernan came to him and said, "We want you to do this stunt, OK? You think you can do it?" VelJohnson was afraid to say no. He was new to big movies, eager to please. "I knew I had to do this part well or it was all over," he says. "[McTiernan] promised me they would strap me in securely, where it would be impossible for me to get hurt. And they did that." In the end, he managed it in two takes. "I did [it], and I'm very proud of that. They strapped me in, I was terrified, but I did my own stunt. People don't believe that I did it, but I really did my own stunt."

TOP AND OPPOSITE *Sgt. Al Powell's police car reversing at top speed after Marco's body lands on the hood.*

ABOVE *Marco meets a grim end, shot through the boardroom table by John McClane.*

INSERT *A set plan offers a bird's-eye view of Fox Plaza's grounds. This illustration was used for planning a number of exterior scenes, including Al Powell's frantic escape.*

Another major vehicle stunt required stunt coordinator Charles Picerni to get behind the wheel of an armored SWAT vehicle. After speeding down the street, the armored vehicle needed to ram up the stairs outside Fox Plaza (before the terrorists blow it up with a rocket launcher). The production team built the central rail that the vehicle crushes as it ascends the stairs and covered the whole area with boards painted to look like the stone flooring, to protect the real surface underneath. With Silver and various Fox executives looking on, Picerni was told not to damage the real Fox Plaza outer railings as he drove the vehicle up the stairs. "If I hit this rail, I'm gone," he says. "I had about a foot on each side." With the evening's darkness impairing vision even further, Picerni refused to delegate to another stuntman. "I wanted to take the responsibility," he says. "And I got up it and it was perfect."

To create the effect of the rocket launcher blowing up the armored vehicle, a fake missile was attached to a solid-fuel rocket engine and fired down a piano wire to the vehicle from a floor above. (The wire was treated with acid so it wouldn't shine and show up on camera.) A gasoline explosion was rigged beneath the tank, and black powder was used to detonate it. The scene was shot several times, but fortunately the vehicle chosen was robust enough to withstand the pyrotechnics. "A tank's a tank," said Di Sarro. "It won't be too affected by a fireball."[16]

OPPOSITE *Driven by Charles Picerni, the SWAT vehicle mounts the Fox Plaza stairs.*

ABOVE *Al Di Sarro's special effects team sets off a dramatic explosion at Fox Plaza.*

LEFT *The SWAT vehicle explodes after a direct hit from a rocket launcher.*

NIGHT TERRORS

As impressive as Picerni's SWAT vehicle stunt was, the production had an even more auda-cious sequence planned for the moment where two FBI helicopters arrive, responding to the unfolding terrorist incident. Flying below the roof level of the skyscrapers, one chopper circles the rooftop of the Nakatomi building, where McClane and the hostages have gathered. Staged at Fox Plaza and the surrounding streets in Century City, it was a remarkably daring stunt. "For those helicopters to fly and make those tight turns . . . that was really dangerous," says Jan de Bont. Nevertheless, it was Silver who encouraged his pilots to get the skids of the helicopters to skim through the water on the street fountains. "I said, 'I want you to get as close to the deck as you can,'" says the producer.[17]

It had taken months of arranging permits and chairing planning meetings to get the local authorities on board. "Century City decided they would give us a week to shoot the scene, every night for a week," says Beau Marks, whom McTiernan credits as the man who planned out the sequence. "And the studio came down and said, 'We do not want you inconveniencing [the local] community, 'cause this is where we live.'"

Because Fox was so worried about upsetting the neighbors, Marks and McTiernan opted to shoot the whole sequence over the course of one Sunday night. The helicopters had an assigned route among and around the buildings. Twelve cameras were stationed along Constellation Boulevard, Century Park East, and Avenue of the Stars. "We had to plan it like crazy," says McTiernan. "And each cameraman had a list of shots he was supposed to get, and we had the time to run the helicopters through the action three times. In order to do some-thing like that, with helicopters that low, you have to clear everything from within five hundred feet of the flight path and every single human being underneath it has to be somebody you are paying, [and they need to have] stunt training and safety training. You don't just fly over the city. So it was an enormous undertaking."

With the FBI helicopters—two Vietnam-era Hueys flown by Picerni's nephews—accompanied by two camera ships, the plan was for the choppers to fly down the street, then

ABOVE *The crew prepares for the FBI helicopter scene, flying two choppers through Century City and over the heads of a group of extras playing hostages.*

OPPOSITE TOP AND OPPOSITE CENTER *The choppers take flight over Century City.*

OPPOSITE BOTTOM *Director John McTiernan looks on nervously as preparations are made.*

up and over Fox Plaza, where extras were gathered on the roof, playing hostages. But after the first take, McTiernan started to get concerned about the safety of the operation. Just five years earlier, a fatal accident involving a Vietnam War–era helicopter on the set of *Twilight Zone: The Movie* had rocked the industry, and the memory was still fresh. "I was on the top of the building, and when the helicopter came in the first time and hovered over the crowd of extras we had in there, it terrified me," says McTiernan. "It just scared the shit out of me. One of the few times of my life in the movie business, I bottled out. I said, 'That's it, we got it!' I knew I had the shots I needed." For the next two runs, the helicopters didn't come near the top of the building.

Because of the short schedule in Century City, the plan had always been to shoot more angles of the helicopter in a less populated location: Marc Veluzat's Diamond V Movie Ranch in Santa Clarita, some thirty-five miles north. The ranch was a remote haven for filming where insert shots of a chopper against a night sky could be captured safely, and without intense time pressure. Scaffolding was erected to place the camera ten feet above the desert floor so that the shot would not be clouded by the dust kicked up by the rotor blades.

While the chopper shots had to be immaculately choreographed, the studio-shot scenes inside the helicopters featuring FBI agents Johnson and Johnson were another matter. Inside the chopper, Robert Davi's Big Johnson whoops and yells, "Just like fuckin' Saigon, eh, slick?"—as McTiernan puts it, "glorying back to his days in Vietnam." Grand Bush's Little Johnson wryly replies, "I was in junior high, dickhead." Bush's retort was an inspired moment thought up by the director, who took Bush aside and whispered the line in his ear. "When I said that line, the look of dismay on Davi's face was solid gold," chuckles Bush. "Davi never broke character, and McTiernan loved every second of it."

OPPOSITE TOP LEFT *Helicopter inserts are shot at the Diamond V Movie Ranch in Santa Clarita.*

OPPOSITE TOP RIGHT AND BOTTOM *The chopper interior shot on the Fox soundstages with Robert Davi as Big Johnson.*

LEFT *Stand-ins for the principal actors on the helicopter interior set.*

BELOW *Director John McTiernan (seated) looks on as the helicopter interior set is prepped.*

HO-HO-HOSE

John McClane's fire hose jump is one of the most iconic moments in *Die Hard*. It comes shortly after McClane arrives on the building roof, where the hostages have been amassed. Realizing that Hans's crew have rigged the top of the building to explode, he fires his gun into the air, scaring the hostages back downstairs. Thinking quick, he grabs a fire hose, wraps it around his waist, and jumps from the roof just as Hans detonates the explosives. The hose's metal spool wedges against the ledge, allowing him to swing into the plateglass window below, which he takes out with bullet fire before crashing feetfirst into a Nakatomi office.

Originally, Picerni remembers, the plan was to shoot the stunt entirely on a soundstage. But after scouting the rooftop of the Fox Plaza building with McTiernan, where they even spotted a fire hose, Picerni became convinced that much of the sequence could be done on location. "I got so excited, I said, 'John, we could do it right here.' I jumped up on the ledge, thirty stories up. He got all upset: 'Get off the ledge, get off the ledge!'"

Sure enough, the main part of the sequence—a long shot of McClane falling and then dangling from the side of the building on the hose—was no special effect. "That was done on the Fox Plaza building and that was real," confirms Picerni. "We jumped right off that. It was a breathtaking situation." Stuntman Ken Bates used a decelerator to actually swing from the top of the building. With the stuntman on wires and his weight controlled by a pulley system, the decelerator safely simulates a free fall. "The decelerator mechanism will kick in about fifty feet off the ground," explains Picerni. "It will slow you down to a position where you can get out of [the fall]."

TOP *Filming the scene in which John McClane smashes through the office window.*

RIGHT *Storyboards illustrated by John L. Jensen show John McClane as he's dragged backward by the fire hose spool after firing his way through the Nakatomi glass window.*

OPPOSITE *Stuntman Ken Bates performs the fire hose stunt, dangling from the real Fox Plaza.*

PAGES 84–85 *Storyboards by John L. Jensen depict John McClane's dramatic rooftop escape.*

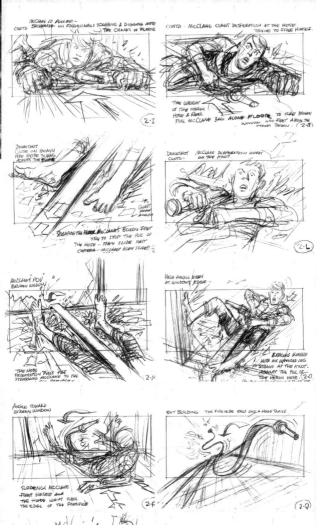

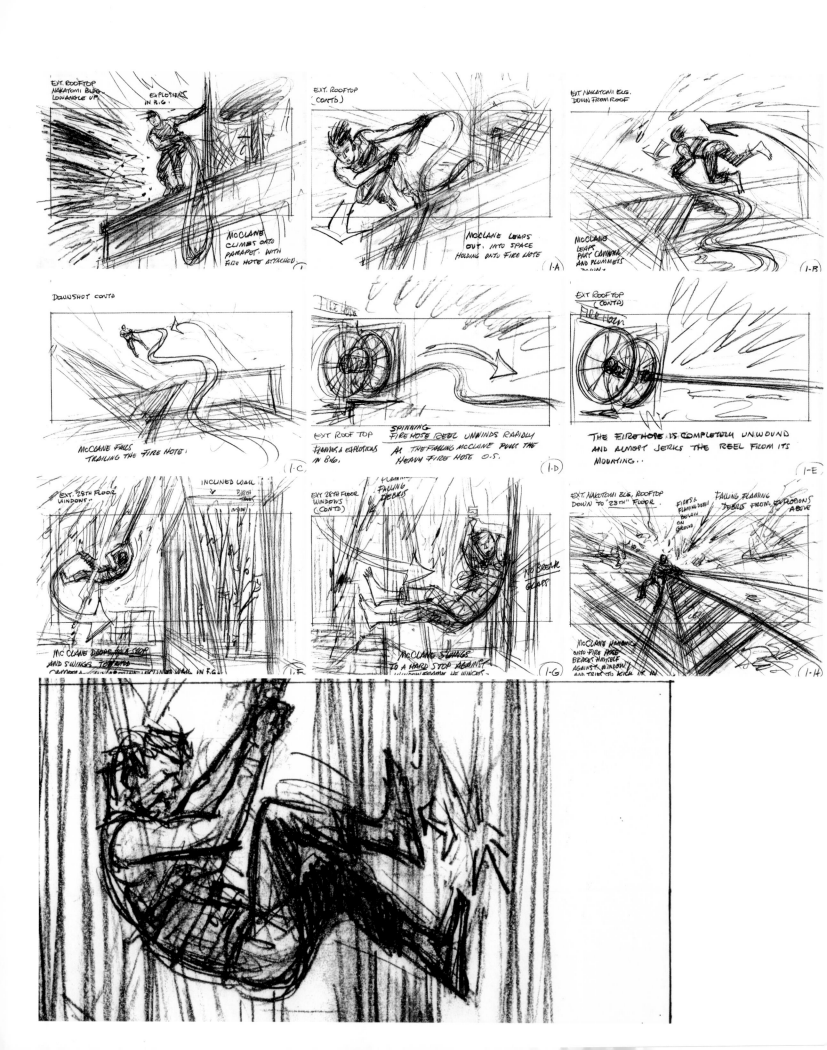

EXT. ROOFTOP
NAKATOMI BLDG.
LOW ANGLE UP

EXPLOSIONS
IN B.G.

MCCLANE
CLIMBS ONTO
PARAPET. WITH
FIRE HOSE ATTACHED.
(1)

EXT. ROOFTOP
(CONT'D)

MCCLANE LEAPS
OUT, INTO SPACE
HOLDING ONTO FIRE HOSE
(1-A)

EXT. NAKATOMI BLG.
DOWN FROM ROOF

MCCLANE
LEAPS
PAST CAMERA
AND PLUMMETS
DOWN ...
(1-B)

DOWNSHOT CONT'D

MCCLANE FALLS
TRAILING THE FIRE HOSE.
(1-C)

FIRE HOSE

EXT. ROOF TOP
FLAMES & EXPLOSIONS
IN B.G.

SPINNING
FIRE HOSE REEL UNWINDS RAPIDLY
AS THE FALLING MCCLANE PULL THE
HEAVY FIRE HOSE O.S.
(1-D)

EXT. ROOFTOP
(CONT'D)

FIRE HOSE

THE FIRE HOSE IS COMPLETELY UNWOUND
AND ALMOST JERKS THE REEL FROM ITS
MOUNTING ..
(1-E)

EXT. "28TH FLOOR
WINDOWS"

INCLINED WALL

BIRCH
TREES

INSIDE

MCCLANE DROPS IN A STOP
AND SWINGS TOWARD
CAMERA. SLAMS INTO THE INCLINED WALL IN F.G.
(1-F)

EXT. 28TH FLOOR
WINDOWS
(CONT'D)

FLAMING
FALLING
DEBRIS

NO BREAK
GLASS

MCCLANE SWINGS
TO A HARD STOP AGAINST
WINDOW FRAME. HE WINCES.
(1-G)

EXT. NAKATOMI BLG. ROOFTOP
DOWN TO "28TH" FLOOR

FIRE &
FLAMING DEBRIS
BELOW
ON
GROUND

FALLING FLAMING
DEBRIS FROM EXPLOSIONS
ABOVE

MCCLANE HANGING
ONTO FIRE HOSE
BRACES HIMSELF
AGAINST WINDOW
AND TRIES TO KICK IT IN.
(1-H)

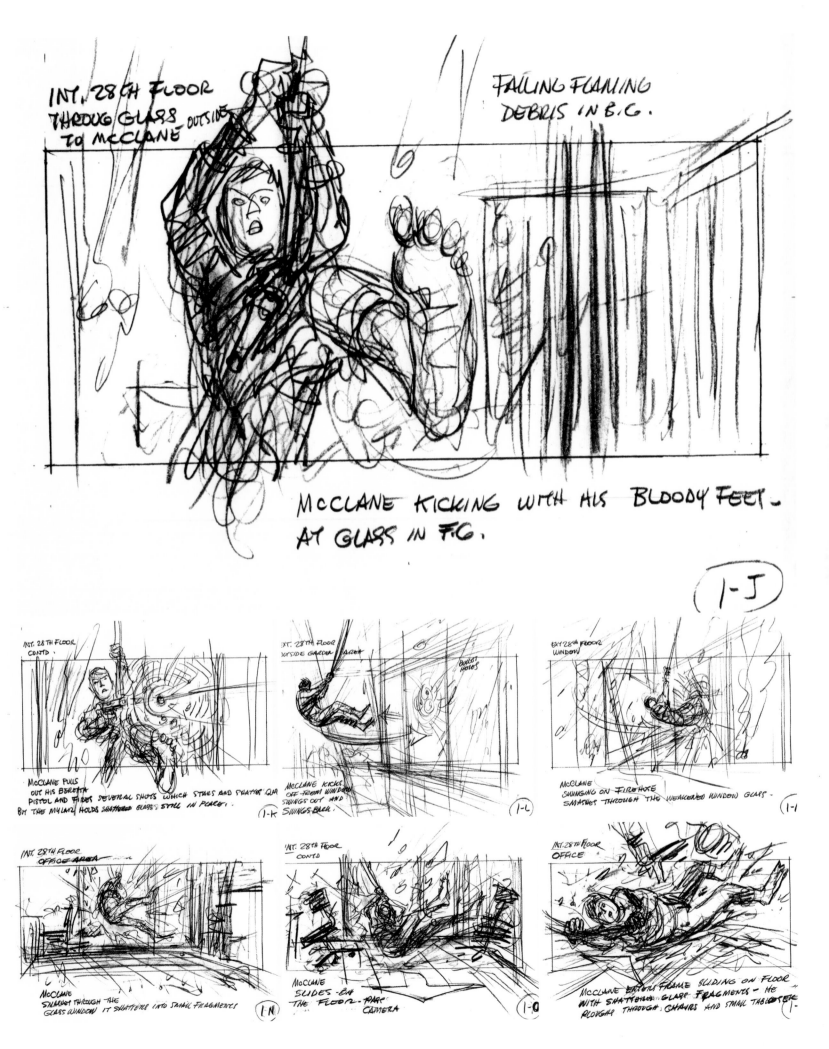

INT. 28TH FLOOR
THROUG GLASS OUTSIDE
TO MCCLANE

FALLING FLAMING
DEBRIS IN B.G.

MCCLANE KICKING WITH HIS BLOODY FEET.
AT GLASS IN F.G.

1-J

INT. 28TH FLOOR
CONTD.

MCCLANE PULLS
OUT HIS BERETTA
PISTOL AND FIRES SEVERAL SHOTS WHICH STARS AND SHATTERS GLASS
BUT THE MYLAR HOLDS SHATTERED GLASS STILL IN PLACE.

1-K

EXT. 28TH FLOOR
OUTSIDE GARDEN AREA

BULLET
HOLES

MCCLANE KICKS
OFF FROM WINDOW
SWINGS OUT AND
SWINGS BACK.

1-L

EXT. 28TH FLOOR
WINDOW

MCCLANE
SWINGING ON FIREHOSE
SMASHES THROUGH THE WEAKENED WINDOW GLASS.

1-1

INT. 28TH FLOOR
OFFICE AREA

MCCLANE
SMASHES THROUGH THE
GLASS WINDOW IT SHATTERS INTO SMALL FRAGMENTS

1-N

INT. 28TH FLOOR
CONTD

MCCLANE
SLIDES - BY
THE FLOOR. PAST
CAMERA

1-Q

INT. 28TH FLOOR
OFFICE

MCCLANE ENTERS FRAME SLIDING ON FLOOR
WITH SHATTERED GLASS FRAGMENTS - HE
PLOUGHS THROUGH CHAIRS AND SMALL TABLES ETC.

Bates was not the only person involved in selling this major stunt. Willis insisted on doing his own stunt work whenever possible. Noting that it adds "a lot of production value" to the film, with McTiernan able to get the camera in close, Willis felt that performing these kinds of stunts took him back to the New Jersey street kid he once was: "On a personal level, it satisfies the little boy who still lives in me who gets to shoot guns, kill the bad guys, and be a hero while doing jumps and swinging from ropes."[18]

Willis filmed the moment where McClane first jumps from the roof with the hose around his waste. This involved the actor leaping from one of the Fox lot's parking structures, which De Govia had dressed to look like the Nakatomi roof. Al Di Sarro rigged the roof with mortars, and Willis's back was padded and his exposed skin covered with protective gel to absorb the heat. The jump was twenty-five feet into an airbag. McTiernan and Silver both jumped first to prove how safe it was. As Willis made the spectacular leap, "All the way down," recalled Di Sarro, "I could hear him yelling, 'G-ddamn you, Aldoooooooo!'"[19]

Willis remembers it all too well. "When I jumped, the force of the explosion blew me out to the very edge of the airbag I was supposed to land on. And when I landed everyone came

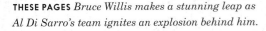

running over to me and I thought they were going to say, 'Great job! Attaboy!' And what they were doing is seeing if I'm alive because I almost missed the bag."[20]

The sequence where McClane, suspended from the fully extended fire hose, shoots his way through the plateglass window was shot on the Fox soundstages. Willis was attached to a large cable, allowing him to freely swing to and from the glass. For the moment where McClane actually comes through the glass, Keii Johnston doubled for Willis. As for the minor but memorable detail of McClane's bloody footprints smeared on the glass, McTiernan says, "It wasn't accidental. We deliberately did it to remind you in the middle of all of that—oh shit, his feet are still all cut up!"

Scott Eddo's makeup skills were also needed, when McClane smashes through the glass and is almost pulled back outside by the weight of the spool. "He's covered in blood, got glass cuts all over . . . there were no [prosthetic] pieces made for that. There was no nothing. Joel just decided that when we were ready to shoot. He said, 'When he comes through here, I want him all bloody. Cuts all over his back and his arms.' I looked at him kind of like, 'Hmm. That's what you want in twenty minutes?' That's how we rolled."

TOP LEFT AND OPPOSITE TOP *Bruce Willis filming on the damaged atrium set.*

LEFT *Willis and Joel Silver on the damaged atrium set.*

ABOVE *The Christmas wrapping tape and Beretta 92F props used for the scene in which John McClane takes Gruber by surprise.*

INSERT *Storyboards by John L. Jensen illustrate an unused scene in the destroyed atrium in which McClane has to dodge a swinging elevator car.*

DELETED
ATRUIM
SCENE

FLAMES
FROM FIRE
BALL

9

INT. 28TH FLOOR

BIG
ROO

FLAMES

TABLE ROCK

FLAMING
WRECKAGE CRASHES
THROUGH OUTSIDE WINDOWS
INTO GARDEN POOL AREA IN B.G. BLOCKS McCLANE'S
WAY PAST

FLAMES

WATER FALL

ROCK

FLAMES
FROM FIRE
BALL

④

LONG SHOT INT. GARDEN AREA - EXPLOSIONS RIP THROUGH CEILING

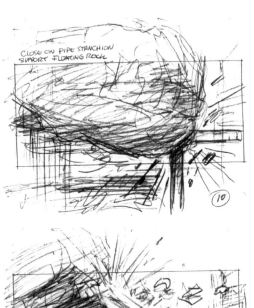

CLOSE ON PIPE STANCHION
SUPPORT FLOATING ROCK

⑩

CLOSE ON (CONTD)
PIPE STANCHION
FLOATING ROCK, AS IT BREAKS FREE
WATERFALL WATER JETS FROM
BROKEN PIPE STANCHION.

⑪

GARDEN POOL
AREA.

MCCLANE
RUNS THRU
POOL
AT THE
HUGE "FLOATING" ROCK FALLS BEHIND HIM

GARDEN POOL
CONT'D

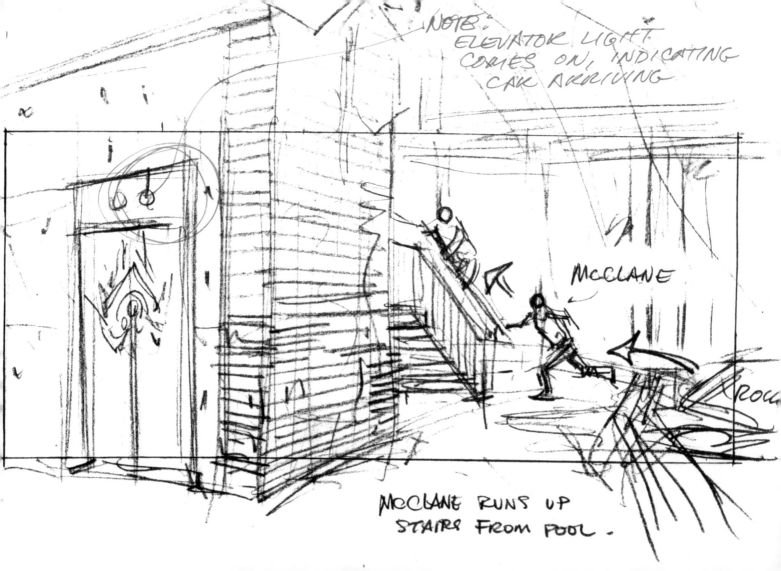

72L CONTD.
TAPE STILL ON GUN

MCCLANE FIRES HITS HANS IN HIS RIGHT NIPPLE. THE BULLET GOES THRU HIM STARRING THE WINDOW

472L CONTD HANS STARES INCREDULOUSLY.
TAPE JAMS MCCLANES GUN?
HOLLY TRIES TO BREAK FREE.

472M CLOSE ON MCCLANE
HE CLEARS HIS GUN
MCCLANE "GET OUT OF THE WAY HOLLY!"

472P
THE BULLET STRIKES HANS IN THE SHOULDER SPINNING HIM BACKWARDS TO THE STARRED WINDOW

472X BLEEDING WRIST
THE WRIST WATCH BAND SNAPS OPEN AND SLIDES OFF HOLLY'S WRIST.

472Z CONTD
HANS FALLS SCREAMING

72Z-1 CONTD

472Z-2 EXT WINDOW MCCLANE UP TO PULLS HOLLY AWAY

472Z-1 CONTD

CONTD
HANS FALLS WITH FALLING GLASS FROM WINDOW
NAKATOMI

FALL FROM GRACE

Like a modern-day *High Noon*, McClane's final face-off with Hans is one of *Die Hard*'s finest moments. McClane arrives to save Holly with his gun strapped on his back with tape (it was McTiernan's idea to use Christmas wrapping tape after he spotted it on a prop cart). McClane grabs the gun from his back and shoots his nemesis and Hayden's Eddie in quick succession. Hans falls backward through the window—grabbing onto Holly's wrist as he falls. When McClane unclasps her Rolex watch, Hans plummets to his death, the camera trained on his face. It's one of the few blue-screen shots in the film. Rickman wasn't actually dangling off Fox Plaza; the stunt was shot on a stage, and the blue background would be replaced by a shot taken from upper floors of the tower.

Unusually, it was the principal actor, Alan Rickman, doing the fall, instead of a stunt double. McTiernan had talked Rickman into performing the stunt himself and falling twenty-five feet as he looked into the camera (and not at where he was landing) into an airbag covered in blue-screen material. "I said, I'll do it, but as I long as I get some training," Rickman recounted. "Indeed, training was necessary because in order to fall backward I had to bring the gun up into frame and then absolutely remember to spread-eagle my arms and legs because if I didn't create a kind of star shape, your body will turn and you're in danger of landing on your head."

Understandably, Rickman was nervous. This was to be his last shot of the film. No longer worried about being fired, he had other concerns—or as he later put it, "Once they've decided you're all right, they'll make sure they've got it all in the can before they do the shot where they might kill you."[21]

"I did it first, demonstrated it," says the director. "You can't say, 'You go over there and get yourself killed!' You have to step up and say, 'Look this is OK, I'll do it, I'll show you how it works.' And I demonstrated it. I hung on the platform and looked in the camera, and on the cue, I let go and let myself fall into the bag. It's big and noisy when you hit the bag but it's not a terrifying experience. But it has to be the actor [doing it] because of the way the gravity changes and your face distorts as you begin to fall and the crazy shit that happens to your eyes, as you realize, 'Oh my God, I am dropping through space!' You can't fake that."

Capturing the moment required the best efforts of nearly every department. Rickman's face would be in close-up and had to stay perfectly sharp, even though he'd be accelerating away from the camera. Fortunately, Jan de Bont knew of the work of Richard Vye, who had created a computerized follow-focus system, originally developed to help track sporting events. Vye shot the tumble with an extra video camera set at a ninety-degree angle to the main camera

OPPOSITE *Storyboards by John L. Jensen map out Hans Gruber's demise.*

LEFT *Stuntman Ken Bates performs Gruber's death fall outside Fox Plaza.*

ABOVE *Hans Gruber (Rickman) plunges to his death in a still from the final film.*

shooting Rickman's fall. The extra camera had a motor on the lens, and an encoder fed positional information into an Apple computer, which in turn controlled the focus of the main camera. Vye practiced on tennis balls before turning to the real thing, keeping his camera trained on Rickman's ear as a focal point.

The camera ran at twelve-and-a-half times the normal speed—three hundred frames per second. When played back at twenty-four frames per second, the shot would be super-super-slow-motion. That meant each frame would be exposed only very briefly, so the shot had to be captured under extremely bright lights.

The fall was performed at 3:00 a.m. "He was a game guy," says Picerni, who had Rickman secured to a quick-release harness. On the first take, Rickman was told that the rig operator would drop him on the count of three. Privately, Picerni told the operator to drop him on "one." McTiernan talked Rickman into a second take, but it's his first, terrified take that made it into the film. "We had four seconds of this terror hitting his face," says McTiernan. "Genuine surprise!"

Fortunately, Vye's focus system worked well, and once the shot was completed, Al Cox, optical supervisor on the film, married the blue-screen footage with the 65mm background shot taken from a window on the thirtieth floor of Fox Plaza. "McTiernan loved the shot so much that he kept asking, 'Can't I get about four more frames?'" says Richard Edlund, the

THIS PAGE *Alan Rickman performs Hans Gruber's desperate death throes.*

OPPOSITE *Bonnie Bedelia and Bruce Willis film the scenes in which Gruber hangs on for dear life.*

film's visual effects producer. "Sadly, that was impossible; only about fifteen feet of the drop could be used before Rickman fell into the lights illuminating the blue screen."[22]

To capture the moment from below, when Hans is seen hanging from the window before he falls, Picerni Jr. was brought in to perform the stunt at the Fox Plaza building. "My son Chuck came out of the window on a cable," says Picerni. And finally, the long, faraway shot of Hans falling from the Nakatomi building was performed by stuntman Ken Bates using a descender; strapped into a harness, which is hooked onto a cable, Bates's fall was controlled by a pulley mechanism. "As you get closer to the ground," says Marks, "it slows you down." With an airbag underneath for additional safety, he fell 318 feet from Fox Plaza without a scratch.

As the shoot marched toward its conclusion, tempers frayed between the production and the Fox Plaza building managers. A scene near the end of the film—as the camera pans down from the top of the building to observe the carnage on the ground, and bearer bonds flutter in the air—became a flashpoint. "That day that we destroyed the whole courtyard, with all the paper coming down, that was a rough day," says Silver. "They didn't want that shit in their place and they were complaining about it."[23]

The scene was to be shot over the weekend, with all vehicles, debris, and paper cleaned up before start of business on Monday. That Friday, the production asked if Fox Plaza residents could turn off their lights before leaving for the weekend. "By the time we shot that scene," says Edlund, "they were so pissed that Joel [Silver] wouldn't get out of there, they said, 'Fuck you,' and a lot of them left their lights on."

OPPOSITE *Alan Rickman in position to film Hans Gruber's fall.*

TOP *Rickman hangs twenty-five feet in the air before letting go and dropping toward a giant airbag.*

ABOVE *John McTiernan* (far left) *discusses the Gruber fall shot with Jan de Bont* (far right) *as Rickman looks on.*

OPPOSITE TOP AND OPPOSITE BOTTOM LEFT *The Fox soundstage is rigged for Alan Rickman's stunt.*

LEFT *John McTiernan (right) offers encouragement to Rickman.*

TOP *Rickman is helped from the airbag after shooting his fall.*

ABOVE *Jan de Bont and Rickman discuss the shot.*

EXAGGERATING REALITY

Die Hard contains only about 150 visual effects, not a large number even by 1988 standards. But that didn't make the task any easier. Before the era of digital effects, all visual effects were practical by nature, shot either during or after the shoot, often away from the main production in a separate facility. What's more, they needed to seamlessly integrate with the physical effects—explosions, for example—orchestrated by special effects coordinator Al Di Sarro.

Silver wanted the effects to be dynamic and spectacular—what he called "exaggerated reality." That phrase became a motto for the production and for those at Boss Film Corporation (later Boss Film Studios), the company hired by Silver to produce the visual effects. Boss had been founded by Richard Edlund after he left George Lucas's effects house Industrial Light & Magic, where he had won Oscars for his work on Lucas's *Star Wars: Episode IV – A New Hope* (1977) and Steven Spielberg's *Raiders of the Lost Ark* (1981). One of the best effects companies in the business, Boss had great expertise in high-speed, large-format cinematography, which was essential in that era of models, miniatures, and in-camera effects.

Edlund was the visual effects producer on *Die Hard*, overseeing a highly experienced team. Brent Boates, the visual effects art director, had been a production illustrator with credits including *Ghostbusters* and *Fright Night* (1985), both of which were early Boss projects. Mark Stetson, the model shop supervisor for *Die Hard*, had overseen models for *Blade Runner* (1982), *The Right Stuff* (1983), and *Ghostbusters*. Thaine Morris was a pyrotechnics expert who already had *The Empire Strikes Back* (1980) and *Star Trek II: The Wrath of Khan* (1982) on his resume. Fresh off *Ghostbusters* and James Cameron's *Aliens* (1986), Patrick McClung joined the production as chief model maker.

One of the first shots to incorporate Silver's "exaggerated reality" vision was the sequence where McClane straps C-4 explosives to a chair and pushes it down an elevator shaft. Highly complex, the scene required both a shot of an accelerating fireball in the shaft and exterior shots of the windows blowing out, as McClane's makeshift bomb wipes out most of the building's third floor. An artful combination of models and pyrotechnics was needed.

TOP *Bruce Willis flashes a smile to the crew during the filming of the chair bomb scene.*

ABOVE *The C-4 "chair bomb" tumbles toward its target.*

OPPOSITE *Storyboards by Brent Boates show the required shots for the "chair bomb" explosion.*

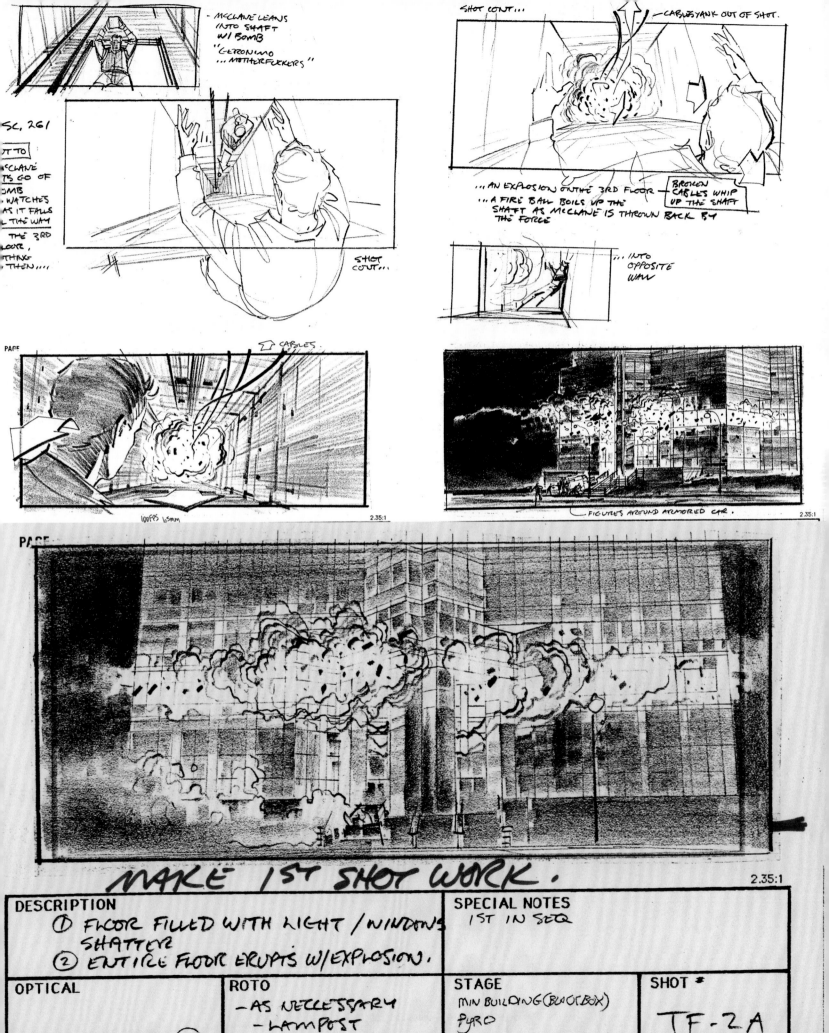

- McCLANE LEANS INTO SHAFT W/ BOMB "GERONIMO ...MOTHERFUCKERS"

SHOT CONT...

CABLES YANK OUT OF SHOT.

SC. 261

T TO
CLANE
S GO OF
OMB
WATCHES
AS IT FALLS
L THE WAY
THE 3RD
OOR,
THING
THEN.....

SHOT CONT...

...AN EXPLOSION ON THE 3RD FLOOR
...A FIRE BALL BOILS UP THE
SHAFT AS McCLANE IS THROWN BACK BY
THE FORCE

BROKEN CABLES WHIP UP THE SHAFT

...INTO OPPOSITE WALL

PAGE

CABLES

100 FPS 65mm

2.35:1

PAGE

FIGURES AROUND ARMORED CAR.

2.35:1

PAGE

MAKE 1ST SHOT WORK.

2.35:1

DESCRIPTION		SPECIAL NOTES	
① FLOOR FILLED WITH LIGHT / WINDOWS SHATTER ② ENTIRE FLOOR ERUPTS W/EXPLOSION.		1ST IN SEQ	
OPTICAL	ROTO - AS NECESSARY - LAMPOST	STAGE MIN BUILDING (BLACK BOX) PYRO	SHOT # TF-2A

Dropping a large quantity of explosives down a thirty-story elevator shaft and filming a full-scale fireball was not an option—not at Fox Plaza or any other building. Instead, Stetson and his team built a miniature elevator shaft on a stage at Boss's headquarters in Marina del Rey, a few miles west of Century City. Standing at around twenty-three feet in height, the shaft was almost as tall as the stage's ceiling, meaning that Bill Neil, Boss's cinematographer, could only just fit a camera above it.

To create the illusion of depth, the funnel-shaped shaft was a forced-perspective design. Measuring four feet by six feet at the top, it tapered down to just six by nine inches at the bottom. Details like tiny lights and pipework were added inside the shaft. Every elevator door and each floor's markings had to be scaled and painted by hand. Even the light fixtures were created in gradually diminishing sizes, all to help fool the eye into thinking the shaft was much larger and deeper than it was. The painstaking work paid off and the effect proved so realistic that one day McClung put his head down into the nearly finished model and had a moment of vertigo. "It scared the crap out of me, because when I looked down, all of a sudden, it looked like I was looking down a real thirty-story elevator shaft," he says.

One tricky part of the effect was that the real-life fireball wouldn't have to travel very far from the bottom of the twenty-three-foot tube to the top, but on-screen it would have to look like it was rising up thirty stories. "So we [didn't] want [the blast] to blow very hard," says Morris, "and we wanted a very slow explosion, so I used chemicals that would burn fairly slowly." Morris prepared a mixture of naphthalene, flash powder, and benzoyl peroxide. Crucially, this concoction burned at a low temperature, meaning that the model—made from Masonite and styrene and coated with fire-resistant paint—sustained only minor damage as the fireball enveloped its interior. With the 65mm camera up on high and operated remotely, the team set about shooting the explosion.

TOP *The Boss team sets up the camera to shoot into the scale elevator shaft.*

ABOVE *John McClane wedges open the elevator doors.*

OPPOSITE TOP *The elevator shaft before and after the explosion is unleashed.*

OPPOSITE BOTTOM *The exterior of the scale elevator shaft.*

The first take was a flop. The shot called for the fireball to rise at a steady rate and stay bright all the way up, but since the tube was funnel-shaped, the fireball spread out as it rose. Its energy dissipated, it dimmed, and its ascent slowed down. The solution, which came from McTiernan and was developed by Neil and his team, was ingenious.

Neil would turn the camera *off* just after the filming of the shot started. The camera would continue to run briefly under its own momentum, slowing down as it ground to a stop. As it did so, the film would move through the camera more slowly, so the frame rate would decrease; the shutter would slow down too, so the exposure time would increase. When the film is played back at regular speed, the fireball seems to move faster and get brighter as it rises. "It was a very gutsy move," says Stetson, "and it worked really, really well." It took five or six takes, each about a day apart, to allow repainting of the inside of the tube, which would inevitably be scorched, despite the low-temperature fireball. Even after multiple attempts, the fireball still tended to dim toward the top of the shaft; several different takes were combined to maintain the brightness of the fiery cloud.

As the chair bomb lands in the shaft, it causes absolute devastation below, blowing out the building's windows in spectacular fashion. "The producers were exploring the idea of actually blowing out the third floor of the real building and doing it live," remembers Boates. "The floor in the real building was vacant anyway, so apparently they were considering what it would cost to replace all of the windows."[24] Thankfully, the Boss team came up with a more cost-effective method, one that had been pioneered on the 1986 comedy-thriller *Legal Eagles* for a shot in which a Manhattan art gallery catches fire.

First of all, Di Sarro contacted the flashbulb division of lighting company Sylvania, who supplied bulbs with a two-second burn, which would create a large flash. Banks of these were rigged inside the third floor of Fox Plaza to simulate the explosion's initial flash of light inside the building. Hundreds of bulbs were set up—so many that there were only enough available for one take. Right up to the night of the shoot, there was lingering concern. "I remember Joel Silver saying: 'Are you sure this is going to look good? There's still a chance we can do this live,'" says Boates.[25] With the sidewalks wetted down to reflect and amplify the flash of light, Bill Neil and his crew captured the bright flash with five 65mm cameras. McTiernan also wanted billowing smoke for the subsequent fallout from the explosion, and so Di Sarro rigged a trough system at the base of the building. "We filled that gutter up with a pyrotechnic composition that we came up with, and detonated it."[26]

To create the actual explosion, as the windows blow out, Stetson and his crew built a scale model of Fox Plaza. A 1:3 scale of the actual third floor, the steel "firebox" contained a pyrotechnic charge made from Morris's naphthalene mix. The real building incorporated reflective surfaces like granite and glass, so the box was sheeted with black Formica for a similar effect. Brittle styrene windows were also created to ensure the desired effect of the glass shattering in dramatic fashion.

After a successful test shot of the model exploding was filmed, there were teething troubles. Subsequent shots of the miniature exploding didn't perform as well. Frank Urioste remembers Richard Edlund bringing him iterations of the shot that weren't quite working. "I said, 'There's no debris,'" remembers Urioste. "'There's fire but there's no wood or glass coming out with it.' He'd say, 'Let me try it again.' Finally Joel said, 'We can't wait any longer, we can't wait any longer.' We were one day away from actually blowing up the third floor of that

building. I said, 'I'm sure he's going to get it, Joel.' And we got it. They got it all in right. That is a great visual effects shot."

Other explosions were shot at full scale. When Hans detonates the explosives on the roof, the giant blast is seen briefly in a long shot, as a fiery Nakatomi Plaza is glimpsed alongside its neighboring skyscrapers. The explosion was set off on the roof of the real Fox Plaza, with a huge propane mortar keg set up by Di Sarro and his team. "It was really spectacular," says Stetson, "and it drifted off so beautifully. It just mushroomed out from the building." Propane fireballs, however, are very short-lived. To combat that, the Boss team shot the explosion with film going through the cameras at five times the normal speed, 120 frames per second. Played back at the normal 24 frames per second, the giant fireball exploded in super-slow-motion.

The Boss team also played a part in the camera pan from the top of the building that captures the fluttering bearer bonds during the finale. The live-action shot filmed by Bill Neil had to match with an identical downward camera tilt on a burning model, created in the parking lot at Boss Film's Marina del Rey headquarters. As so-called miniatures go, this one was particularly sizeable: a twenty-three-foot facade made of plywood, plastic, and tape, with plexiglass for its windows. So the model's facade would mimic the real marble exterior of the Fox Plaza tower, it was covered in photo prints. "Virgil Mirano, the staff photographer at Boss Film, shot textures of the marble facade of [Fox Plaza], which we then printed," says Stetson. "We just went down to a one-stop photo place and had hundreds of prints of that

made in scale. [When they were stuck to the model they] gave us the gloss we wanted, and it was a fast way to replicate that texture." But Boss's location near the ocean complicated those plans; humidity from sea breezes would make the photos bubble and buckle and frequent replacements were required.

Even the bonds floating through the air were miniatures: half-inch squares of Japanese tissue paper, shot at high speed against a black background, then slowed down to look larger and heavier and optically composited into the model shot. "McTiernan wanted everything to look real and gritty," says Edlund, "and it did."

The Century City helicopter scene also required the Boss touch. After the FBI choppers fly to Nakatomi Plaza, Hans detonates the explosives on the roof, causing one of the whirlybirds to crash into the side of the building. Boss used radio-controlled helicopters crafted by Patrick McClung on a 1:7 scale. A model of the roof of Fox Plaza and its top floors was also built, and housed in the parking lot at Boss's Marina del Rey headquarters, standing at around seventeen feet tall and matching the scale of the helicopters. The faux tower-top had a steel frame and plywood sides, since it would have to hold up in an explosion, probably for more than one take.

Stetson calls those remote-controlled helicopter shots "probably the most challenging" of the picture. Much of the burden for executing the crashing-and-burning helicopter would fall on pyrotechnics expert Thaine Morris, who decided to hire remote-control helicopter pilot Larry Jolly after trying—and failing—to control the model copters on his own. Jolly was highly skilled, says Morris, who remembers him demonstrating his abilities by adjusting the engine of a model helicopter one-handed while he made it hover "about four feet above his head."

Boss was located in an area zoned for heavy industry, so setting off pyrotechnics in the evening was legal. However, its Marina del Rey neighborhood was also home to lavish private apartments right across the street. One take, shot at around 10:00 p.m., brought a neighbor out from the apartments yelling about the noise. "One of the ladies from across the street comes stomping in and ran into the big Irish fireman that we had there," recalls Morris. "He told her that she was on private property and she'd better get off." After

being escorted off, she called a reporter from a local TV station. "So I got to be interviewed on TV over that thing," says Morris. The segment finished with the reporter in the middle of the street, explaining into the camera that one side was zoned, so Boss could set off bombs all night, adding, "But Mr. Morris says he will do his level best not to do that after ten o'clock."

The helicopter explosion required a fairly complicated rig. The idea was for the model chopper to burst into flames at the side of the scaled-down Fox Plaza model and then for

the tail boom to come off. The whole wreck would then fall to the ground below. A trigger wire ran to the helicopter model, so as it fell, the tail would come apart and a series of small bombs would go off, each set with electronic timers to detonate thousandths of a second apart. The whole thing would be shot with a high-speed camera and played back at regular speed; slowing down the shot would add the illusion of weight and mass to the model.

"Joel Silver had told us we'd never get the shot," remembers Morris. And on the first take, sure enough, the helicopter did not explode—at least at the start of the shot, that is. "I put too fine a cable on the trigger," says Morris. It fell straight to the ground where it blew up on impact, shooting fire around special effects cinematographer Bill Neil's feet. "Scared everybody pretty good," deadpans Morris.

Thankfully, the second take worked, although it took a rather rudimentary piece of equipment to help the model helicopter on its way. "Basically the helicopter comes over," remembers Edlund, "and it hit the edge of the building and it wasn't going to go over and [Thaine Morris] shoves it over the edge with a broom stick."

The next day, Edlund's phone rang. It was Joel Silver. He'd seen the dailies of the effects shot. "Edlund," he yelled down the receiver, "that shot is totally legitimate!"

OPPOSITE *Storyboards by Brent Boates depict the FBI helicopter crashing into Nakatomi Plaza.*

TOP *The remote control helicopter is piloted over the Nakatomi Plaza roof model.*

ABOVE *The model helicopter is rigged for its flight.*

RIGHT *Explosions engulf the Nakatomi Plaza roof model.*

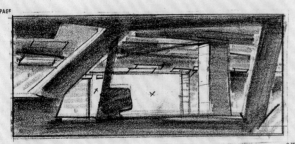

DESCRIPTION			SPECIAL NOTES	
CHAUFFEUR'S POV			- INSERT 35mm PRODUCTION FTG. * 65mm FG. MATTE PASS. SOFT EDGE	
OPTICAL -COMP. REDUCED PROD. FTG. 35mm -65mm FG. MATTE PASSE READY FOR COMP ◯	ROTO -ROTO GARAGE PILLARS / LINTEL		STAGE	SHOT # GT-1
MATTE	ANIMATION		MODEL/CREATURE	FRAMES
				SCRIPT
				PLATE 65mm ◯

(handwritten at right of storyboard: CHECK STATUS RE: CUT 500.)

2.35:1

PROBLEMS IN POST

The shoot for *Die Hard* wrapped in the last week of January 1988. "We finished on time. There wasn't time to run over!" remembers McTiernan. Indeed, the production had just five months to complete postproduction before the proposed US release on July 20. "We were scheduled down to the last possible days to give us enough time to get the cut done and get the prints made," adds McTiernan. "It was very different then. . . . This was in the olden days where they had physical copies of the film and you had to strike them. It took a long time to strike that many prints." Urioste was left with precious little time in the editing suite. "The schedule was terrible," he says.

Although McTiernan had handpicked Urioste and respected him greatly both personally and as an editor, the two sometimes butted heads. It was their first time working together, and McTiernan thought that Urioste was Silver's guy, taking his instructions from the producer. "But I don't do what anybody says," states Urioste. "I do what I think I should do." Things became heated enough between Urioste and McTiernan during dubbing that Lawrence Gordon had to

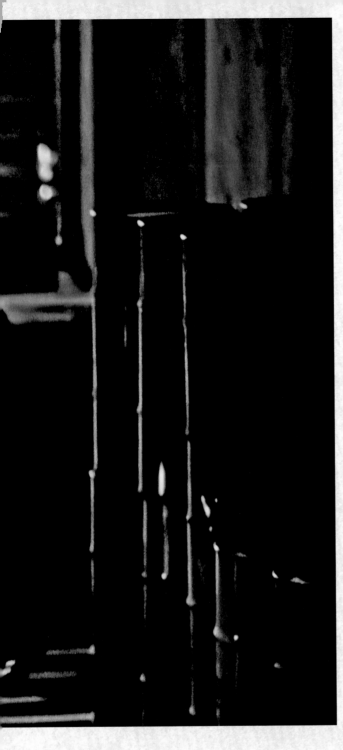

intervene. Moreover, Fox's creative executives had notes Urioste didn't agree with. "They kept saying it's too long," he recalls. "I kept telling everybody if we don't develop the opening that way, if you don't care about John and Holly, the rest of the movie just won't work. It was the first time I ever had to deal with a creative executive. And I didn't have the time to deal with it."

With three weeks to go before the film's delivery date, John Link, who had cut *Predator* for McTiernan, was brought on as the additional editor. Urioste, who had known Link since the mid-1950s when they were both apprentices at NBC, wasn't keen on the idea at first, as he was accustomed to cutting alone. But the addition of Link proved a godsend. Urioste continued to cut alone, while McTiernan was able to work with Link on segments he wanted to refine.

Urioste wouldn't show the film in its rough edit form. Not for Bruce Willis, not for anyone, even threatening to quit if he was forced to. "One night Joel said, 'We have to show the studio something,'" he recalls. "He meant everybody. So I showed them the scene where they shoot [Takagi] in the head." Urioste added some music from *Lethal Weapon* to give it some atmosphere and showed it to Silver. "He says, 'Oh my God, we've got to show this to everybody.'" The sequence went down a storm. "They didn't bother me after that," says Urioste.

When the first cut of the movie was finally assembled, Silver was even more excited. At a party with Willis and wife Demi Moore, Silver urged them to see it. The group went from the party directly to Lawrence Gordon's house, watching the film at midnight. By the time it was over, the assembled audience was ecstatic, fully convinced they had something special on their hands.

✱ ✱ ✱

The sound team was also hustling to make the *Die Hard* soundscape as compelling and fluid as the footage. Wisely, Silver gathered together several key collaborators with whom he'd worked before. "He's a huge proponent of good sound and he really expects everyone to bring their A game," says Ron Bartlett, who was fresh off *Action Jackson* when he joined as *Die Hard*'s Foley editor, adding atmospheric sounds to bolster the audio captured on set. "He's a very intense man and he expects a lot," Bartlett continues. "He's very demanding, but in a good way."

Leading the sound team was supervising sound editor Stephen Hunter Flick, whose relationship with Silver went back several years to *48 Hrs.* He had also just won an Academy Award, shared with John Pospisil, for his work on *RoboCop*. "I'd cut an important sequence, then hand it off to another editor, Richard Shorr," says Flick. "He'd recut it, hand it back to me, and I'd recut it again. By passing it through a different set of hands and a point-of-view, Richard and I would work in tandem . . . improving upon each other's work. Nothing was sacrosanct."[27] Also on board the *Die Hard* sound team were Don J. Bassman, Kevin F. Cleary, Richard Overton, and Al Overton Jr. All were veterans of several Silver productions with the exception of sound mixer Overton Jr.

Flick was inspired by his colleague Alan Murray's work on *Lethal Weapon*. "It was dangerous and interesting. . . . That's the way I wanted my movies to sound." His focus was entirely on realism (with the exception of the nighttime traffic heard in the rooftop scenes, as the LA ambient noise he found "sounded like a nasty traffic wash," so he jettisoned it in favor of recordings from the New York streets).[28]

Bartlett credits Flick for creating the distinctive sound of the guns, a crucial component of *Die Hard*. "He really went to town by getting things recorded fresh just for that film, cutting them himself, and they sounded fantastic." For *Die Hard*, Flick also returned to the library of gun sounds he'd recorded in Texas during his work on *RoboCop*.

Flick's work was meticulous. Vanessa Theme Ament, a Foley artist on the film, recalls creating additional sounds to amplify the moment Marco's body lands on Powell's cop car. "Steve Flick had his editors cut in most of the crash, but we sweetened it with some Foley stage hits against the car, crunching of the metal and squeaking of the car door. . . . This was a married effect."[29] One thing never made it, though. "We had made a sound of glass in McClane's feet, for the moment where he digs it out," remembers Flick. Some on the production team felt it was too gruesome, though. "We had to take it out," he adds.[30]

ABOVE *Hans Gruber leads his crew from the van—minus the ambulance.*

OPPOSITE BOTTOM *A sketch showing Argyle's point of view in the basement car park.*

BLOODY MESS

A crisis arose once the film was submitted for ratings. The studio expected *Die Hard* to get an R rating because of its violence and strong language—with fifty f-bombs, there was no way it was going to be rated PG-13. They were right about the latter point. When the Motion Picture Association of American (MPAA) reviewed the cut, they said that it was too violent even for an R rating, with one scene in particular causing an issue. To avoid an X rating—commercial poison for a film of this size—the scene where Hans shoots Takagi in the head, splattering blood and brain on the window behind him, needed to have a few frames of that splatter removed.

The existing cut was gruesome, admits Urioste, but he insists, "The way I had it cut was the softest way." The filmmakers assembled, and Urioste argued that the MPAA's plan would only make matters worse. "It'll look even more gross," he said, "because it'll be wham! Right in your face." But they didn't dare defy the MPAA and risk being saddled with an X rating, as some theaters wouldn't even book X-rated films. Urioste recounts a meeting in the cutting room: "Joel said, 'Here's what we're going to do.' This is vintage Joel. [He said,] 'Take out the four frames . . . show them the shot without the four frames. Then [later] put them back [in the film].'"

"I said, 'I can't do that Joel,'" says Urioste with a laugh. "And Larry Gordon said, 'Joel, do you want to ruin this guy's reputation?' It was the only trouble [Joel and I] had on the whole movie." Eventually Silver relented and the frames were cut from the film for good.

With the MPAA's notes taken in, the time finally arrived for Urioste to show a final cut of the film for Silver, Willis, and the other producers and studio executives, albeit with a temp score, as composer Michael Kamen's work was yet to be completed and wouldn't be recorded until the first two weeks of June. There were just twelve people in the screening, recalls de Souza. "We're all watching, we're excited, and twenty minutes in, John McTiernan says, 'Oh shit!'"

The director had spotted a major issue. When Hans's gang arrives in the green Pacific Courier truck, it is clear that behind the men, the vehicle's interior is empty. This was a major continuity error, as the truck was supposed to contain the gang's getaway ambulance that would roll out of the back of the truck in the movie's finale. It was a typical result of major plot elements being reworked even as the shoot drew to a close. "The ambulance idea came three weeks before the movie wrapped," confirms de Souza.

Decades later, visual effects artists would have digitally added an ambulance behind the gang. In 1988, that wasn't an option. All McTiernan and Urioste could do was edit the shot shorter so the audience wouldn't get a good look in the back of the truck.

Unfortunately, that edit had a ripple effect. The cut scene included Hans and his gang synchronizing their watches on arrival. The shot established that they had the same watch, and later on McClane would notice that the "terrorists" he killed all wore the same timepiece. More importantly, during the Bill Clay scene, McClane would notice that Hans was wearing one of those watches when he lit the villain's cigarette, leading him to realize he's talking to a terrorist, not a hostage.

In the final cut, McClane still notices the watches on the dead men, and on Hans, but without the setup shot, there's no way for the audience to make the same connection McClane is making. "I guess he's psychic," says Steven de Souza, sardonically, "but the original explanation made total sense, in a detective kind of way."

ABOVE *The blood-splattered glass in Joseph Takagi's office, destined to cause problems with the MPAA censors.*
LEFT *Hans Gruber shoots Takagi as Karl looks on.*

Despite these plot issues, the final cut played sensationally. "When the last reel finished, and the song 'Let It Snow!' played," Urioste recounts, "Four people jumped up, and Joel was in front: '*It's a hit!*' they shouted."

The reaction was equally euphoric from the first public audience to see *Die Hard*. With the movie in the final sound-mixing process, a test screening was held in Mountain View, California. The test scores were sky high, with people standing on their seats in excitement. One young man even yelled, "Show it again!" Fox became so confident in the film that the same creative executives who'd thought the film was too long now wouldn't let Urioste touch it again.

Urioste wanted to tighten the final cut, arguing that a minute could be lost and wouldn't be missed. Silver disagreed. "Joel said, '*What* do you want to do? Are you crazy?'" recalls the editor. "So that's the movie that went out. We didn't touch a frame."

SCORING *DIE HARD*

McTiernan began formulating his vision for the *Die Hard* score long before the film entered postproduction. He wanted to integrate Ludwig van Beethoven's "Ode to Joy," a piece from the composer's Ninth Symphony, as the villains' motif. Urioste agreed, believing it the perfect choice to accompany the moment where the vault finally opens. "It was just fantastic," says the editor. "And it actually helped the editing because you cut to the tempo of the music."

Composer Michael Kamen, on the other hand, was less pleased. "I thought it was sacrilegious," said Kamen, whose resume already included scores for David Cronenberg (*The Dead Zone*), Terry Gilliam (*Brazil*), and Silver's *Lethal Weapon*. "I told him I'd make mincemeat out of Wagner and Strauss but why Beethoven?"[31]

A huge Stanley Kubrick fan, McTiernan had an answer. "That particular piece of music was in [Kubrick's 1971 film] *A Clockwork Orange* in the Korova Milkbar when Alex hears the sophisto sing that piece of music a cappella." In his eyes, the *Die Hard* terrorists were the descendants of Alex and his gang of droogs; McTiernan says he'd forgotten the title of the piece of music by the time he came to work on *Die Hard*. "I was quite shocked [when I remembered]," he says. "I was already building it into the movie all over the place. I didn't realize it was 'Ode to Joy,' which was the essence of what I'd been selling to Joel and Larry—can we make this fun instead of hostile?"

Fortunately, Kamen too was a big Kubrick fan and swiftly came round to the idea, telling McTiernan that if he was going to use Beethoven, he should also license *A Clockwork Orange*'s other famous track, "Singin' in the Rain." Kubrick used the wonderfully cheery song from the 1952 Gene Kelly musical as Alex and his droogs indulge in some "ultra-violence." Subtly wound into Kamen's eventual score—notably in the SWAT team's attack on the building and the missile destruction of the armored vehicle—it was also linked to the gang's hacker, Theo, who even hums it as he shuts down the Nakatomi elevators, ripping out a clutch of wires and kicking a metal panel in time to the song.

With other familiar tunes (including "Winter Wonderland") sprinkled in, Kamen took less than four weeks to write the entire score, although McTiernan and the editors made some major changes to the placement of certain cues throughout the scoring process. "Some music was repurposed in a significant way," says author and film historian Eric Lichtenfeld. "There are cues that were recorded for one scene and used in others." Take the track "Tony and John Fight." It's used when McClane and Tony tumble down the stairs, but it's also heard when the terrorists gatecrash the party and during the shoot-out in the computer room, even though Kamen wrote other music for those scenes. Also, the cue heard when Takagi is killed was actually recorded for the scene where McClane radios for help from the roof before fleeing the terrorists' gunfire.

At the very last minute, another problem threatened to derail the entire picture. It was a week before release and the music for the final reel—which starts on the big special effects panning shot down the Nakatomi building and continues through the closing credits—hadn't arrived. The picture had to be delivered the next day, and Kamen's last part of the score was the final missing piece. When Urioste, who had been involved with the integration of the score into the picture, received the music for the final reel at eight o'clock that night, his heart sank.

"It was awful," he says. "It didn't work. It ruined the movie." It included "Ode to Joy" at the end instead of the Vaughn Monroe song "Let It Snow!"—a change that spoiled the ending in Urioste's view. Overall, he felt it was too heavy and not at all funny. Urioste called Silver at home and explained the issue. The producer rushed in and arrived at 9:00 p.m. to watch the ending reel with the music added. He agreed with Urioste: It wouldn't work. But it was too late to revise the score, and the reel had to be delivered to the labs in time to strike release prints. At this late date, delaying release of the movie was impossible. With everything seemingly under control, McTiernan had left for a badly needed vacation. Urioste and Silver had to decide the next step. They opted to go with the temp music that Urioste had used in editing. "We used to call it the mish-mash reel," he says. The temp music included pieces from the scores of *Cocoon* (1985) and *Man on Fire* (1987) and—most crucially—reinstated "Let It Snow!" "Joel had all his people from Fox going absolutely nuts to find the rights to all these pieces of music," Urioste says. "But they got it."

According to Urioste, Kamen was not happy with this meddling. But ultimately it was the right decision. "Ode to Joy" worked as a motif for the classically educated Hans, but was hardly suitable to accompany the McClane family reunion. "If you listen to it, you can hear the difference," says Urioste. "In fact, when we put in 'Let It Snow!' at the end, it just felt good." Despite their differences of opinion on *Die Hard*, Urioste and Kamen remained on good terms and soon worked together again on *Road House*.

ABOVE *Composer Michael Kamen.*

OPPOSITE *Unidentified* Die Hard *promotional art circa 1988.*

Twelve terrorists. One cop. The odds are against
John McClane… That's just the way he likes it.

BRUCE WILLIS
DIE HARD

TWENTIETH CENTURY FOX Presents A GORDON COMPANY/SILVER PICTURES Production A JOHN McTIERNAN Film Bruce Willis DIE HARD
ALAN RICKMAN ALEXANDER GODUNOV BONNIE BEDELIA Music by MICHAEL KAMEN Visual Effects Produced by RICHARD EDLUND Film Editors FRANK J. URIOSTE, A.C.E.
and JOHN F. LINK Production Designer JACKSON DeGOVIA Director of Photography JAN De BONT Executive Producer CHARLES GORDON Screenplay By JEB STUART and STEVEN E. de SOUZA
Based upon the novel "Nothing Lasts Forever" by RODERICK THORP Produced by LAWRENCE GORDON and JOEL SILVER Directed by JOHN McTIERNAN
Color by DeLuxe®

40 STORIES OF SHEER ADVENTURE!

High
above
the city of
L.A. an army of
terrorists has seized
a building, taken hostages,
and declared war. They were
ready for anything… Except
an off-duty cop trapped inside.

BRUCE WILLIS
DIE HARD

TWENTIETH CENTURY FOX Presents A GORDON COMPANY/SILVER PICTURES Production A JOHN McTIERNAN Film Bruce Willis DIE HARD
ALAN RICKMAN ALEXANDER GODUNOV BONNIE BEDELIA Music MICHAEL KAMEN Visual Effects RICHARD EDLUND Film Editors FRANK J. URIOSTE,
and JOHN F. LINK Production Designer JACKSON DeGOVIA Director Photography JAN De BONT Executive Producer CHARLES GORDON Screenplay JEB STUART and STEVEN E. de SOUZA
RODERICK THORP Produced by LAWRENCE GORDON and JOEL SILVER Directed by JOHN McTIERNAN

OPPOSITE *Final art for what would become the most iconic of
the posters created to promote* Die Hard.

TOP LEFT *A sketch concept for the* Die Hard *theatrical poster.*

TOP RIGHT *An alternative theatrical poster bearing the effusive
tagline "40 stories of sheer adventure!"*

POSTER PARADE

Before the electrifying test screenings, *Die Hard*'s release had not been on the viewing
public's radar. "The expectations for the movie were quite low," remembers Hart Bochner.
Willis himself shrugged and moved on after the shoot came to an end. "I never gave it much
thought," he admits. "I thought, 'Well, that happened.'"[32]

According to Jeb Stuart, the Fox marketing department didn't know what to do with
the film at first. The early one-sheet featured a shot of the tower with its roof exploding (Joel
Silver's marketing instincts vindicated) and a wide-eyed Willis with half his face in shadow. The
tagline was "40 stories of sheer adventure!"

"Everybody scratched their heads," Stuart says. "Who makes adventure movies? It's
not *Tarzan*." Later, the "adventure" tagline was dropped, and the one-sheet changed to a
fiercer shot of Willis, his entire face clear, pistol at the ready.

Even after the positive test screenings, the studio still wasn't sure how best to market
the film. Willis was still perceived as a comic actor, they believed, so they weren't sure how
much they should feature him in promotional materials. "Two weeks before the movie opened
[they] took Bruce's friggin' picture off the poster," sighs McTiernan. "They're the ones who
run the studio and they're the ones who have the responsibility for marketing the movie. . . .
That's their business and it was their conclusion that they needed to take him off the friggin'
poster, which was quite shocking."

At the film's big Hollywood premiere, Steven de Souza got a reminder that while *Die Hard* was designed to be pleasing summer entertainment, it was a change from what audiences were used to. "It was the first one of my movies I took my kids to see in a movie theater, because they were [previously] too young for my R-rated movies," says de Souza. When McClane sees the terrorists with their formidable weapons and gear, then looks at his gun and runs away, de Souza's eleven-year-old son grabbed his father's arm and said, "Dad! Your hero's chickenshit!" But after the film, viewers also gave de Souza what he felt was a great compliment: They told him they thought McClane was going to die. "If people thought he was that vulnerable, that showed the movie worked," he says.

A lot of critics (though not all) also thought the movie worked. *Variety*'s review, one of the first to appear, was generally enthusiastic, saying, "*Die Hard* is as high-tech, rock-hard, and souped-up as an action film can be." Newspaper reviews were generally mixed to positive. The *New York Times*' Caryn James managed to mention Willis's salary in her first sentence and had plenty of complaints, saying it had to be "the most excessive film around" and calling the story "flimsy" and the first half hour "slow." But she loved Alan Rickman and wrapped up by conceding "*Die Hard* turns out to be everything action-genre fans, and Bruce Willis's relieved investors, might have hoped for."

De Souza remembers that the early reaction was so good that just before *Die Hard* opened, Fox gave the film an unusual vote of confidence: They called Universal, which planned to open *Midnight Run*, a Robert De Niro–Charles Grodin action-comedy, on July 20, the same date as *Die Hard*, with a friendly warning. "[Fox] said, 'You really oughta move your movie,'" says de Souza. "And [Universal] said, 'What are you talking about?' But we were tracking really it closely [and were sure it would be a hit]."

Fox decided on a limited platform release for *Die Hard*, opening it July 15, 1988, on just twenty-one screens, then taking it to 1,276 screens the next weekend. It's unusual for major films to get the platform treatment, which is often used to build word of mouth, but it was a shrewd move for *Die Hard*. The film took in over $3 million in its weeklong limited release and garnered a lot of buzz by the time it opened wide.

Grossing over $10 million the next week, *Die Hard* managed to sustain its popularity. (Two weeks after the movie opened, Fox's marketing department put Willis's face back on the poster.) It never was number one at the box office, but it was in the top five every week for the rest of the summer, topping out at number two in its tenth week, at the end of September. In short, American audiences loved it. It finished with $83 million at the domestic box office. When it completed its international engagements, it had grossed $140.7 million worldwide.

That gave Fox, the Gordons, Silver, and Bruce Willis the last laugh on the star's big salary. Three years later, Fox's new president of marketing and distribution, Tom Sherak, told *The Hollywood Reporter*, "The old management was very smart in making *Die Hard*. I remember the controversy about 'how could you pay Bruce Willis so much money?' There was a lot of controversy over that. Then you saw the movie and said wow!"[33]

When the Academy Award nominations were announced the following year, *Die Hard* got the nod in four categories: best sound effects editing, best visual effects, best film editing, and best sound. The Oscars took place on March 29, 1989, but the seminal animated live-action movie *Who Framed Roger Rabbit* beat *Die Hard* to the prize in the first three categories; Clint Eastwood's Charlie Parker biopic *Bird*, meanwhile, claimed best sound.

Time would prove a greater vindication than any award. *Die Hard* became a watershed moment in Hollywood, changing the face of action movies and creating an often imitated, rarely equaled, and certainly never bettered template. For the better part of a decade, variations of *Die Hard*, or at least what writers and producers understood *Die Hard* to be, became not just a Hollywood staple, but a cliché. Many of those lone-hero-trapped-with-the-bad-guys, "*Die Hard* in a . . ." films got made, replacing the office building with other settings: *Under Siege* (an aircraft carrier), *Passenger 57* (an airliner), *Air Force One* (the president's plane, with the president as a McClane-style hero), and more.

Steven de Souza recalls that in 2000, after he'd written and directed a horror movie called *Possessed* for Showtime, he got a call from a producer who'd liked it. "I have a picture that needs a production polish," he was told. "If you can rewrite this movie, you can direct it. I'll write you a complete blank ticket, it's right up your alley."

His curiosity piqued, de Souza answered, "All right, tell me what it is."

"*Die Hard* in a building!"

He passed.

But that was a dozen years after *Die Hard*. In the short run, it was clear that audiences loved McClane and wanted to see more of him. Before the first prints of *Die Hard* could wear out in theaters, before the first week's box office receipts were even fully tallied, the producers had already begun talking about how to bring back John McClane.

FOR YOUR CONSIDERATION
BEST SOUND
RE-RECORDING MIXERS: DON BASSMAN, KEVIN F. CLEARY, RICHARD OVERTON
PRODUCTION MIXER: AL OVERTON
DIE HARD

FOR YOUR CONSIDERATION
BEST ART DIRECTION
PRODUCTION DESIGNER: JACKSON DeGOVIA
ART DIRECTOR: JOHN R. JENSEN
SET DECORATOR: PHIL M. LEONARD
DIE HARD

OPPOSITE *Alan Rickman* (top left), *Reginald VelJohnson* (top right), *and Alexander Godunov* (bottom left) *attend the* Die Hard *premiere.*

RIGHT *"For Your Consideration" advertisements used in the build-up to the Academy Awards.*

PART 2 DIE HARD 2:
DIE HARDER

"Another basement, another elevator . . . how can the same shit happen to the same guy twice?" —JOHN MCCLANE

The magnitude of *Die Hard*'s success would take the whole summer of '88 to reveal itself, but *Die Hard 2* was already in the works. A week after the first film opened, burgeoning screenwriter Doug Richardson was summoned to a meeting with Lawrence Gordon and Lloyd Levin. Richardson had recently sold *Hell Bent . . . and Back*, a script he'd cowritten with friend and former agent Rick Jaffa, although the film had yet to be made. "I was a baby writer, I was unproduced," says Richardson. In other words, no matter how good he was, he would be relatively cheap by Hollywood standards.

At the meeting, Richardson was asked if he was a fan of *Die Hard*—he was, he'd already seen it twice—and if he'd like to write the sequel. Just like its predecessor, *Die Hard 2* was to be based on a preexisting novel, this time Walter Wager's *58 Minutes*, an airplane-hijacking thriller first published in 1987. Levin had discovered the book and approached Wager's literary agents, Curtis Brown, to option it back in June 1988, before *Die Hard* was even released.

There was no mention to Wager that his book could serve as the basis for a *Die Hard* sequel, but once Levin secured the book, the Gordon team saw that it was the perfect source material for a follow-up film. While he'd received no official word from Fox about developing a second *Die Hard*, Gordon knew it was only a matter of time, so getting the ball rolling with the Wager book was a preemptive move. "Because he was Larry Gordon and I was nobody," says Richardson, "he could call the studio and say, 'Hey, I've got this great action movie, I've got this writer, we already own the book. It's gonna cost no money. Make the deal.'"

Larry Gordon would produce again, along with his brother Charles, with Levin overseeing development. In a series of meetings that followed, though, Richardson learned there was an underlying aspect of the plan; the Gordons wanted to evolve a *Die Hard* sequel without Joel Silver. Richardson was told in no uncertain terms: "Joel is great at putting the money on the screen, but he wouldn't know how to develop anything." Silver's contract guaranteed that he would produce *Die Hard 2*, but as long as the script was called *58 Minutes*, and as long as its hero wasn't named John McClane, that clause wouldn't kick in. So by keeping this script under the radar, the Gordons could develop it without Silver.

With Silver left out the loop, Richardson got to work. He read Wager's *58 Minutes* just once, in a single afternoon. "I read it with a John McClane perspective," he says. He found the story to be like a modern-day version of *Airport*, which is to say, a very stock action melodrama. The book's hero, Frank Malone, was a New York cop waiting in John F. Kennedy International Airport (JFK) for his daughter to fly in for a Christmas visit, only to have a terrorist take over air traffic control and hold the planes waiting to land for ransom. As a blizzard approaches, Malone has just fifty-eight minutes to save everyone, including his daughter, who is onboard one of the planes. Like the original *Die Hard*, the action plays out in almost real time.

Richardson kept Wager's antagonist, Willi Staub, but changed several details. In the book, Staub is "one of the three most notorious terrorists alive," and his attack on JFK is part of a plan to free seven political prisoners. Richardson changed the target to General Esperanza, a deposed Chilean despot that the writer named after his grandmother's house-keeper. At the time Richardson was hired to write the screenplay, the US was trying to extradite Panamanian dictator Manuel Noriega. The writer took some aspects of Esperanza's character and situation straight from the news headlines, giving the story a touch of topical relevance.

Per his instructions, Richardson didn't name McClane in the first draft. Instead, he renamed Wager's hero Frank Zelinski. Richardson also kept Malone's imperiled daughter in the script, knowing that she would later be changed to Holly McClane. As he constructed the first draft, Richardson focused on what he felt made *Die Hard* unique: "This kind of hyperbolic action in a realistic situation, à la terrorism, à la thievery, but the action being bigger-than-life."

While researching the mechanics of airport life, Richardson spent a few days in the control tower at JFK shadowing air traffic controllers. He also sat down with members of the Federal Aviation Administration (FAA) to quiz them on how it might be possible for terrorists to

. . .RAP RAP RAP RAP. What?
looks up and out the window.

POV

Smearing a view for himself
windshield is FRANK ZELINSKI
He clears a wider circle and

PUNK
Okay, man. I ge
So I won't steal

FRANK
Gettin' smarter
          (finger to
Cold air feeds t
Here, don't want
death.

And he zips up the boy's j
and over his eyes.

ABOVE *Walter Wager's book* 58 Minutes, *published by MacMillan, which became the basis for* Die Hard 2.

OPPOSITE *Bruce Willis returns as John McClane in* Die Hard 2.

overrun an airport. "That was the approach," he says, "to come at it from a realistic standpoint, learn how planes fly, how you could put them in danger, and then how you could realistically create a situation where a terrorist was trying to shut down the airport."

He also underlined that the airport would be covered in snow, an echo of the Wager book, in which wintry conditions play a big part in ensuring the planes can't fly to another airport. Still, it was a decision that would later have huge ramifications for the production. "Snow," he deadpans. "That's probably my greatest contribution to *Die Hard* [2]."

Richardson finished work in August 1989, and his timing proved perfect. During this period, there was a shakeup at the top of the studio. Joe Roth, founder of mini studio Morgan Creek Productions, replaced Leonard Goldberg as chairman of Fox Film Corporation, "almost the exact same weekend I was done with the script," says Richardson. "One of the first things [Roth] said was, 'I want *Die Hard*, I want a sequel.' Larry said, 'Here's a script,' and it was green-lit like that."

Within a week of turning it in, Richardson became aware of the next inevitable phase. "Chuck [Gordon] took me to lunch," says Richardson, "and said, 'Here's what's gonna happen. The movie's gonna get green-lit, Joel's gonna come onboard, he's gonna fire you and bring on [Steven] de Souza.' Because that's what he did to Jeb [Stuart] on the first one, and Joel was going to repeat himself." Everything went as Charles Gordon predicted. The two screenwriters would share credit on the final film.

* * *

When Silver read Richardson's script, he was concerned. "I remember . . . thinking, 'How can the same thing happen to the same guy twice?'" He wanted to replicate the experience of the first film but tell it in a way that was fresh. Once again, McClane would be fighting a Christmastime terror attack, but it would be very different from taking on Hans Gruber and his European crew.

As de Souza began his rewrites, Richardson's script began to morph. "Thematically, it didn't change," Richardson says. "Tonally, it changed a notch." He cites the scene where McClane gets into a snowmobile chase with the bad guys: "It got a little bit more into James Bond at that point. My version was a little more serious, a little more reality-based." From there on, he continues, "The movie took off more into de Souza land." Putting his own stamp on the script, de Souza even identified Esperanza's South American home as Val Verde, a fictional country he had already invented for use in *Commando* and *Predator*. He also turned Willi Staub into *Die Hard 2*'s Colonel William Stuart, an ex–US Special Forces commander turned mercenary who'd been hired to free Esperanza.

Richardson's idea to invent a Noriega figure was embellished. The bad guys would be domestic terrorists instead of foreign terrorists, right-wing zealots trying to free the dictator and pocket a big haul of cash at the same time. "It was an Oliver North kind of thing," says de Souza, referring to the White House aide who'd gotten caught up in the Iran-Contra scandal and was known to support Noriega. Indeed, when de Souza received feedback from Fox creatives, dated October 10, 1989, concern was raised that Stuart "may come off too much like an Ollie North parody than a flesh-and-blood villain."

As the revisions continued, JFK Airport became Dulles International in Washington, DC, and Carmine Lorenzo, the head of the airport police, was fashioned like *Die Hard*'s LAPD Deputy Chief Dwayne Robinson, an uncooperative local cop. This time, though, that local cop would eventually join the fight and prove a valuable ally. Replacing the cocksure and largely incompetent FBI agents in the first film would be antiterrorist Special Forces commandos led by one Major Grant—but instead of being useless, they'd not only be hypercompetent soldiers but also key accomplices in the crime.

Perhaps the most memorable and certainly the most disturbing moment that de Souza added was a sequence where the terrorists deliberately crash a passenger plane on the runway, as McClane tries but fails to wave the plane off. All aboard the plane die in a fiery wreck. "I said, let's put a little girl on the plane," says de Souza. "No one will believe it'll crash." Beyond its shock value, the sequence had an important storytelling purpose: It left McClane wounded and vulnerable, as he'd been in the first *Die Hard*, and also introduced the idea that the film's hero could fail. It was a ploy to "totally mind-fuck the audience," says de Souza. "We thought we were very clever."

ABOVE AND OPPOSITE TOP *Concept designs for the insignia of Major Grant's military task force.*

OPPOSITE BOTTOM *A crest created for Steven de Souza's fictional country, Val Verde.*

Despite the confidence in their story, one issue haunted the filmmakers from day one: the budget. They had planned for *Die Hard 2* to cost $48 million, well up from the $28 million spent on *Die Hard*. The original film was considered expensive, but not overly so, and the sequel's budget was not necessarily exorbitant by late-'80s standards. At the time, the norm was for sequels to underperform at the box office compared to their predecessors. Asked to spend more on a film that was projected to earn less, Fox started looking for ways to economize.

Silver recalls being summoned by Roth, who was worried he would lose his job if the film's budget crept into the $50-million bracket. With typical bravado, Silver told him it was more likely to fall into the $60-million range. Silver had good reason to shock Roth: Shooting in snow was always liable to inflate a budget. This was long before visual effects artists could digitally render snow with the click of a mouse. "These days, that wouldn't be a thirty-second conversation," he says. "We'd just put the snow in and move on."

Nevertheless, Silver had to play the game. Before shooting started, de Souza got a call from the producer, who told him that the studio had proposed a new budget-saving idea: move the setting of the picture from the East Coast to Los Angeles, and instead of a blizzard threatening the planes, make it fog.

"Fog?" said de Souza, baffled.

"Yes. It's the worst fog ever. So I need you to change all the snow to fog."

De Souza protested that the change would be more complicated than that. But Silver said, "It's never gonna happen, it's a complete jerk-off. These things happen. I know it's a waste of time. But please, you gotta do this for me." So de Souza dutifully wrote up a draft where Los Angeles (which is, in fact, prone to occasional heavy fog) was inundated by its densest, most impenetrable fog ever. "And as soon as they looked at it," says de Souza, "[the studio executives] go, 'We don't believe this.'" The fog promptly lifted, and the setting returned to the snowy East.

De Souza also remembers a meeting with studio brass, including Joe Roth, where a junior executive opined that the real story of *Die Hard 2* didn't start until Esperanza arrived at the airport, about thirty pages into the script. So why not just cut those pages entirely? McClane would arrive at the airport at the same time as Esperanza's plane landed, and that's where the film would begin, potentially eliminating days of filming from the schedule and hundreds of thousands of dollars from the budget.

Silver and de Souza were stunned. The script had been carefully constructed, first by Richardson with Gordon and Levin, then by Silver and de Souza, and the opening thirty pages had a number of essential story beats. These included a key battle between McClane and Stuart's men in the baggage area of the airport and a deadly fight between the airport SWAT team and the terrorists in the concourse.

What happened next, says de Souza, was "a real Hollywood tantrum, but done for a purpose." Silver lost his cool. "Joel, to his credit, says, 'You know, I came up here, I didn't know what we were going to talk about. I actually was going to surprise you people with some storyboards, because I think there's a sequence in this movie, it's one of the best sequences in any movie I've ever done, and it's a sequence that happens to be in the pages you're throwing out.'"

Growing ever more heated, recounts de Souza, Silver continued. "But maybe I'm wrong. I could be wrong. But I'm not. So, you guys know what you're doing. Here, why don't you take a look at this and tell me what to do with it, since it's not in the movie anymore." At that, he threw down a binder with sixty pages of storyboards in it, the binder popped open, and storyboard pages flew about the room as it slid the length the table, stopping near Roth. The room fell silent. "Look Joel, it was just a suggestion," said Roth, trying to break the tension. "You're the producer." On their way out of the meeting, Silver turned to de Souza and said conspiratorially: "Well, that worked."

KEEPING THINGS TICKING

After *58 Minutes* was green-lit as *Die Hard 2: Die Harder* in August 1989, the target release date was set for June 29, 1990—less than a year away. It was a tight schedule for such a big film, but the new regime at Fox was eager for a hit. Willis and Silver had been scheduled to make another action film, *Hudson Hawk*, first, but fortunately TriStar Pictures was willing to postpone it long enough for them to squeeze in *Die Hard 2*.

John McTiernan was the logical choice to direct the sequel, although at this point he was in postproduction on his 1990 submarine adventure, *The Hunt for Red October*. Moreover, he just wasn't feeling the sequel. "I didn't want to do it," he says. McClane had turned Willis into something more than the original character was meant to be. "I don't know," he sighs, "Bruce was suddenly cool and suave and sophisticated and a superhero."

That opened the door for Renny Harlin, a hot young director at the time. A native of Finland, Harlin's first Hollywood film had been 1988's successful horror sequel *A Nightmare on Elm Street 4: The Dream Master*. His next assignment was to be *Alien³*, but after a year of development, he became disenchanted with the project. "I quit, very fearfully," he says, "and the next day Fox offered me another movie, *The Adventures of Ford Fairlane*. After having spent almost a year in the dark and slimy world of aliens, this kind of rock 'n' roll comedy-action film felt like a breath of fresh air, so I jumped on it."

While shooting *Ford Fairlane*, a Lawrence Gordon–Joel Silver production, Harlin was visited on set by Silver and Willis, who invited him to lunch. "I thought it was just one of those social things," says Harlin. "It wasn't until the next day that Joel came to me and said, 'Bruce really liked you, and me and Fox, we've decided to offer you *Die Hard 2* to direct right after *Ford Fairlane*.' And I was like, 'Wow! That's pretty awesome! Yeah, I'm in.'"

Harlin was soon collaborating with de Souza on development of the script, but unfortunately their working relationship was an awkward marriage of talents. Harlin became frustrated with what he felt was de Souza's inattention to detail, and de Souza, in turn, felt that Harlin didn't "know his way around a script."

De Souza says Harlin ticked several boxes for Silver. He was under contract at Fox, and he owed the studio a picture. Since he was young, and early in his career, he didn't command a big salary, an important consideration since Silver was under pressure to control costs. "And Joel wanted a malleable director," says de Souza. "Joel basically said, 'This kind of movie is like a Swiss watch with the second unit, and stunts and stuff like that. So I need somebody the department heads can support and who will be straight-ahead. I don't need somebody coming in here with a vision.'"

De Souza remembers Harlin coming into his first meeting with long blond "rock star" hair, cowboy boots, pants with a bold stripe down each side, and a script loaded with sticky notes. According to the screenwriter, the meeting did not go well.

"Renny," said Silver, "Number one, you don't speak English. Number two, I've got a star who's going to push our limits because it's a sequel. Number three, I've done nine, ten scripts this year [with de Souza]. I've lost count. The script is on schedule and it's on budget. Number four, Bruce doesn't want notes. He doesn't want changes. We like it the way it is. So if you want to give notes, you've got to take another movie; the studio will be happy to give you another one."

"Alright, fine," said Harlin. "We'll talk later." And with that, Harlin put away his notes, although he never did give up on influencing the development of the script.

"I was the logic police," the director says. "I worked tirelessly, in the very few weeks that I had between *Ford Fairlane* and starting shooting *Die Hard 2*, in figuring out how we create a logic. How does he lose his gun? When it exactly happens. How does he get a new gun?" De Souza, Harlin says, "couldn't care less" how McClane acquired his weaponry from one scene to the next. "He just couldn't be bothered with that kind of thing."

Harlin was also concerned that it should be clear how McClane gets from one part of the airport to another, something he felt wasn't explained in de Souza's script. In a tense story with a ticking clock, where the hero has to cover some significant distance on foot, those details would really matter. To solve the problem, Harlin says, he came up with the idea that the various areas of the airport could be accessed by underground maintenance tunnels.

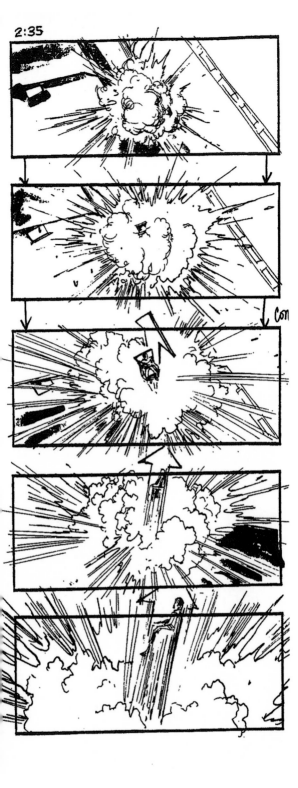

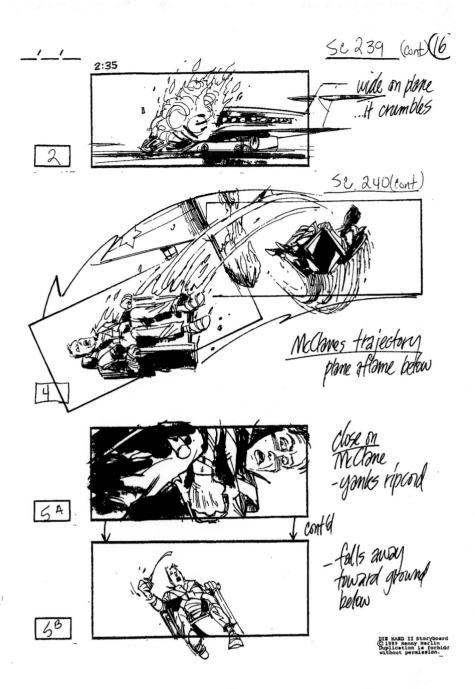

Harlin also states he invented one of the film's signature moments: the ejector seat escape. Trapped inside Esperanza's cargo plane, McClane is surrounded by Stuart's men, who are raking the aircraft with automatic weapons fire, even throwing grenades into the cockpit. "Steve writes McClane into this impossible situation . . . and then he somehow gets away," says Harlin. According to the director, he quizzed de Souza, who simply shrugged, saying that McClane escaped out the back door. Harlin says he invented a more compelling resolution: "I came up with the ejection seat." De Souza, however, claims ownership: "What Renny has confused in his mind was when the picture was budgeted, there was no money shot of that ejector seat coming all the way up to the sky and falling back to the ground." An "incredibly expensive shot," it was initially rejected by the studio. "Renny went to war to get that shot. I think in his mind, it's become that he's invented the idea of that moment."

Despite sometimes being at odds, Harlin and de Souza remain respectful of each other's abilities. "Steven de Souza was a great writer for *Die Hard 2* because he has a great sense of humor, and he has lots of great ideas," offers Harlin, while de Souza says of the director, "I think he's a great shooter."

Regardless of who came up with the shot—and despite its implausibility—the sequence would become one of the highlights of *Die Hard 2*. "If you plant things strongly enough, the audience will buy it," Harlin says. "Instead they enjoy the hero's resourcefulness and cleverness. They'll celebrate it."

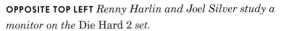

OPPOSITE TOP LEFT *Renny Harlin and Joel Silver study a monitor on the* Die Hard 2 *set.*

OPPOSITE RIGHT AND ABOVE *Storyboards for the dynamic ejector seat sequence.*

REUNION TOUR

As preproduction got underway, Jackie Burch came back to handle casting for *Die Hard 2*. This time, there wasn't a problem getting actors interested. "*Die Hard* was such a success," she says. "All these people want to be in movies that they think are going to be great."

Bruce Willis returned, earning $7.5 million for the role, and there was no more Hollywood snark about his salary. He was bullish about reprising McClane. "I have the same goals in this one that I had in the first one in that I don't want John McClane to be a superhero," he said. "I don't want him to be invincible." His mandate was to "play him as a guy who is vulnerable and who is afraid to die and who does get tired and hurt and beat up. If he has his choice, he wouldn't get involved, but he has no other choice."[1]

In Richardson's script, Al Powell did not return. But Silver demanded that de Souza find a way to shoehorn him in. Silver even personally called Reginald VelJohnson to recruit him back to the franchise. VelJohnson was shooting the first season of *Family Matters*, a new ABC sitcom, and remembers Silver telling him, "You should do this movie. Get rid of that terrible TV show that you're on and come do this movie." Although VelJohnson was already contracted to ABC, executives there were kind enough to let him shoot two small scenes for *Die Hard 2*, but no more.

Bonnie Bedelia signed on to play Holly again. "It'd look pretty stupid if he had a different wife," she says. "I couldn't do that to them. Also, how often do you get to be in a hit that big, no matter what you do in it? . . . Why not do it? You'd have to be some kind of pompous fool not to."[2]

William Atherton's narcissistic TV reporter Richard Thornburg came back with an even juicier part and more scenes with Bedelia, a prospect that was particularly appealing as the two actors happened to be good friends off-screen. Initially, Thornburg was not in Richardson's script either. "I had to fight hard to have him in the movie," says Harlin. "In the original script, Bonnie Bedelia's character was on the plane and that's it." While pairing "Dick" with Holly required the audience to suspend disbelief that the two characters could end up on the same hijacked flight, the conceit added a lot of juicy story potential. "I felt that it was dramatically an essential part of the picture," says Atherton. "And my agents loved that idea."

The role of villain Colonel Stuart went to William Sadler, a New York stage actor who would be playing his first major part in a high-profile film. He was shooting a smaller part in Dennis Hopper's *The Hot Spot* in Texas when casting on *Die Hard 2* started. On his return to Los Angeles, he met with Silver, Harlin, and Willis. "Sadler was relatively unknown at that point," says Harlin. "He came in to read for the part. I loved what he did. I loved his facial structure and his icy blue eyes."

It was a role Sadler was raised to play. "I grew up on a farm outside Buffalo," he says. "I spent my entire childhood running around the barn with a BB gun, and with my friends diving out of haylofts and coming up shooting. We were acting out all of these action movies that we loved. I realized I'd been rehearsing for [*Die Hard 2*] my entire childhood." Still, Sadler was apprehensive about taking over as the Die Hard villain. "Alan Rickman was brilliant," he says. "He was slimy, and dangerous, and funny, and a completely delicious villain. Trying to out-Rickman Alan Rickman would have been a terrible idea."

When casting General Ramon Esperanza, Burch steered Silver toward Franco Nero, the Italian actor famous for playing the titular coffin-dragging gunslinger in the 1966 spaghetti Western *Django*. "I had seen him in enough stuff," she remembers, "and then just said [to Silver], 'Will you go for Franco Nero, and make it very international?' And he's so handsome!" Nero, as it happened, had the same Los Angeles business manager as Silver, Fred Altman, whose office walls were adorned with posters of Nero's European movies. Already encouraged by Burch, Silver took one look and said: "I want him."

Renny Harlin loved the idea; the Finnish director had grown up watching Franco Nero movies. Silver sent the actor the script, but Nero was due in Sicily to shoot a drama, *Breath of Life* (1990). Nero remembers Silver calling him in Italy. "He said, 'So, are you going to be with us?' And I said, 'I don't think so, because I don't think I like my role.'"

Silver wasn't taking no for an answer, but Nero demurred, saying he had to be on set for *Breath of Life* because he was also a producer on the film. Finally, Silver called again and offered a plan: Nero would fly to Los Angeles, shoot two days, fly back to Italy for *Breath of Life*, then return to finish *Die Hard 2*. "He said, 'I tell you what to do . . . you go back and do your fucking movie, and then when you're through with the movie, you stay with us,'" says Nero. That worked for Nero, and Silver got his general.

For the third major bad guy, the treacherous Major Grant of the antiterrorist unit, Burch suggested John Amos, a familiar face from the 1970s TV sitcom *Good Times*, the blockbuster miniseries *Roots* (1977), and the hit Eddie Murphy film *Coming to America* (1988). "I've always thought he was so talented, and he's a wonderful man, too, so it's always fun when you can put in people that you really like," Burch says.

The casting of Samantha Coleman, a TV reporter who recognizes and helps McClane, was more convoluted. Burch considered hiring the physically striking Rene Russo, who had just appeared in the Charlie Sheen baseball comedy *Major League* (1989). "Then I realized, wait a second, we can't have Rene Russo on the ground with Bruce while Holly's up in a plane. It just wasn't smart," she says. "I said, 'No, we can't do this. We need a different girl as a character actress.'" If audiences saw McClane interacting with an overtly glamorous character on the ground while his wife was in peril aboard a hijacked plane, they might lose sympathy for the film's hero.

Sheila McCarthy was the next to be considered. A rising star in her native Canada, she had won a Genie—the Canadian equivalent of an Oscar—for the 1987 feature *I've Heard the Mermaids Singing*. Willis had casting approval, so McCarthy flew to New York to meet him at

THIS PAGE *(clockwise from top left)* Sheila McCarthy as TV *reporter Samantha Coleman; a storyboard shows McClane* *giving Coleman the slip; concept art for the logo of Coleman's* *news show; Dennis Franz and Fred Dalton Thompson as* *Carmine Lorenzo and Ed Trudeau.*

OPPOSITE *(clockwise from center left)* Vondie Curtis-Hall as *Miller; John Leguizamo as Burke; Art Evans as Leslie Barnes;* *a storyboard depicts Marvin giving McClane a ride; Tom* *Bower as Marvin.*

his hotel. Shortly after arriving back home, however, she heard that the part had been cut. Determined to the last, she decided to write a letter to Willis at his New York hotel, lobbying to have the role reinstated.

"I said very plainly that the part probably couldn't mean anything to him, but that it was a big deal to me, and I had won the Canadian equivalent of the Oscar for a movie, but I was kind of forging a new path in the States, and I just thought *Die Hard 2* would be really fun to do," she says. "So, maybe someone had given him a break many years ago when he did *Moonlighting*, and maybe he could give me a break." She didn't expect him to get the letter, but he did. The part was restored, and Willis pushed for McCarthy to play it.

For Ed Trudeau, the head of air traffic control at Dulles International Airport, the team turned to Fred Dalton Thompson. A former Washington insider and Senate staffer, Thompson had started acting in the mid-'80s, initially in two films for director Roger Donaldson, *Marie* (1985) and *No Way Out* (1987). Thompson would later become a US senator, run for president, and play a regular role on NBC's long-running *Law & Order*, as the Manhattan district attorney. "He was a real natural," says Harlin. "He carries weight, and he feels like a true authority."[3]

Art Evans, a veteran of the New York stage with a growing list of TV and film credits, landed the role of Leslie Barnes, the air traffic control engineer. "It's hard when you're doing a sequel, and the first one was so good, so I was trying to bring in interesting actors," says Jackie Burch, "like the Art Evans, the Fred Thompsons, that were all talented, and different, so that it made the movie interesting." Evans took his role seriously, spending time with real air traffic controllers. "It taught me a great deal about air traffic control," he says, "but I could only take it for five hours. . . . It's a stressful job."

For airport police chief Carmine Lorenzo, Burch went to one of her favorites, Dennis Franz. Best known for his role as Lt. Norman Buntz on the hit NBC drama *Hill Street Blues*, the actor would later gain even greater acclaim as Andy Sipowicz on *NYPD Blue*. "I had put him in *Psycho II*," says Burch, "so I had a history with Dennis, and I always loved him." Playing Lorenzo's brother Vito, the airport cop who gives McClane a hard time early on, was Robert Costanzo, another actor who'd spend time on both *Hill Street Blues* and *NYPD Blue*.

Harlin wanted Burch to cast Colonel Stuart's crew as a diverse-looking group so they would be easy for the audience to differentiate without much dialogue. "I wanted to get a group of men who would look strong, powerful, capable, and also very different from each other," he says.[4] The team ended up being a remarkable collection of rising talents, many of whom would go on to be prominent in the industry, including Robert Patrick, Vondie Curtis-Hall, Mark Boone Junior, Tom Verica, and John Leguizamo. "All those guys are multifaceted," Burch says. The casting director remembers walking Patrick to Silver and telling him: "Joel, we got to hire this guy." Silver did so on the spot. Years later, Patrick confided that he went to his car and cried after that moment because he was so broke and needed the job so badly. Later, James Cameron cast him as the liquid-metal villain in *Terminator 2: Judgment Day* (1991); only then did he have the cash to send Burch flowers. "It was very sweet," she says.

John Leguizamo, a Colombian American actor who had just appeared in Brian De Palma's Vietnam drama *Casualties of War* (1989), auditioned on video in New York. "I rocked it hard, and they gave me the part of the lead terrorist," he says. But when he turned up on set, all of his costars were "six-two, pumped out of their minds, and I was just this scrawny little guy." He was instantly demoted to Terrorist #7, his part getting smaller and smaller and his character suffering a much earlier death. "Eventually I got cut down to one single line of dialogue," he adds. To make matters worse, the line ("all systems tapped, Colonel") would need to be fixed in auto-

mated dialogue replacement (commonly known as ADR, the postproduction process in which actors rerecord lines to augment the audio captured on set). Leguizamo had already returned to New York after shooting. "The part was so small, they didn't want to pay to fly me back to LA to record the line."[5] To save money, the production rerecorded the line with another actor.

Even the smallest roles were great "discoveries," says Burch, like Irish actor Colm Meaney, soon to gain widespread fame on the television show *Star Trek: The Next Generation*. Meaney was brought in to play the pilot of Windsor 114, the British plane that is guided to its doom after Colonel Stuart and his men take control of Dulles air traffic control communication. Then there was Tom Bower, a Colorado-born performer who had been working since the mid-1970s. Bower was cast as Marvin, the janitor who helps McClane through the bowels of the airport. "I loved his face," says Harlin, "and loved him as a character actor and loved that character."

WEATHE
(on a weath
This Arctic blas
to sweep and kee

BEFORE TAKEOFF

For Harlin, preproduction on *Die Hard 2* was manic. He wrapped *Ford Fairlane* in August 1989 and went straight into prep for the biggest film of his career. With just three months before shooting was due to start in November, he was also diving headlong into postproduction on *Ford Fairlane.* "I don't know how I prepped *Die Hard 2*," he reflects. "Somehow I managed to make two movies at the same time." Still, he went into the film extraordinarily well prepared, storyboarding every shot himself.

Harlin brought two key collaborators straight from *Ford Fairlane*: production designer John Vallone and cinematographer Oliver Wood. Vallone was a Silver favorite who had designed a number of his films, including *Commando*, *Predator*, and *48 Hrs.* Harlin had handpicked Wood for *Ford Fairlane*, the cinematographer's first feature film, and felt he would also be perfect for *Die Hard 2.* "I wanted to find somebody with a really fun, flashy style, and Oliver Wood had been shooting the TV series *Miami Vice*," says Harlin.

An ALARM SOUNDS. Willi sh
down.

                    WILLI
     Time to get up.

She stirs only slightly to

                    WILLI
     The day has come

EXT. BROOKLYN STREET -- N

Residential area. A tight
side. Parking here is at

And stepping out from the
in and out of the cars, co
his ears. Turning, he mal
Easy mark. He slides a s

ABOVE *Renny Harlin and Bruce Willis discuss a scene on the set of* Die Hard 2.

OR (cont'd)
)
ust going
weeping.
n states
ure...

eyond his years. Eyes that ha
ecially death. And by his ow
e world's most dangerous man.

er. Made more for couch
sculined figure. Tatooed.
  And hair, thinning to his

window. And there, pulling b

nel. A sheet of white.

kind that might fool the most

t off. There lays a WOMAN.

for work.

wake-up call.

'D)

e with cars crammed in on eit
mium.

way is a PUNK. Moving quietl
high. Cap pulled down around
choice. A non-descript sedan.
m out from his waistline and

Also recruited were a number of *Die Hard* veterans, including costume designer Marilyn Vance, makeup supervisor Scott Eddo, special effects coordinator Al Di Sarro, composer Michael Kamen, and stunt coordinator Charles Picerni. New to the Die Hard family was English-born editor Stuart Baird, who had cut Silver's *Lethal Weapon* as well as *Gorillas in the Mist* (1988), which earned him an Oscar nomination. Joining him in the cutting room was Robert A. Ferretti, fresh from editing *Tango & Cash* (1989) with Baird over at Warner Bros.

Costume designer Vance faced new challenges on *Die Hard 2*. The first film focused on a limited number of characters inside a single office building. While the exterior scenes had many extras, especially uniformed first responders, the sequel would require hundreds, including passengers on planes, civilians in the airport, air traffic controllers, and police. There would be uniforms for airport police and airport SWAT, Colonel Stuart's ex-military terrorists, and Major Grant's Blue Light Special Forces team. Many of those characters and extras would need heavy winter outerwear to film snow scenes in freezing conditions.

Some of those outfits could be bought, but many looks would have to be sewn from scratch. "We created a lot of things," says Vance, "because you can't get authentic military [uniforms] in the right quantities and the right amount of time, especially for action movies." Real fatigues can vary from unit to unit, so special care would have to go into making them appear authentic. Vance was also aware that Defense Department approval might be required to use real uniform designs—approval that was not always easily obtained. To navigate the issue, she based her designs on real-life uniforms but made them different enough that they would not require Pentagon sign-off. That also gave her leeway to create special uniforms adapted to meet the needs of the stunt team, which might have to fight in them, fall in them, or use them in conjunction with safety harnesses.

Stewart's band of terrorists would get a different sartorial treatment than Hans's thieves did. The Gruber gang had European flair, and that had launched a Hollywood trend that was quickly turning a once-fresh idea into a cliché. "I didn't want to go with the typical terrorist look which [would come into] vogue in the early '90s, terrorists in fancy suits," says Harlin, "so I decided to go with utilitarian outfits for the terrorists."

William Sadler experienced a particularly memorable costume fitting. With Vance and Harlin looking on, he tried on one outfit after another, covering all of Stuart's scenes. Seemingly about to wrap up, he realized he hadn't tried a costume for his first scene, which according to the script would feature him doing tai chi in a hotel room with his shirt off. Sadler asked what he'd be wearing.

There was a pause before Harlin answered. "I said, Bill, will you promise me that you will go on a super diet and train eight hours a day like a maniac? I want you to be in unbelievable shape." Why? "Because I want you to be naked in the movie. I think our villain should be introduced naked." Mulling it over, Sadler asked if the production could push the scene to the end of the shoot, to give him time to hit the gym.

"I wasn't in terrible shape," Sadler says, "but I didn't want to watch the film when I was sixty and think, 'Ah shit, I wish I'd done a few sit-ups.' When you're going to be in the sequel to *Die Hard*, it's surprising how motivated you get."

Written by de Souza, the scene was a perfect way to introduce Stuart to the audience. "I wanted to show that this is a guy who is a fighting machine," says Harlin. "He lives and eats and breathes this world."

De Souza had also penned the film's much-talked-about teaser trailer. Created "before I even wrote a word on the screenplay," de Souza says, it was also the first thing Harlin shot. The trailer was the perfect way to surprise audiences: Over a black screen, a voiceover lists off key statistics about the running of Dulles airport for almost a minute before intoning, "But tonight, on Christmas Eve, it will all come to a complete stop. And one man is the only chance anyone's got." It suddenly cuts to a gun-toting Willis running through a dark tunnel, illuminated by flashing red emergency lights. "How can the same thing happen to the same guy twice?" he yells.

That line, or a variation upon it, would make it into the sequel, but the trailer footage wouldn't. Still, in the days before movie news and trailers were launched with huge amounts of publicity on the internet, the reaction was phenomenal, says de Souza: "It was in theaters before it had really percolated into the mainstream media that there was going to be another Die Hard movie. It was a big reveal."

BEGINNING IN LA

Die Hard 2 started shooting on November 28, 1989, just three months after Joe Roth's official decision to move ahead and less than eight months before the film's release date. The shoot was set to be split between interior work (on three soundstages at the Twentieth Century Fox studios in Los Angeles) and location work (mostly in Denver, Colorado, where the snow scenes were to be captured). Unfortunately, the production faced challenges from the get-go. Originally, only a small amount of money was set aside for the requisition of planes. The plan was to strike a deal with an airline or maybe rent an aircraft. But no self-respecting airline wanted to come near a story about terrorists blowing up planes.

With no airline willing to grant permission for its name to be used, logos had to be invented for fictional aviation companies like Windsor, Northeast Airlines, and Fuji Air. These were painted onto hired 747s and later stripped off. Silver at least managed to negotiate the use of Denver's Stapleton Airport and, for brief scenes in the bar and concourse, Los Angeles's Tom Bradley International Terminal.

Harlin was determined to deliver a movie in the same vein as *Die Hard*, while injecting something fresh into the proceedings. "I kept talking about 'replicating the experience,' in the sense that when you sit down in the movie theater, you're not faced with a completely new kind of character," he says. "You feel that this is the familiar Bruce Willis that you met in the first movie. His attitude, his sense of humor, and his troubles in life are still something you can relate to. But at the same time it was my responsibility to try to come up with something new,

something more exciting, something more surprising, something bigger, and make it worth the audience's while to pay for a ticket."

Willis had followed the first *Die Hard* with a part in director Norman Jewison's well-received drama *In Country*, playing a disillusioned Vietnam vet. "I needed to know after five years of television work whether I could still find a character who wasn't me, who didn't smirk, who wasn't wisecracking, and who didn't get the girl in the end," he says.[6] Thus, returning to McClane didn't sit easily with him. "He wanted to be taken seriously," remembers Harlin. "He didn't want to be the guy from *Moonlighting* anymore. He looked at the script and said, 'I want all this humor out of there. I want the movie to be real. I want my character to be real. This is a serious movie.'" He initially resisted lines from the script like, "Just the fax, ma'am," said jokingly to a flirty female car rental clerk when McClane is faxing Al Powell a set of fingerprints.

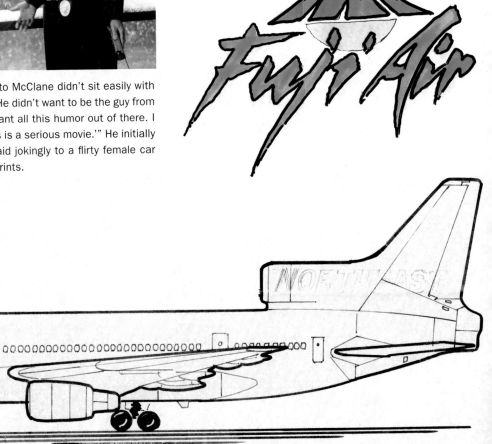

OPPOSITE CENTER LEFT *John McClane looks on in disbelief as Colonel Stuart takes control of the skies.*

OPPOSITE TOP RIGHT *Panic breaks out at the air traffic control tower in this storyboard frame.*

OPPOSITE CENTER RIGHT *A logo design for the fictional airline Fuji Air.*

OPPOSITE BOTTOM *Concept art for a plane owned by fictional airline Northeast.*

ABOVE *A miniature airport built outside the air traffic control set to give the illusion that real planes were taxiing along the runways in the background.*

Harlin told Willis he thought the star was off the mark: "I said, 'We're making a sequel because the audience loved *Die Hard*. What did they love about it, that it's a terrorist action story? No, they loved your character. They loved this blue-collar guy who's got marital problems, who still has this wry, witty, sarcastic sense of humor.'" Silver intervened, just as he had done on the first *Die Hard*, requesting that Willis always do one take Harlin's way to humor the young director. Reluctantly, the star agreed.

The plan was to leave LA for Colorado in mid-January to shoot snowy exteriors, once winter had really set in. In the meantime, the early part of the *Die Hard 2* schedule would mostly focus on interiors that could be shot on soundstages in Los Angeles: airport scenes with no view out the window, the control tower scenes, and the airliner interiors. Both production designer John Vallone and the film's art director Christiaan Wagener were qualified pilots whose knowledge of the world of aviation and airports informed the design process.

One of the most important studio sets was the air traffic control tower, where much of the action plays out as McClane and the airport officials communicate with Colonel Stuart, who plans to take over the runway, land Esperanza's plane—due in fifty-eight minutes, of course—and then take off in a commandeered 747. "We had to figure out the scale of an actual airport," noted Vallone during production, "and then shrink it down to a size that would fit on a stage that's about 130 by 207 feet."[7]

SC 249   R2 ②
OTS McClane
Grant fwd. "maybe
they're more creative
than you think!" etc.

...you're the wrong guy
in the wrong place, at
the wrong time!"

Squad Rm.
MC
Pull-back
w/mcClane
exit
"story of
my life."

Cont'd

dolly to profile

Engineering
Rm.

SC 250
Barnes takes McCl.
aside, "...you could th
showed up out there
in" etc.

DIE HARD II Storyboards
©1989 Renny Harlin
Duplication is forbidden
without permission.

TOP *The control tower set as seen from outside.*

INSET *Dennis Franz and Bruce Willis argue it out in Carmine Lorenzo's office set.*

ABOVE *McClane butts heads with Major Grant in this storyboard sequence.*

OPPOSITE TOP *A stuntman performs a backward fall for the Annex Skywalk sequence.*

OPPOSITE BOTTOM *Willis cracks a smile on the Annex Skywalk set.*

INSERT *A storyboard sequence illustrates the moment when McClane uses a conveyor belt to retrieve his gun, just in the nick of time.*

The control tower set was a huge two-story edifice constructed at the center of Stage 16 on the Fox lot, a space almost identical to the one used to build the atrium for *Die Hard*. The size of the set allowed Harlin to elaborately take in both levels of the build in one sweeping shot. "I wanted to have a set where the camera could crane from the bottom floor to the upper floor in one continuous move," he says. Outside the windows, miniature runways were built in forced perspective, and model airplanes were fitted with radio-control engines allowing them to taxi, giving the illusion of a functioning, albeit snowed-under, airport. The special effects team mounted huge drums in the rafters that dropped fake plastic snow to simulate a blizzard outside the windows. The drums would drop bigger flakes nearer the window and smaller flakes farther away to give a sense of depth to the panorama.

Top-of-the-line video equipment, monitors, radars, and so forth were also installed to give the impression of a real air traffic control facility. So impressive was the set that it attracted some esteemed guests. "A lot of filmmakers and executives from different movies made sort of a pilgrimage to our set," says Harlin. "I remember it was the first time I met one of my heroes, Martin Scorsese. He walked around and was shaking his head looking at the size of [it]."

He might have been shaking his head harder if he'd known how much creative license had been taken with the design. "Believe me," says Harlin, "real air traffic control towers are not this big and not this spectacular. I did a lot of research. I went to a lot of air traffic control towers. They looked really boring. So we decided that fiction had to be more important than reality." The clutch of monitors that move up and down on a rig in the center of the room, for example, was dreamed up to look great on film. "This was not a very popular movie among air traffic controllers or airlines," laughs Harlin.

Other sets on the Fox soundstages included the airport police station. This set would be used for a key scene where Chief Lorenzo learns that Major Grant and his men are traitors when McClane demonstrates the bullets they've been firing at Stuart's gang are blanks. Also, the Annex Skywalk, a part of the airport's new under-construction terminal, was built for a scene where Barnes and the SWAT team set out to reestablish communications with the planes circling overhead before being ambushed by Stuart's men. The Annex set included a working travelator for the scene where McClane, trapped under some collapsed scaffolding, activates the walkway to bring a gun into his reach just in time to shoot an attacker.

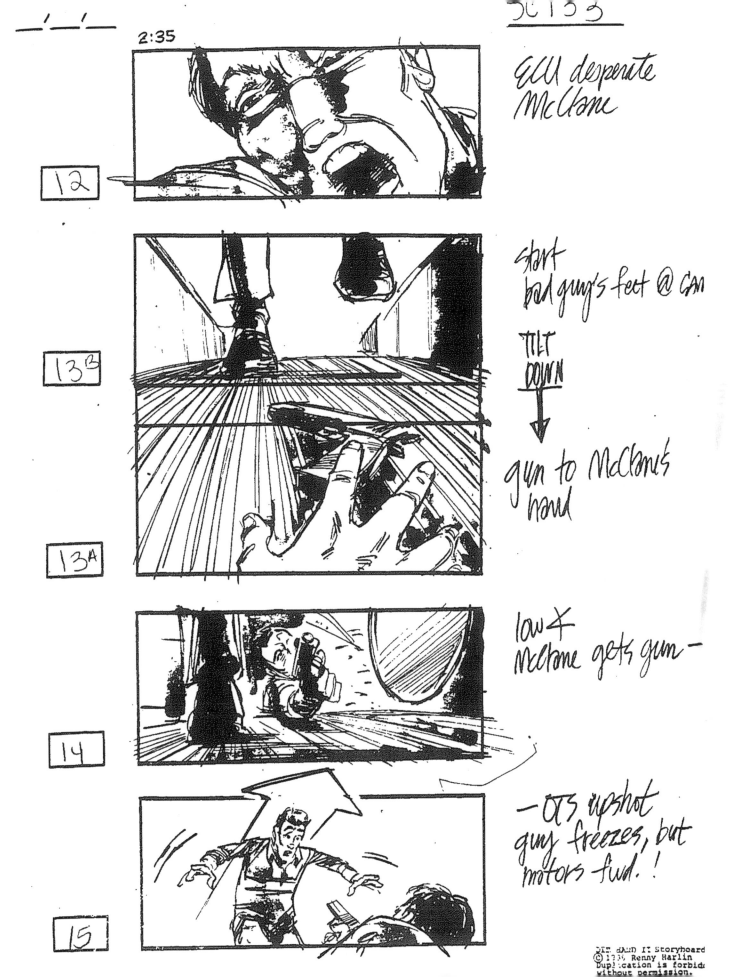

Sc 13 S

ECU desperate
McClane

12

start
bad guy's feet @ cam

TILT
DOWN
↓

gun to McClane's
hand

13B

13A

low &
McClane gets gun —

14

— OTS upshot
guy freezes, but
motors fwd. !

15

- down on dangling
(& victorious) McClane

63

Cochrane scrambling
- still snagged on be[l]

64

- tries to shed top coa[t]

(longlens over roller
out @ Cochrane

65

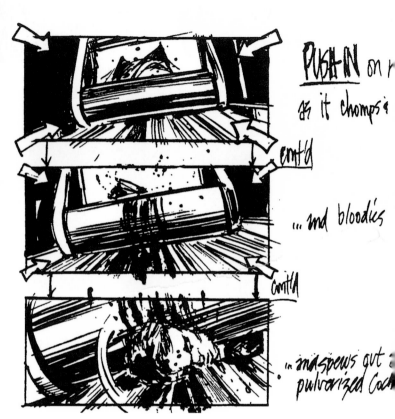

PUSH IN on [r]

as it chomps [&]

cont'd

... and bloodies

cont'd

... and spews out
pulverized Coc[h]

SC 53

"INTO THE HATCH
HEADFIRST."

56

(closer on
McClane)

For the film's first major set piece, a brawl in a luggage-handling area between McClane and Stuart's men, the production converted a warehouse in downtown LA. The initial plan was to shoot in a real airport luggage area, but the internal conveyor belts weren't safe enough to use in a fight scene. A labyrinth of moving ramps, catwalks, and mechanical equipment was constructed. "We ended up designing an area where these belts moved in certain ways that would serve our action," says Harlin, "and could be controlled in a very safe way."

Stunt coordinator Charles Picerni helped stage the fight. "I had it pretty well mapped out for [Harlin]," says Picerni. "And he saw it and liked it, and we shot in that way." The sequence sees McClane and one of Stuart's henchmen, Sgt. Oswald Cochrane (John Costelloe), tussling violently on a moving ramp. Managing to pin his opponent, McClane sees what Cochrane doesn't: a large cylindrical baggage press up ahead. He jumps to safety by grabbing onto a scalding pipe as Cochrane's head gets caught in the machinery.

Harlin was particularly pleased with the moment when McClane takes a golf club to Cochrane's accomplice, Miller, played by Vondie Curtis-Hall. "What in general makes action films complicated," he says, "is that you want to have a certain amount of firefights and a certain amount of hand-to-hand combat. You are always looking for the new weapon."

Other locations in Los Angeles included the Wilmington Harbor Generating Station, which doubled for the airport's basement and boiler room. "[It] had very little to do with an airport," says cinematographer Oliver Wood, "but just looked so dramatic and spectacular that it was well worth doing. When you entered the place, it just felt subterranean. We decided that underneath the airport should be a kind of orange-warm hell. The lights were gelled, and we used a lot of steam."[8] Likewise, the Jensen Treatment Plant in Granada Hills stood in for the tunnels under the runways. Mojave Airport—now known as Mojave Air & Space Port—became a tropical airfield that is shown on-screen in a news report about General Esperanza.

The airliner interiors of the plane carrying Holly and Thornburg were shot at Stage 27 at Universal Studios, using a preexisting jetliner set. Despite the usual secrecy surrounding a production of this size, the *Die Hard 2* shoot became an attraction on the Universal Studio Tour. Tourists would swarm the door to the soundstage, and the clicking of their cameras would fill the air. "Everybody knew all of us were in there doing *Die Hard 2*," says William Atherton. "I just remember the tour guide was always saying, 'Bruce Willis! Bruce Willis!' in very loud Japanese. We'd just be hysterical on the inside."

OPPOSITE *Storyboards illustrate the luggage room fight and Cochrane's grisly demise.*

ABOVE *Bruce Willis on the luggage room set.*

TOP RIGHT *A storyboard panel shows McClane wielding a golf club in the luggage room fight.*

CENTER RIGHT *Franco Nero's General Esperanza surveys his troops alongside William Sadler's Colonel Stuart on location at the Mojave Air & Space Port.*

BOTTOM RIGHT *Renny Harlin (center) on board an Esperanza tank at the Mojave location.*

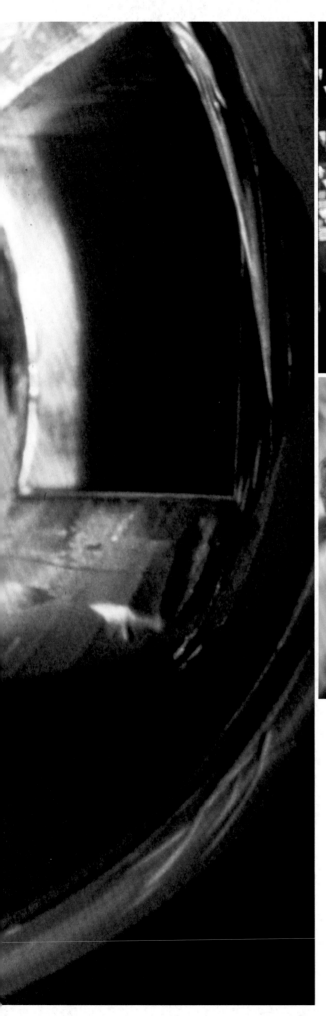

When the tourists departed and the cameras rolled, Atherton and his friend Bonnie Bedelia would riff off each other, although few of his extra lines made it into the movie. "I made up too much," he says. "It was funny at the time, but I think it wasn't appropriate for the film, so the editors probably saved my ass." The actor says he admired Harlin as a technician and shot designer. "When you're in a plane like that," observes Atherton, "you have to keep it all visually moving, and I remember him doing that extraordinarily well." Lighting rigs were mounted outside the windows to simulate an orange sunset glow for scenes set just before nightfall.

For Harlin, these sequences with Holly were crucial to the success of the film. "The movie is not really so much about saving the world and saving hundreds of people; it's about the simple thing of saving somebody you love. Without this relationship, I think the film would be much, much less effective."

LEFT AND TOP *John McClane explores the airport's underground tunnels.*

ABOVE LEFT AND ABOVE RIGHT *Good friends William Atherton and Bonnie Bedelia reunited for* Die Hard 2.

CHASING THE SNOW

After almost two months in Los Angeles, *Die Hard 2* moved on to location shooting in Denver in mid-January 1990. At the city's main airport, Stapleton International, Silver and the *Die Hard 2* company were officially greeted by Denver's mayor, Federico Peña, and his wife, Ellen Hart Peña. "They know how much moolah a film company brings to town," said *Variety*.[9] And indeed, the production spent as much as $50,000 a day just on food, lodging, cars, and other routine expenses. Hundreds of extras were outfitted for winter, and the airport was dressed with festive decorations and lights. The production even shipped in real reindeer (something the Finnish Harlin was very proud of) for the opening scene in which McClane's mother-in-law's car is towed away.

If Silver had been under budget pressure before shooting, things quickly began to spiral out of control when the production left Los Angeles. The cause wasn't poor planning or creative differences, but a true act of God: January and February 1990 proved unusually warm and dry in Denver. When the cast and crew arrived, they were greeted by rapidly melting snow. The actors were left killing time as the production figured out what to do. "Everybody was in a holding pattern," says actress Sheila McCarthy, who managed to read the entire works of author Anne Rice during her downtime on set. Willis did what he could to keep spirits up. On January 28, the Denver Broncos were playing the San Francisco 49ers in the Superbowl. The actor rented a basketball court and threw a viewing party for the cast and crew, with giant-screen TVs at either end. "It was fish, meat, and vegetables, and pastries, and drinks, from one end to the other," says Art Evans. "Bruce really took care of his staff and his cast. He was a very sharing person."

Just about every way of faking snow was considered. Plastic flakes could only be used on soundstages (and FAA regulations prevented their use in the vicinity of aircraft) so other solutions were sought. Special effects coordinator Al Di Sarro instructed the production to buy a large ice-chipping machine. Loaded onto a forty-foot trailer, it needed to be towed to the

location, where huge refrigerated trucks containing three-hundred-pound blocks of ice were on standby. Often starting six hours before call time, the crew would blow the chipped ice onto the set with hoses. "We literally snowed in the whole approach and drive-in to Stapleton Airport with crushed ice," said Di Sarro.[10]

The unit then decamped to Mead, a small farming community thirty-two miles outside of Denver, to shoot exteriors at a local church. In the film, Stuart sets up his base at a church near Dulles Airport and hacks into the airline systems from the location. The Highlandlake Church in Mead was fitted with a false front and steeple to play the part, while outside, dozens of trucks, motor homes, vans, cranes, lighting, and equipment lined the roads. The site had been chosen in anticipation of the picturesque winter wonderland look, but once again, nature had come up short.

"In Mead alone, we probably chipped two hundred thousand pounds of ice a day to dress the set," Di Sarro estimated.[11] A local fire department was even hired to spread fire-retardant foam on the ground around the church to also simulate snow. Moreover, with temperatures as low as fifteen below zero, the filming equipment began to suffer. Film became brittle, lenses stiffened up, and cameras froze. Batteries also needed to be kept warm. "Cooking" the equipment—surrounding a camera or a lens with space heaters—was a primitive solution, but it worked.

Ironically, during the shooting of a scene where McClane fights with Stuart's sentry outside the church, real snow did fall, as Denver was hit by the Front Range blizzard of 1990, one of the worst snowstorms in decades. Over three feet of snow fell in two days. Conditions were so severe that the lights and camera equipment that had been set up at the church had

OPPOSITE TOP *John McClane endures a blizzard.*

OPPOSITE BOTTOM *Silver chats with Willis during an airport terminal shoot.*

TOP *Joel Silver and Bruce Willis share a joke outside Stapleton International Airport.*

ABOVE *Renny Harlin directs a scene.*

to be broken down and stowed for their protection. "You could see six feet in front of you, maximum, and other than that it was just a whiteout," says Harlin.

The director calls it the toughest night of the shoot. "I looked at Joel, who was next to me, and he was absolutely pale. He looked at me and he said, 'Renny, I've been through a lot of movies and a lot of challenges, but I think this time I just took too much on my plate, and I don't know how to solve this.' And that's when I realized, I'm in really big shit, because if Joel—Joel who is bombastic, Joel who can go through anything—if *Joel* feels like we might not be able to survive this one, then how am I going to do it?" Eventually, the storm passed and work resumed.

The fight itself provided one of *Die Hard 2*'s signature moments, with McClane dispatching Stuart's lookout, Baker (Tony Ganios), in hand-to-hand combat by stabbing him in the eye with an icicle. Harlin tried to do it as "tastefully" as possible so as not to turn off audiences. Scott Eddo's makeup team created a gory appliance with a stub of plastic icicle embedded in the center that was then fitted into the eye of Willis's opponent. During the fight, says Eddo, "They cut to another angle where he's made impact. Bruce pulls his hand away as if the icicle broke in his hand and left him with a stub." A prosthetic head was also created for certain shots.

The sequence where Stuart's men escape on snowmobiles and McClane pursues them was also partly shot in Mead and on a nearby frozen lake. Once again facing issues of diminishing snow, Charles Picerni, who was also now shooting second unit as well as working as the stunt coordinator, had a flash of inspiration. He'd worked on the 1989 comedy *National Lampoon's Christmas Vacation* and shot in Breckenridge, Colorado. "There was a snowmobile run up there called Tiger Run, and I said, 'Let's go up there and scout that location. We might find snow up there.' Sure enough, there was. And the next night I had a unit going up there with me, a second unit, and we shot that snowmobile sequence up there."

With the stunt team using ten Yamaha Exciter snowmobiles, Picerni plotted the scene out without storyboards. "It was difficult to orchestrate," he says. "I took stuntmen up there. They sent me actors up there to shoot—Franco Nero and a couple of others—and I shot them." For the spectacular moment when Willis's snowmobile explodes as it leaps over a truck, Al Di Sarro's team took over. First, the engine from a snowmobile was removed, and a dummy replica of Willis was attached. A tow vehicle was used to pull the engine-less snowmobile at speed, making the leap over the truck with the snowmobile following behind. The explosion was activated via a rip cord trigger, and another cable was used to pull the dummy off the vehicle just before the explosion. For shots involving close-ups of McClane, Harlin came in to shoot. "I had him rolling down a hill where he finds out the bullets were fake," says Picerni. "And Renny shot Bruce on a close-up there."

Eventually, the producers gave up on shooting in Denver, and the *Die Hard 2* company became a troupe of nomads, crisscrossing the continent. "We had to chase the snow," says Willis.[12] After Denver, the team went to Moses Lake near Spokane, Washington, to shoot on the runways surrounding the Grant County International Airport, landing with eight airplanes, three helicopters, and three hundred cast and crew. To begin with, it was relief. "There's a beautiful cover of snow everywhere," Harlin says. "I go to sleep and I wake up the next day. . . . I go to the window, and I open the curtains, and I scream in horror. It's green grass on the yard. There's not a flake of snow on the ground." An overnight rise in temperature had caused the snow to melt. With the airport reserved, and planes hired, it was an utter disaster for the production.

The crew started brainstorming. What about bringing in twenty refrigerated trucks from Canada full of snow? A good idea, but it would take a day for the vehicles to arrive. In the meantime, a plan was hatched to hire thousands of local schoolchildren to help nail "snow blankets," essentially white fabric sheets, to the ground with wooden pegs to create the illusion of a snowy landscape. Potato flakes were also used, blown by wind machines and fans to create a blizzard. After a day's preparation, the snow-laden trucks from Canada arrived. "We got the first truck on the runway," recalls Harlin. "And a giant cube of ice, the biggest cube of ice you've ever seen, slides onto the runway." The snow had melted during the daytime, turned to slush, and then refrozen again. Worse still, potato flakes got caught up in the heaters installed to keep the actors and crew warm. "Now we have the smell of fried potatoes in the air," adds Harlin.

At least the scene where Stuart, Esperanza, Grant, and their men board the 747 to make their escape could be shot in the airport's giant hanger. Outside, Harlin was looking

OPPOSITE *The terrorist Baker is stabbed through the eye with an icicle. This prosthetic head, a dead ringer for Baker actor Tony Ganios, was intercut with footage of Ganios fighting with Bruce Willis.*

TOP *John McClane gives chase on a snowmobile.*

ABOVE *Willis, Ganios (wearing the prosthetic eyepiece created by Scott Eddo), Renny Harlin, and Joel Silver.*

to complete the film's climactic stunt, in which McClane jumps from the WNTW news crew's helicopter onto the wing of the 747 housing Stuart and his gang as the plane gathers speed on the runway. After preventing takeoff by jamming his coat in the aileron, McClane stays on the wing to fight Major Grant and then Colonel Stuart. Unfortunately, when the real 747 started its engines, the exhaust blew all the carefully pinned snow blankets away. "So now no snow blankets, no snow from Canada," says Harlin. "Only potato flakes that smell like fried potatoes."

Understandably, tempers were fraying and emotions rising. "Tears were not far from our eyes. It really seemed hopeless," says Harlin. Silver remembers the crew working all day to chip the ice, only for another mini spike in temperature to ruin their work. Hardened visual effects veterans were brought to tears because all their hard work was melting away in front of them.

Yet, somehow, they managed to shoot the stunt, or at least a portion of it. Oliver Wood lit the mile-long stretch of runway, doing his best to keep the snowless ground in the background out of shot. For some shots, a camera vehicle ran alongside the plane, although the best footage came from a camera helicopter flying parallel to the 747. Despite the spacious nature of the setting as it appears on film, in practice it was anything but. "Out on the runway, where we would have 150 people, cameras, lights, flags, and snow machines, it began to feel a little tight," notes Wood.[13]

Back again after *Die Hard*, Willis's stunt double Keii Johnston leaped ten feet from the helicopter to the wing of the moving plane. "That was all done practical," says Picerni, who was leading the second unit, "with the doubles going down the runway, [while I was] freezing my ass off!" With the camera helicopter shooting the scene, there could be no mistakes. "Everything had to be set," says Picerni, "because that plane, that 747, was scheduled to take off right after that and go to Hong Kong. If it didn't work, we were gone." Thankfully, it did. Flying "a real helicopter over the wing of a real 747," as Willis puts it, was a true Hollywood moment. "I don't think that's ever been done."[14]

TOP LEFT *The WNTW news helicopter is prepped for a shot.*

CENTER LEFT *McClane runs across the airfield.*

BELOW *Concept design for Esperanza's plane.*

OPPOSITE TOP *Stunt doubles portraying John McClane and Colonel Stuart fight on the wing.*

OPPOSITE BOTTOM LEFT *Renny Harlin shooting from underneath the wing of a plane.*

OPPOSITE BOTTOM RIGHT *General Esperanza's plane lands.*

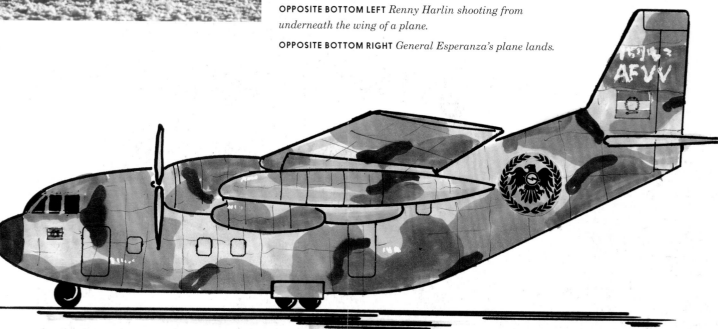

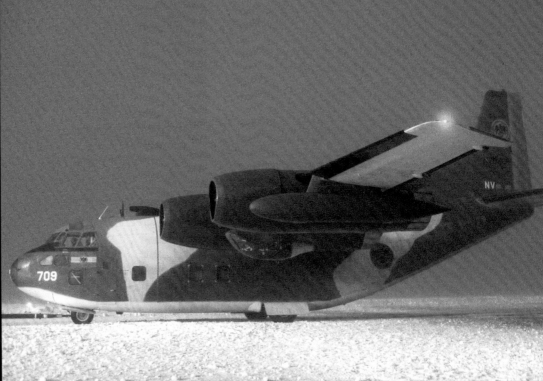

CALIFORNIA OR BUST

After Moses Lake, the production returned to Los Angeles to film the interior of the church on Stage 14 of the Fox lot. But there was a long way to go, with much exterior snow-related work still to be done. "It was incredible pressure," says Harlin. "I spent more sleepless nights on that movie than any other movie in my career. I was literally scared out of my wits." With location scouts all over North America, reports of snowfall would be flooding in. At certain times in the production, *Die Hard 2* quite literally had its own fleet, utilizing a full-scale 747, an L-1011 passenger plane, a C-123 military plane (modified to look like its successor, the C-130, for the scenes in which it ferries Esperanza), and A-Star and Bell 206 helicopters, all perfect for transporting equipment and personnel in an increasingly outlandish search for snow.

The production next moved to Alpena, Michigan, a town about 250 miles north of Detroit on the shores of Lake Huron, to shoot some exterior airport sequences. There was snow, at least, but filming at the small-scale Alpena County Airport was logistically difficult. Planes aside, the crew needed support equipment like a deicing truck, a tug plane to tow the "hero" planes into shooting position, power units to run the electrical systems when the airlines were parked, and even air stairs to allow cast and crew to board the planes. Shooting continued for a few nights before the weather turned again, first to freezing rain and then to fog.

Biodegradable soap flakes became a temporary solution, thanks to the work of Bob Graham, whose company Graham Enterprises specialized in design and development for film studios. With the soap industry no longer making flakes, Graham discovered they would need special machinery to create them. A factory was retooled to work around the clock for four weeks, producing nothing but soap flakes. After forty thousand pounds were shipped to Michigan, "They went through the first batch very quickly, so we made another forty thousand pounds and then another ten thousand pounds after that," says Graham.[15]

One of the major shots captured at Alpena was the postcrash wreckage, after the Windsor 114 plane is guided to its doom by Colonel Stuart. Around six truckloads of scrap airline parts were brought in by Al Di Sarro and spread over a half-mile area. For each take, the material was set on fire. "Then between takes we would try to put it out so that we would have something to burn for the next take," said Di Sarro.[16] The shots where the L-1011 carrying Holly McClane finally lands safely, and the passengers disembark via inflatable slides, were also filmed at Alpena.

So desperate was the search for snow, "we even considered going to Greenland," says Willis.[17] While the idea of leaving the country was nixed, the second unit was sent farther north to the former Kincheloe Air Force Base, since redeveloped as Chippewa County Airport, in Sault Ste. Marie on Michigan's Upper Peninsula. There, the production shot a scene in which McClane brandishes makeshift torches in a vain attempt to prevent the Windsor 114 plane from crashing on the runway.

The main unit next headed back to Los Angeles, where they took over Stages 15 and 16 at Fox. In the studio, they completed further shots of the church exterior and the shootout around the cargo plane that lands with Esperanza. The remaining footage needed for the fight sequence on the wing of the 747 was also completed in the studio, with Willis, Sadler, and Amos acting out their choreographed combat moves on an eighty-foot prop wing. Suspended twenty-two feet off the ground, this wooden, silver-painted wing was attached to a section of prop fuselage, hooked to scaffolding. "It was amazing to go into a Fox stage where they've built cathedrals and cities and find that this wing filled it up," says Wood.[18]

Even more ambitious were the efforts to chill the set. "We wanted to see the actors' breath," explains Wood. "Refrigeration units were brought in and left on overnight to get the stage down below 32 degrees. So we would arrive on a beautiful day, 80 degrees outside, and put anoraks on, and scarves and pants, and all go inside."[19] It didn't quite work, as William Sadler recalls: "When they turned on the ever-present gigantic fan that was blowing chipped ice in our faces the whole time, you couldn't see our breath anyway, so they backed off doing that."

While the main unit had been working frantically, the process was no less stressful for the effects crew at Industrial Light & Magic (ILM). After six weeks' negotiating to win the contract to produce *Die Hard 2*'s visual effects, the team had only five months to complete nearly forty major effects shots, including many of the sequences involving aircraft. While the production had already been forced to hire real aircraft, at $60,000 to $75,000 a day, it was far more cost effective to build miniatures for many of the scenes, particularly those involving multiple planes circling, unable to land. The action scenes involving planes, particularly the crash sequence, would also require miniature work. Made of fiberglass and aluminum, these

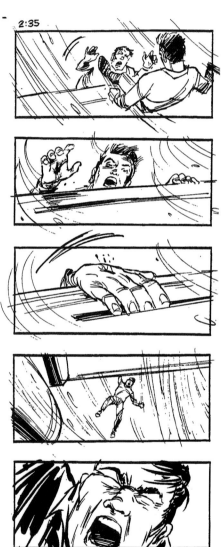

OPPOSITE *The climactic fight on the wing is shot in the studio, complete with falling snow.*

TOP *Filming Holly McClane's jump to safety.*

ABOVE *A storyboard shows McClane hanging on to Esperanza's plane for dear life.*

LEFT *Another reunion for the McClanes.*

scale models included an F-4 Phantom jet, a modified C-130, one 727, three 747s, five DC-8s, and two L-1011s. Sizes varied, but the 747s were twenty-three feet long and forty inches high.

Early in March, the effects team—cheekily nicknamed Crash and Burn Productions—left their Marin County base. Among them were visual effects supervisor Mike McAlister and visual effects art director Paul Huston, who had both worked in various effects departments on the *Star Wars* and Indiana Jones films. The team traveled to a remote airstrip in the Mojave Desert valley. With swirling winds, the conditions were ideal to help simulate shots of the planes circling in wintry blizzards. While they were not quite facing the trials that the main unit had endured, it was still tough. "It was very cold at night. It was extremely unpleasant. Lots of dust," remembers Huston. Tents were set up so that the team could prep their planes in shelter, but the wind hitting the canvas was so loud that crewmembers had to wear earplugs. Outside, in the storms of dust, the models were suspended by cranes in the air, secured by wires, and attached to a radio-controlled rig that allowed each plane to tilt or bank over the smoke clouds (created by Navy foggers, used to hide battleships at sea). Cameras and lights were also hung from the cranes.

Some shots, such as one featuring Esperanza's plane being escorted by two F-4 Phantom jets, were captured using a different approach. McAlister and Huston were flown in a rented Learjet to shoot plates of "the clouds, the sky, the motion, and the speed," says Huston. "[Mike] took a VistaVision camera [which provided a higher-resolution variant of 35mm film] and just stuck it up against the window of the Learjet and shot film out the window." This was then composited together with footage of the three model planes, shot against a traditional blue-screen backdrop.

When it came to the crash of Windsor 114, there had been much debate throughout the shoot about the nature of the scene, with Fox executives expressing concern that killing so many innocent people would alienate audiences. Studio chief Joe Roth convened a meeting to propose a more sanitized version, in which the terrorists crash a nonpassenger cargo plane. Harlin sided with Silver and de Souza in favor of the original scripted version. "I felt very strongly that these terrorists had to do something extremely evil and horrendous in order to make their threat real," the director says. "As terrible as it seems, I felt that they had to bring a plane down in order to make us believe they are capable of doing this. It's not empty threats but a real situation, and the stakes are extremely high."

The original concept stayed. To make the scene as convincing as possible, Harlin studied footage photographed by the FAA during crash tests, as well as data from real crash tests. The interior of the plane was shot at Universal, attached to a rig that could turn 360 degrees, upside-down or sideways. With the camera on a long crane, the setup also included an air blower to create jets of air on the faces of actors playing the doomed passengers. The overhead baggage compartments were even rigged to spill out contents during the crash. "The only problem was it was too effective," says Harlin. "We all agreed it was too much, too cruel, and that the audience would have trouble settling in after that."[20] The final film showed only minimal footage of the victims.

To create exterior shots of the crash, ILM used a 747 model during the miniature shoot in the Mojave. The team needed three shots: the plane hitting the runway and its nose rising upward, the plane sliding down the tarmac, and the plane exploding. The crash was shot at two hundred frames per second using a model packed with gunpowder, kerosene, and flammable liquids and rigged to break apart in a series of blasts. "It was all choreographed to extend the action, to give the audience so many chances to believe that these people were going to make it," says McAlister.[21] To add to the atmosphere, smoke was deployed to hang in the air, and white gypsum was placed on the ground to simulate snow.

ILM was also involved in the finale. As Stuart and Esperanza take off in the stolen 747, McClane pulls the handle on the fuel dump. He then sets fire to the trailing gasoline, engulfing the plane in flames as he utters "yippee-ki-yay, motherfucker." This was fantasy, of course; the powerful exhaust from the plane would easily extinguish any fire. But no matter: ILM delivered an incredibly convincing denouement. The effects team shot various elements for the sequence, including the fire trail, created by filming a long pipe pumping out ignited propane gas, as well as the moment the flames leap and catch the wing of the plane—an effect realized by filming a flamethrower being fired into the air. These pieces would later be composited with shots of the model plane exploding.

OPPOSITE *In the Mojave Desert, the ILM team films a model plane coming in for a landing.*

ABOVE *Building an F-4 Phantom jet model.*

BELOW *McClane observes the fuel trail leaking from Esperanza's plane.*

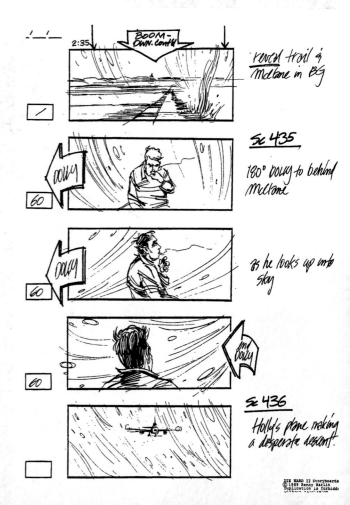

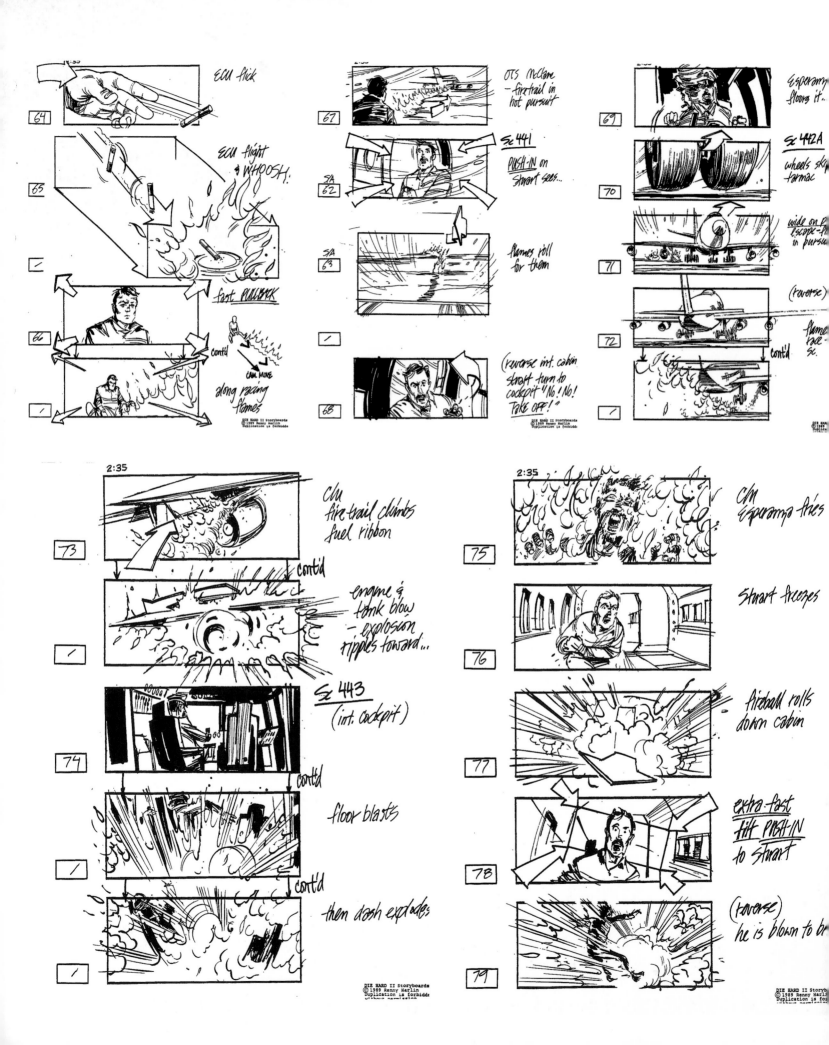

To capture the airborne explosion of the escaping villains' plane, a 747 model was rigged to hang twenty feet from the ground at the Mojave location. A combination of kerosene, gunpowder, and three hundred to four hundred pounds of explosives was used to detonate the model. "It was the biggest pyro explosion ILM had ever done," says Huston. "They threw everything at it! I remember hearing the pyro guys bragging about how big it was." With the explosion visible from a freeway several miles away, the airport was getting calls asking if a plane had crashed.

For Harlin, one of the film's most pivotal moments was the ejector-seat sequence, in which McClane escapes from the cargo plane that transported Esperanza to Dulles Airport. As the plane explodes beneath him from grenades lobbed by Stuart's men, McClane parachutes away to safety. "There are some shots that are worth the money because they're the ones that sell the movie," he says. "They're the shots for the trailers, the shots the audience will be talking about when they go home. I was very persistent. I wanted ILM to do it somehow."[22]

OPPOSITE *A storyboard illustrates the sequence in which Esperanza, Stuart, and their gang meet a fiery end.*

TOP *Navy foggers are used to create clouds during the Mojave Desert miniature shoot.*

FAR LEFT *Filming the Windsor 114 crash in Mojave.*

LEFT AND ABOVE *Filming Esperanza's plane model in Mojave and against a blue screen at ILM.*

The sequence was anything but easy to accomplish. McAlister was worried. "You have to execute the shot with twice the normal fidelity because everybody's looking for the clues that tell you that it's fake," he says.[23] A further problem arose when ILM learned that to accommodate Willis's shooting schedule, they needed to shoot the blue-screen plate of the actor *before* filming the plane's explosion—forcing the team to guess how Willis should be lit so the shot would seamlessly match the background-plate explosion.

For the blue-screen element, shot at ILM in San Rafael, California, Willis was strapped into an ejector seat that was attached to a motorized rig that rotated him head over heels, as the camera moved in on his facial grimaces. "Bruce was strapped in with a harness, and we had him tumbling very slowly as the camera dollied in on a one-hundred-foot-long track until we were tight on his face," says McAlister.[24] The shot was then composited with the explosion below as the plane is blown to smithereens.

To complete the sequence, a quarter-scale puppet and parachute was created and thrown off a construction crane, forty feet in the air, to simulate the moment McClane glides to safety as Stuart and his men look on.

The same level of ambition went into the film's final shot. After the villains' 747 explodes, leaving a fiery trail that gives the passenger planes the runway light they need to land, Harlin and Wood wanted to pull the camera back from the happily reunited McClanes to reveal the snowy runway. Involving six jumbo jets, police and emergency vehicles, plus passengers and airport crew, the scene would be far too expensive to set up for real. A giant matte painting, created by ILM artist Yusei Uesugi, was the answer. The methodology presented a major challenge, however. Usually mattes were incorporated into shots lasting just a few seconds, the brief exposure on-screen allowing the illusion to hold. The *Die Hard 2* finale shot was going to be thirty-five seconds long, allowing the audience ample time to scrutinize the visuals. The sequence would also need to blend six live-action plates featuring actors and vehicles, all shot at night on ILM's backlot.

"We dressed up the ground with calcium carbonate for snow," explains Huston, "and we had a bunch of different tow vehicles, transportation, a golf cart that Bruce Willis was driving in the film. We had a lift that the camera was on so it could shoot at different heights. I created a diagram for what the different heights and lenses and distances would be from the different groups."

Uesugi had already figured out the composition of the painting using model airplanes set up on a board, with nails used to represent people. After the live-action plates were shot, he began constructing the matte painting on an eight-foot panel. "He took color prints from the plates that we shot, and he positioned [them] on [the] panel, and then painted in the airplanes," explains Huston. Using still photography of the large-scale airplane models as reference, Uesugi spent five weeks completing the project.

In a groundbreaking move, digital techniques were used to blend live-action plates and the matte painting. "That was the first digitally composited matte painting shot that ILM ever did," adds Huston. Data from the matte painting was fed into a Macintosh II computer, allowing Uesugi to play with and blend the colors of the image using the then brand-new Adobe software Photoshop, designed in part by ILM's John Knoll.

In addition, to bolster the illusion that the matte was actual live-action photography, the filming rig was set up to perform what looked like a natural camera move. "When the shot starts, the motion-control film camera that shot the matte painting was on a track, and it pulled back maybe ten feet," says Huston. This simple effect immediately brought verisimilitude to the scene.

As the ILM team frantically worked to deliver their shots, somehow Harlin and his team made it through to the final days of shooting without collapsing. It was now early April, just three months before the film was due in theaters. "I remember vividly that these were the last two days of shooting when I was shooting in the cockpit of the plane, and I could feel everyone was breathing very heavily down my neck," says the director. He credits Joel Silver with shielding him from the studio despite frequent visits from stressed executives. "You keep shooting," he remembers Silver telling him. "If it takes a day, if it takes two days, if it takes three days, whatever it takes, you make your sequences as good as you can. You don't worry about anything, because I tell you one thing, when this movie comes out, if it's a hit, nobody cares what it took to get there. If it's not a hit, we look like idiots. So you just make a great movie, and that's all you have to worry about."

TOP *ILM artist Yusei Uesugi at work on his meticulous matte painting for the complex final shot of* Die Hard 2.

ABOVE *Bruce Willis films the ejector-seat sequence against a blue screen at ILM.*

OPPOSITE BOTTOM *John McClane uses an ejector seat to escape certain death in this final frame from* Die Hard 2.

"Excellent" Ratings	Total %	Males Under 25 %	25 and over %	Females Under 25 %	25 and over %	NRG Norms %
Performances						
John McClane, played by Bruce Willis	70	71	66	73	70	40
Col. Stuart, played by William Sadler	44	46	36	53	40	25
Barnes, played by Art Evans	38	41	33	40	28	25
Lorenzo, played by Dennis Franz	36	36	28	46	37	25
Sgt. Al Powell, played by Reginald Veljohnson	35	41	21	44	36	25
Dick Thornberg, played by William Atherton	34	37	23	42	34	25
Captain Grant, played by John Amos	33	36	20	45	31	25
Holly McClane, played by Bonnie Bedelia	32	32	16	46	35	25
Trudeau, played by Fred Dalton Thompson	32	38	21	39	32	25
Esperanza, played by Franco Nero	20	21	14	30	15	25
Elements						
The action	69	76	63	78	60	25
The pace	55	56	51	68	45	25
The ending	51	50	46	56	52	25
The story	45	49	44	54	33	25
The settings	44	43	44	55	32	25
The music	34	34	32	40	31	25

III.   ADJECTIVE SELECTIONS

-- The movie was described, through the selection of adjectives from a list, by almost all audience members as action packed and entertaining and at high levels as funny, fast paced and suspenseful. Other positive description at moderately good levels were interesting characters, well acted, appropriately violent and high quality.

RED ALERT

The shoot finally wrapped on April 6, 1990. Accounts of the film's delays and cost overruns were leaking to the show business press. *Variety* reported the shoot was three weeks behind schedule. *The Hollywood Reporter* called it "panic time at Fox."[25] By the end of the month, the story heated up in the general press. Syndicated gossip columnist Marilyn Beck wrote that Harlin had conceded the film was over budget—"we had a lot of bad luck"—but wouldn't confirm or deny that the picture was going to be $20 million over its $48 million budget. Fox officials denied the figure, but the story wouldn't go away.

Rightly or wrongly, Silver was frequently identified as the cause of the problems. The *Los Angeles Times* weighed in, noting that Silver had "a long-standing reputation as a free-spending producer." The *LA Times* article recounted stories of an especially lavish birthday party for Willis, though the studio insisted the weather, not irresponsible spending, was behind the cost overruns. In early May, *Variety*'s Michael Fleming reported the final cost would be $62 million.[26] Studio chief Joe Roth had already called a "red alert" to get control of *Die Hard 2*'s costs and ensure it would make its release date, which had been moved back from June 29 to July 4—not a huge change, but enough to fuel gossip about delays and costs.[27]

Harlin maintains to this day that, despite the frantic search for snow and all the jetting around the country, shooting never got too far off schedule. To help the production stay on track, editors Stuart Baird and Robert A. Ferretti had been working in the cutting room twelve to fourteen hours a day, seven days a week since the first day of filming. "There wasn't even enough time to have a director's cut and a producer's cut," says Ferretti. "It was just one cut, in the theaters, that's it."

Harlin didn't see eye to eye with Baird on how *Die Hard 2* should be assembled. "I had huge cat fights with Stuart," the director says. Harlin felt that he and Oliver Wood had emulated some of the techniques McTiernan introduced on *Die Hard*, including restless camera movement and shots set up to flow from one moving shot to another. According to de Souza, Baird felt that Harlin was too protective of his shots and unwilling to trim them. He insisted to Silver that Harlin be banned from the editing room and instead asked that Silver or de Souza cut the film with him. De Souza ended up with the assignment.

The edit even led to a legal dispute. The production had secured a $20,000 product placement deal with Black & Decker that called for McClane to use a Univolt cordless drill in a scene where he removed an air duct grill in one of the below-ground tunnels; the power tool company in turn began a promotional campaign featuring Willis as McClane. But with Harlin itching to add another stunt, the moment got moved to an elaborate sequence that sees McClane open up a hatch with the drill to discover a narrow girder above a pit of fire which he must cross. "It's like *Indiana Jones and the Last Crusade*, where Indiana Jones has to take the leap of faith," says de Souza, who wrote it. Eventually, the sequence was cut for delaying the film's momentum and the drill disappeared with it. Black & Decker Corporation filed a civil lawsuit against Fox and a division of the Young & Rubicam ad agency. The company demanded $150,000 in damages for "loss of credibility" with its customers, since the promotional campaign connecting the brand to the movie had already started. The matter was later settled out of court.

Audio issues were also causing headaches. "One of the biggest problems was sound," says Ferretti. The noisy fans installed on set to create blizzards had rendered much of the on-set audio recording unusable and the crunched schedule left no time for normal ADR spotting sessions. To try and get ahead of the issue, the team had been ADR-ing footage during the actual shoot, meaning lines were being rerecorded on the spot to improve the quality. "That's a monumental task," says Ferretti. "The actors would go during their lunch hour and [perform] ADR, and then the sound guys had this nightmare of waiting until the scenes were cut to match it all up. I've never seen that happen before or since."

Other actors were called in for emergency ADR sessions. Franco Nero, who'd journeyed on to film a movie in Chile after wrapping his scenes in *Die Hard 2*, was on his way to yet another

THESE PAGES *The test screening report for* Die Hard 2, *conducted by the National Research Group.*

he National Research Group, Inc.
une 7, 1990
age 7   XR-4859

- Dennis Franz as Lorenzo received an above average 36% "excellent" rating with younger females giving him the highest and older males the lowest rating.

- Other supporting performances which received above average "excellent" rating were: Reginald Veljohnson as Sergeant Al Powell (35%), William Atherton as Dick Thornberg (34%), John Amos as Captain Grant (33%), Bonnie Bedelia as Holly McClane (32%), Fred Dalton Thompson as Trudeau (32%). The only performance which received a below average "excellent" rating is Franco Nero as Esperanza (20%).

- All of the elements received well above average "excellent" ratings (the norm of all elements is 25%).

- The highest rated element was the action, which received an outstandingly high 69% "excellent" rating, with higher ratings from younger than older audience members.

- The pace received a high 55% "excellent" rating, with younger females highest and older females lowest (though still above average) in rating this element.

- The ending received a high 51% "excellent" rating with older males slightly lower, though still well above average, than the other groups.

- The story received a well above average 45% "excellent" rating, with younger females highest and older females lowest (though still above average).

- The settings received a similarly well above average 44% "excellent" rating, with again younger females highest and older females lowest but still above average.

- The music was the lowest rated element but still received an above average 34% "excellent" rating, with only younger females rating this element higher.

shoot when he found himself making a quick stop to rerecord Esperanza's dialogue. "I stopped in Rome for one day," he says. "I had to do it in two hours because the next day I had to go to Leningrad to shoot *Young Catherine*. It was all boom, boom, boom!"

When it came to the music, Harlin had a big influence on Michael Kamen's score. Brainstorming with Joel Silver, the director came up with the idea to incorporate Finland's most popular composer, Jean Sibelius, and his famous composition "Finlandia." "We talked to Michael and he said, 'Yeah, that's a fantastic idea,' and it really is the score for *Die Hard 2*. . . . For anybody who knows music, it's 'Finlandia.' It's composed into different segments, but in the end when the planes are coming down, it is full-on 'Finlandia'

playing." Harlin remembers at the premiere in Finland, "there wasn't a dry eye in the theater" when that played.

Like *Die Hard*, the sequel incorporated some old standards into its soundtrack: Christmas perennial "Carol of the Bells" is being played in the festively decorated airport, while Vaughn Monroe's "Let It Snow!" once again features over the final shot and into the end credits. There's also an evocative use of Patti Page's "Old Cape Cod," which is playing on Marvin's record player when McClane first discovers the janitor's underground hidey-hole.

When it came to screening the film, Harlin's most nerve-racking moment was showing it to Barry Diller, the chairman and chief executive officer of Fox, Inc., the parent company of Twentieth Century Fox and the Fox network. Harlin was "horrified" at the set up: a big theater on the Fox lot, with just a handful of people in attendance. "It's the worst way to watch an action movie because there's no audience," says Harlin. "I remember Barry Diller standing up at the end of the movie, walking past me, and saying, 'I'm sure there's a good movie in there somewhere.' That was all he ever said."

Thankfully, audiences were more enthusiastic. On June 6, 1990, a test screening was held in Mountain View, California, the same location as the original *Die Hard*'s first public screening. The film scored extremely high, with 55 percent of the audience rating it "excellent" (25 percent is the norm). Even the contentious scene when the jetliner crashes and kills innocent passengers did not affect the scores. Indeed, in this particular screening, it was the icicle-in-the-eye moment that was "disliked" more.

Achieving an R rating took some back-and-forth with the MPAA. The film featured its fair share of violent scenes—including Major Grant's demise, sucked into a jet engine—and it was a process of trimming away the worst excesses. "I think it went back to the MPAA seven, eight, nine times," says Ferretti. "Each time we had to reduce the blood splatters." The film was eventually rated R, like its predecessor.

The National Research Group, Inc.
June 7, 1990
Page 10   XR-4859

Confusion

-- Most of the audience did not find anything confusing in the movie which was not cleared up by the end of the movie.

-- The minority who found something confusing and not cleared up, had the following questions:

- Why did not the government get involved?
- Why were not artificial lights used?
- Is there a Pacific Bell Phone in Washington, D.C.?
- Why was not airphone use sooner?
- Why not land at another airport?
- Why did not other planes collide?
- How did John McClane know that there were blanks in the gun?
- Why did the church not explode?

What Would You Tell Your Friends

-- Most of the audience indicated that their word-of-mouth to friends would be favorable. They would stress that the movie had a lot of very good action, that it was suspenseful and exciting and that it was as good as or better than the first movie, Die Hard.

-- Other positive comments were that the story was good, that they enjoyed the plot twists, the jokes/one liners, the special effects, the good acting, especially by Bruce Willis and the fast pace.

-- The violence and the movie being bloody/gory were mentioned both in positive and in negative ways, with older females mentioning these aspects mainly as a negative while the other sex/age groups mentioned them positively.

HARDER SELL

Die Hard 2 was expected to be a hit, and having gone so far over budget, it needed to be. To aid its success, it was released with a different strategy than its predecessor. Where the *Die Hard* release had been platformed—opening on a few screens a week before going wide—*Die Hard 2* was given a six-day "weekend" including a preopening on 1,800 screens (*Die Hard* wide-opened on less than 1,300) ahead of its official July 4 opening date, when it expanded to 2,000 screens.

Around the time *Die Hard 2* opened, *Vanity Fair* published a profile on Joel Silver, focusing on the scandal over the film's costs. Silver did not speak to the magazine, but many close to him did. Some defended him; McTiernan called him "a javelin catcher who buffers directors against the insecurities of inexperienced management—the most capable and focused producer I've ever met." And Roth was diplomatic, while not dodging his budget concerns. "The production was moving so fast, it was impossible to catch up to the costs," he said. "Later, we had to figure out why information was slow and how experienced people didn't know what was happening. . . . It just happened too quickly for everybody. For me, *Die Hard 2* was a systems check and, in part, a systems failure. I hope the system won't be tested this badly again." He also added, "We manage entirely differently now," suggesting Fox would never again give any producer such a long leash. After working with TriStar Pictures on his next picture, *Hudson Hawk*, starring Willis, Silver soon signed a deal with Warner Bros., parting ways with both the Gordons and Fox for good.

When it finally arrived in theaters, *Die Hard 2* opened big, making $21.7 million on its first weekend. By the end of the week, it had grossed $46 million, nearly surpassing its original budget. It stayed in theaters for ten weeks, defying all expectations. Instead of delivering a smaller gross than the first *Die Hard*, *Die Hard 2* finished with $118 million in the United States, comfortably up from the first installment's $81.4 million. It was an even bigger hit outside the US, grossing $122 million internationally. The story of the *Die Hard 2* budget seemed to dominate entertainment news coverage at the time, but like Willis's "scandalous" deal on the first *Die Hard*, the success of the film ultimately justified the considerable expense and silenced naysayers.

Critics generally embraced *Die Hard 2* for its action-movie merits, though some groused it was dumb and wildly unbelievable. It also came in for censure for its violence and high body count. The *New York Times*' Vincent Canby calculated that 264 people died in the film, including 230 on the crashed British airliner, compared with 18 character deaths in the original film. "It's one of the most brutal acts ever committed in the name of entertainment," added the *Washington Post*'s Desson Howe. Says Harlin, "I got the reputation of having killed more people in one action movie than anybody else. I'm sorry to have that label, but I felt it was important for this film."

Despite the critical griping, *Die Hard 2* was successful enough to leave little doubt the studio and star alike would be looking for a third installment, although Willis was coy in public. "I think we've pretty much said everything there is to say about John McClane and terrorists," he said at the time. "Where's he going to go from here?"[28] He was right: It couldn't happen the same way again. The next *Die Hard* would go in a different direction . . . eventually.

OPPOSITE *Final art for the* Die Hard 2 *theatrical poster.*

ABOVE LEFT *Bruce Willis catches up with old* Die Hard *nemesis Alexander Godunov at the premiere of* Die Hard 2.

ABOVE RIGHT *John McTiernan, Bonnie Bedelia, and Alexander Godunov attend the* Die Hard 2 *premiere.*

PART 3

DIE HARD WITH A VENGEANCE

"I am a soldier, not a monster."—SIMON GRUBER

After the success of *Die Hard 2*, there was little doubt there would be a third installment of the franchise, although its path to the screen would be a difficult one. Though Silver was out, Gordon was still keen to produce *Die Hard 3* with Willis returning as McClane. Forming the basis of the story was *Troubleshooter*, a spec script by James Haggin purchased by Gordon's newly formed Largo Entertainment in March 1990. Gordon's intention was to coproduce the film with Fox. With the action taking place on a Caribbean cruise liner, the franchise was following a clear pattern: "The first one is *The Towering Inferno*. The second one is *Airport*. So the third one has to be *The Poseidon Adventure*," says Steven de Souza, who—like a number of other writers—would be brought in to help develop potential stories for *Die Hard 3*.

Gordon turned to newcomer Peter Iliff in the summer of 1990 to rewrite *Troubleshooter*, placing John and Holly McClane on the liner seized by bomb-wielding terrorists from Haggin's original script. "I said I'd do it if they let me sink the boat," Iliff says.[1]

Unfortunately, by then, Die Hard–inspired action films were lighting up the box office. Already in the works was *Dread Naught*, another thriller set at sea, written by Jonathan Lawton. Iliff was even asked to work on the *Dread Naught* script; he passed, but it meant that both sides were aware of each other's projects. Iliff took a crack at the Troubleshooter script, handing in his draft in April 1992, by which point *Dread Naught*—now called *Under Siege*—was shooting with Steven Seagal in the lead. Beaten to the punch, John McClane would never get to take that Caribbean cruise he so desperately needed.

Curiously, Gordon had commissioned another cruise-based script from Walter Wager, the author of the book *58 Minutes*, which had become *Die Hard 2*. Set on British ocean liner the *Queen Elizabeth 2* (QE2), the story saw the McClanes sailing to Italy on a vacation to rekindle their romance, only to have their trip ruined when terrorists smuggle atomic weapon detonators aboard. "Their plan is to sail the ship out to sea, transfer the detonators to a

OPPOSITE *John McClane slips back into the A-shirt for* Die Hard with a Vengeance.

TOP RIGHT *Samuel L. Jackson and Bruce Willis as Zeus Carver and John McClane.*

fishing boat, and sink the ship," said Wager. How does McClane win? He fires a Rolls-Royce stashed on the ship out of the loading door, "so it crashes onto the fishing boat, killing everybody."[2] But again, the arrival of *Under Siege* torpedoed Wager's script.

While the producers struggled to find the right story, other issues were keeping *Die Hard 3* from the screen. Bruce Willis, by then one of the biggest stars in the world, was reportedly asking $17 million to reprise John McClane. In addition, Rupert Murdoch, the owner of Fox's parent company, News Corp., had balked at the studio putting up the entire $60 million budget for *Die Hard 3* after several recent Fox films, including David Fincher's *Alien³* (1992), had underperformed. The possibility of seeing McClane back in his A-shirt seemed remote.

A solution arose in September 1992, when Fox chairman Joe Roth struck a deal with the Disney-based Cinergi Pictures, led by Andrew Vajna, to partner on *Die Hard 3*. The Hungarian-born Vajna had formed Cinergi after selling his stake in Carolco, the highly successful company behind the Rambo pictures. Cinergi's first production was John McTiernan's 1992 film *Medicine Man* with Sean Connery, soon followed by the Willis-starring erotic thriller *Color of Night* (1994).

"Fox had tried to put [*Die Hard 3*] together," recalls Vajna. "But they were unable to make a deal with Bruce; they were just unable to bring the pieces together. I was very friendly with Bruce's agent, Arnold Rifkin, who said, 'You know . . . why don't you try and put this thing together?' So we made a deal with Fox that I would attempt to put it together, and they would get certain distribution rights." Fox had Japan and America; Disney, where Vajna's company was based, had the rest of the world.

Of course, Vajna still needed a script. Coming up with a second sequel was a challenge, he says, noting that the third film in a series is "always the most difficult one to make," with the characters already established and needing fresh challenges. First under consideration for screenwriting duties was *Lethal Weapon* writer Shane Black—who had inadvertently given the Die Hard franchise its title via Joel Silver all those years earlier—but he turned down the offer.

John Milius, who had *Big Wednesday* (1978) and *Red Dawn* among his directorial credits, was approached. He agreed to write a nonnautical version with Barry Beckerman, a producer on *Red Dawn*, noting, "We're off the boat."[3] Aptly, from the man who coscripted Francis Coppola's Vietnam War masterpiece *Apocalypse Now* (1979), Milius describes his involvement with *Die Hard 3* using a Vietnam metaphor: "I'm an American adviser on this script. In fact, I'm really an American adviser in Laos." In other words, it was all hush-hush.[4]

But, the Milius-Beckerman script went nowhere. It was now early 1993, almost three years since *Die Hard 2*, and momentum was waning. To try to get things back on track, Vajna brought in *Die Hard 2* screenwriter Doug Richardson. "I was told that they were having problems getting a version of it made that Bruce wanted," Richardson says. Richardson's script took McClane back to Los Angeles, pitting him against cops planning to steal cash from the Federal Reserve using the newly built subway tunnels.

Little did Richardson know, he wasn't the only one on Die Hard duty: Vajna had also brought in John Fasano, cowriter of *Another 48 Hrs.* (1990), to write a treatment. In Fasano's story, John McClane went up against kidnappers who abducted his daughter, believing her to be the child of a wealthy, powerful industrialist. Vajna later dismissed the idea as "too predictable," but his strategy was always to present Willis with script options.

"Since Bruce had kiboshed a couple of Die Hard scripts prior to that," says Richardson, "while I was writing the official *Die Hard 3*, [Vajna] hired John Fasano to write another version, with a different story, so he could present Bruce with both scripts at the same time and say, 'Bruce, make a Die Hard, any Die Hard.'" But word came back to Richardson that Willis didn't like the choose-a-script gambit and had soured on doing a Die Hard movie with Vajna. "Bruce didn't trust Vajna at all at that point."

Vajna needed to regain Willis's faith. His solution was to try to recruit original *Die Hard* director McTiernan, who was in many ways responsible for the birth of the franchise. Although McTiernan was interested in the prospect of directing another Die Hard film, he knew that the blueprint for the film had to be just right. "John and I both had agreed that we would not come back and try to do a new Die Hard film unless we had a really good script," says Willis.[5] With no sign of the script issue being solved soon, McTiernan jumped ship. He planned to reteam with Arnold Schwarzenegger (with whom he'd just made 1993's *Last Action Hero*) on a remake of the 1935 Errol Flynn pirate adventure *Captain Blood* for Warner Bros.

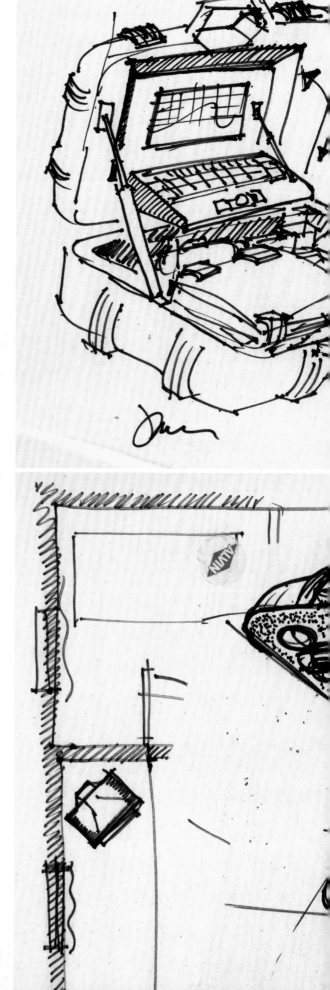

FEB 07 1994

The current "draft" isn't a draft at all. We flat out weren't done enough to have anybody read anything. But FOX had to have something that looked like a script on Jan. 31... so out of the word processor it came. It had no characters whatsoever and the last 25 pages was something we'd rejected as long ago as the last meeting at Sun Valley. But it was the only thing we had on paper. I thought all this had been made clear, but evidently not. Here's what we've actually got in mind....

CHARACTER

McCLANE is something of a burnt-out case, but now we understand why. He is a blue-collar street cop whose marriage to an educated, independent, up-scale woman has failed. He is an ordinary Joe who has nothing in common with his college-bound son. He is, in short, a family man whose family doesn't need him--a protector with no one to protect.

This "lost man" aspect of McClane's character is established in three beats: in our first view of him, sleeping off a hang-over while his fellow cops work; in an early scene with Linda when she asks him if he's married and he replies, "I was once. But it didn't work out"; and in a later scene where he confesses to Linda that he and his wife split up not because they didn't get along, not because they didn't love each other, but because she simply didn't need him.

LINDA is still a strong, self-sufficient woman, but her bias now is more against men than against whites. She is strong and self-sufficient because she has had to be. All her life, men have let her down. They have come to her, used her, and then disappeared, often when she's needed them the most. The prime culprit is the father of her child, who bedded her and then ran as soon as her stomach started to swell. Linda wants a knight, but she always seems to get a knave.

When she meets McClane, she is certain that he is like all the rest. In fact, the first thing he does, however inadvertant it may be, is bring her trouble. But in the end, he will not only come through for her, but will prove ready to sacrifice himself both for her and for a school full of children he has never met.

Each will fill the other's need. Each will complete the other's character.

RHYMIN' WITH SIMON

McTiernan's time on *Captain Blood* was short-lived. Despite Schwarzenegger's enthusiasm, the project rapidly sank. But it did introduce the director to Jonathan Hensleigh, a former attorney who was beginning to make a name for himself as a screenwriter after George Lucas hired him to pen several episodes of his TV series *The Young Indiana Jones Chronicles*. Hensleigh had been tapped to write the script for *Captain Blood*, and after that project collapsed, McTiernan asked if the writer had anything else in his locker. As it happened, he'd written a spec script called *Simon Says*, which Fox had bought for $1 million earlier in 1993, around the same time Richardson and Fasano were creating competing *Die Hard* scripts.

Borrowing a page from the award-winning 1958 drama *The Defiant Ones*, *Simon Says* centered on an NYPD cop forced into a reluctant partnership with a civilian shopkeeper to take on a villain who terrorizes the city with a series of bombs. Hensleigh's inspiration for the story stemmed from an incident in his childhood in which he injured another boy with a rock. The other boy recovered fully, but Hensleigh was haunted by the memory. He imagined what might have happened if the boy had been permanently maimed. What if he returned years later to take revenge on the culprit, who is now a New York cop? A similar stone-throwing incident was not only the *Simon Says* bomber's motivation, but also the source of his obsession with childhood rhymes and riddles; all his twisted games were supposed to take the hero back to his childhood and the incident that ruined Simon's life.

Despite a promising start for the script, *Simon Says* soon started to flounder. "I sold it to Fox after they told me they didn't want to change anything," Hensleigh says. "Then at the first meeting, they said they wanted to change everything."[6] Particularly troubling to the studio was the scene in which the villain forces Hensleigh's hero, Alex Bradshaw, to stand on a New York street wearing a sandwich board emblazoned with a racist slur, quickly putting him in danger with the locals. It was an all too familiar Hollywood tale. "They didn't do anything with it; they fired me and started rewriting me. I was not very pleased by all that," says Hensleigh.[7]

But when McTiernan read Hensleigh's original script, he immediately thought it was the perfect blueprint for a Die Hard movie: a buddy story with the store owner as McClane's worthy companion. He contacted Vajna, who loved the idea, but there was still the matter of convincing their leading man. "We FedExed the script overnight to Bruce Willis, who was at his place in Ketchum, Idaho, and Willis responded immediately," says Hensleigh. The actor liked the script's relentlessness: "The film starts in chaos," Willis says. "It's just this big, rumbling freight train going down the tracks."[8]

Everyone was in agreement: The first half of the script was perfect for a John McClane adventure—so much so, you could practically just swap out Bradshaw and replace him with McClane. Recalling films like Clint Eastwood's *Dirty Harry* and *In the Line of Fire*, where the villain manipulates the hero via phone, the plot would see Simon send McClane across New York, running between locations to solve nursery rhyme–like puzzles in order to prevent bombs being detonated.

With the action taking place across one day, Hensleigh's script fit the Die Hard formula. "Die Hard is a guy in trouble in a box," says Vajna. "Whether the box is the building, whether that box is an airport . . . we broadened it to a city, but it's still a box." Willis sees it in more expansive terms: "It's like going to Disneyland. You're going to travel through this great amusement park, only it's real life . . . and it's called New York City."[9]

Although the filmmakers were off to a good start, issues remained. "It was the back end of the script we needed to figure out," says Hensleigh. An early breakthrough came after Hensleigh rewatched the first *Die Hard*. It was 5:00 a.m. when he had what he calls a "lightning-bolt" moment. "I called John [McTiernan] and said, 'What if [Hans] Gruber had a brother, and that brother is extremely pissed at John McClane?'" It was a clever conceit, linking the third installment to McTiernan's original film not only through the Grubers, but also through the brothers' similar methodology. Like his brother, Hans who used a terrorist siege to cover up a robbery, Simon crafts an elaborate plot about avenging his fallen sibling to distract authorities from a planned heist.

THESE PAGES *Concept sketches by Jackson De Govia for the briefcase bomb used by Simon Gruber.*

INSERT *An extract from an early treatment that includes a reference to Linda, McClane's female sidekick, who was ultimately dropped from the script.*

But what heist? Briefly, it was mooted that Simon and his gang would steal all the paintings in the Metropolitan Museum of Art. But the idea of villains carrying rolled-up canvasses was swiftly dismissed for lacking drama. A diamond theft was also considered and then dropped. Eventually, echoing Richardson's LA-set idea, Hensleigh settled on Gruber's team robbing $140 billion worth of gold bars from the Federal Reserve Bank on Wall Street. The heist would hinge on a scene in which Simon Gruber would send McClane and the store owner, Zeus, to the Wall Street subway station. There, on a subway train, McClane would find one of Simon's bombs. The bomb would subsequently detonate, causing devastation and allowing Simon and his henchmen to dig into the nearby Federal Reserve.

The character of Zeus was reshaped drastically. In Hensleigh's first draft of his *Simon Says* spec script, the store owner was "a Eurasian grocer." The writer had even wanted Brandon Lee to play the role, but the actor died in March 1993 after an accident on the set of *The Crow* (1994). Following that tragic event, "I changed [the character] to an African American," he says. He also changed the character's gender, as McClane's partner became Linda, a mother in Harlem whose kids became endangered by one of Simon's bombs. That idea was eventually rejected in favor of Harlem-based hardware store owner Zeus, a locksmith, electrician, and former cab driver. After intervening when McClane is spotted wearing the racist slur sandwich board, Zeus becomes embroiled in Simon's game.

McClane and Zeus made for an intriguing pairing. "The specific thing was . . . the black guy was the Republican, in effect," says McTiernan. "The black guy was a square, button-down, disciplined man, and [McClane] was the wild fuckup—a complete reverse of most of the racial stereotypes of the time."

McTiernan brought on producer Michael Tadross, a former Paramount executive, to help shepherd the production, and began to assemble his core creative team, bringing in both fresh and familiar faces. Among the returnees was Jackson De Govia, McTiernan's production designer from *Die Hard*, who had just come off *Speed*. Arguably the most successful of the *Die Hard*–flavored action films, *Speed* was perhaps not surprisingly directed by McTiernan's former *Die Hard* cinematographer, Jan de Bont. The Dutchman's transition to director meant that McTiernan needed to look elsewhere for a DP; he brought on the Australian-born Peter Menzies Jr. "[McTiernan] saw the first film I did as a cinematographer, *White Sands*, and he liked how free I was in the camera movement," says Menzies, who had been set to work with McTiernan on *Captain Blood* until that project fell apart.

Despite progress being made by Hensleigh, McTiernan still felt the script wasn't there. Steven de Souza was called in to contribute some ideas, ultimately unused, including the suggestion that the villains should smuggle the gold away from the Federal Reserve by melting it down and storing it on a stolen school bus (mirroring Hans's fake ambulance from *Die Hard*).

Unfortunately for de Souza, he wasn't able to take on the script because of his commitments on *Beverly Hills Cop 3* at Paramount. He was eager to put the job behind him and get onto *Die Hard 3*, but he owed one more rewrite on *Beverly Hills Cop 3* before it started shooting in September '93. That film's director, John Landis, insisted he stay on. His agents pressed him to stay, even if he didn't like the project, reasoning that if he was going to make someone angry, it should be the upstart, Cinergi, not the established major studio, Paramount. "So I got talked into that decision," he says, "to my regret." Without de Souza's help, the script for *Die Hard 3* was in desperate need of a rewrite.

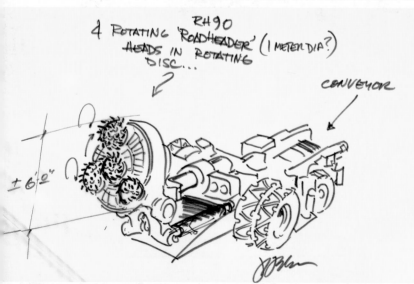

4 ROTATING 'ROADHEADER' HEADS IN ROTATING DISC... RH90 (1 METER DIA?)

CONVEYOR

± 6'0"

CASTING ALCHEMY

Although the script was far from locked, casting proceeded for the new characters. Unlike *Die Hard 2*, *Die Hard 3* brought back none of the supporting cast from the original film. This included Bonnie Bedelia—McClane and Holly would be separated in the story.

The big task was finding an actor to play McClane's companion. Angela Bassett had been mooted to play Linda, according to *Variety*.[10] But by April 1994, when Hensleigh handed in a new draft that replaced Linda with Zeus, the search was on for a male star. Laurence Fishburne was briefly in the frame, but the role eventually went to Samuel L. Jackson.

Bringing in Jackson was a no-brainer. The rising star had won best supporting actor at the Cannes Film Festival for Spike Lee's *Jungle Fever* in 1991, a one-off award that was created just to honor his performance. He'd also just shot Quentin Tarantino's *Pulp Fiction*—as had Willis, although they share no dialogue exchanges in the film—delivering a role that would win him an Academy Award nomination. Producer Michael Tadross had worked with Jackson on John Landis's comedy *Coming to America*, where he played a small role as a fast-food store robber. "When Sam said he wanted to do it, they dropped everybody else and ran right for Sam," he says. "For obvious reasons: He's brilliant."

Vajna concurs. "Bruce had someone to play off, and [the Zeus character] gave it a racial tension." This dimension was new for the franchise, Zeus's background creating a combustible dynamic between himself and McClane. "Zeus has a huge chip on his shoulder about cops," says Jackson (the film's novelization by Deborah Chiel expands on this, revealing that Zeus's brother was accidentally killed during a police raid on a crack house).[11] "Sam is such a good actor," says McTiernan. "He just electrified every scene. He's a wonderful foil for Bruce. The more they fought, the better it was."

English actor Jeremy Irons, an Academy Award winner for *Reversal of Fortune* (1990), won the part of Simon, echoing the casting of Alan Rickman as the German Hans. "I went looking around for who was there on the skyline who could be Hans Gruber's relation," remembers McTiernan. "Jeremy is an extraordinary actor, a chameleon. He can become all sorts of people. . . . He can be a bad guy, but you still like him somehow—he's fun, cool, interesting."

OPPOSITE *Jeremy Irons as Gruber wearing the character's respectable Wall Street attire.*

TOP *Samuel L. Jackson as Zeus Carver.*

ABOVE *Irons wearing Gruber's streamlined combat outfit.*

for tea. The director remembered him from his
...ugh's *Brideshead Revisited*. *Die Hard 3* was to
...was attracted by the anarchic nature of Simon
...own way of finding wealth. And the brazenness
...eply attractive. He made me laugh. I thought he
...t for Bruce."

...Katya, McTiernan originally wanted Grace Slick,
...ioneers Jefferson Airplane. "I wanted to get her,
...uite see her as the female lead in a movie," he
...'t work. "I couldn't figure out how to do it." Still,
...m; he went with rock singer Sam Phillips, whom
...*tinis & Bikinis*. Since Phillips couldn't perform a
...acter mute. McTiernan calls Katya "an archetypal
...oddess, with a terrible scar on her neck which is

...he deep pool of New York character actors. Larry
..., Inspector Walter Cobb. The casting of Bryggman
...aytime Emmys and had twice been nominated for
...t often seen in feature films. Kevin Chamberlin, a
...ebut as Charlie Weiss, an explosives expert who is
...s at the Chester A. Arthur Elementary School—it's
...imon's plan to keep the police occupied while he's

OPPOSITE *(clockwise from
top left) Sam Phillips
as the psychotic Katya;
Larry Bryggman as John
McClane's boss, Inspector
Walter Cobb; Kevin
Chamberlin as bomb
disposal guru Charlie Weiss.*

CENTER LEFT *Colleen Camp
takes to the streets as
Detective Connie Kowalski.*

CENTER RIGHT *Graham
Greene as Detective Joe
Lambert.*

INSERT *Concept sketch of the
police station by Jackson
De Govia.*

Former child actress Colleen Camp added the role of Detective Connie Kowalski to
her already long credit list, while Graham Greene, an Oscar nominee for *Dances with Wolves*
(1990), landed the role of cop Joe Lambert. "He's just such an extraordinarily genuine gentleman," says McTiernan of Greene. This posse of police formed another key element that
distinguished this third film from its predecessors. In the earlier films, the authority figures
were often shown to be foolish, but here they work as an effective team. "I wanted to make
them genuine and decent people," adds McTiernan. Intriguingly, it's McClane that's the
screwup, at least at the beginning. As Inspector Cobb says, "His own wife wants nothing to do
with him, and he's about two steps shy of becoming a full-blown alcoholic."

As the cast took shape, costume designer Joseph G. Aulisi got to work. Aulisi was new
to the *Die Hard* team but had just worked with Willis on the Paul Newman comedy-drama
Nobody's Fool (1994). He dressed McClane in khaki pants and his famous A-shirt (some
things never change), which required twenty-five duplicates, all in various states of distress.
Zeus was fitted in a plain white shirt and dark pants, which also needed multiples. More
noticeable was the apparel given to Simon Gruber, particularly his sleeveless blue T-shirt and
tinted sunglasses. "John McTiernan had the idea of giving him a rock star type of look," says
Aulisi.[12] Irons worked out in preparation, to bring definition to his body and make himself a
worthy opponent for McClane. It was also his decision to dye his hair blond. "I wanted a sort
of Aryan-ness to him," says Irons, a nod to the fact that Simon was "an obscure colonel in the
East German army," as McClane is told.

STARTING WITH A BANG

On July 30, 1994, shooting on *Die Hard 3* got underway, although it didn't begin smoothly. Willis and McTiernan were at odds over certain segments of the script. "For the first two weeks, the director and the star didn't talk to each other," reveals Andrew Vajna. "And that's a little difficult to make a movie that way. So we brought in Arnold Rifkin to do a little bit of negotiating on behalf of Bruce and McTiernan to make sure they ironed out whatever the differences were."

It didn't help that Hensleigh was increasingly distracted by his scripting duties on Joe Johnston's adventure fantasy *Jumanji* (1995), which was gearing up to shoot in Vancouver. "That was a very difficult time for me to try to handle the responsibilities of both films," he says.

The solution was to bring in another writer, William Wisher Jr., who cowrote the screenplay for *Terminator 2: Judgment Day* as well as the Vajna-produced *Judge Dredd* (1995). The producer rang him up, asking if he'd be willing to work for a couple of weeks in Manhattan polishing Hensleigh's script. Wisher had just gotten married and was reluctant to leave his bride in California, but the assignment was too tempting to refuse. On the plane, he read Hensleigh's latest *Die Hard 3* draft. "I remember thinking, 'I don't know if I can fix this in a couple of weeks.'"

The full extent of the task didn't dawn on him until he landed in New York during the first week of the shoot. "I realized that McTiernan hated the script, its current state. . . . He was pretty darn unhappy." When Wisher arrived, McTiernan and company were on location filming one of the story's signature action sequences in which McClane and Zeus cut across Central

TOP *John McTiernan plots a shot for the taxi sequence with Bruce Willis.*

ABOVE *John McClane and Zeus Carver solve Simon Gruber's water fountain puzzle.*

OPPOSITE BOTTOM *Jackson De Govia's concept sketch for the elephant fountain at Tompkins Square Park.*

OPPOSITE RIGHT *Samuel L. Jackson discusses a scene with McTiernan and Willis.*

INSERT *A more developed concept for the elephant fountain by De Govia.*

Park in a commandeered taxicab, trying to reach the Wall Street subway station inside thirty minutes per Simon's demand. During a break in shooting, Wisher approached McTiernan. "He was aware of who I was," says Wisher, "and he knew I was coming, but he didn't know me." Curious, Wisher asked the director why he was shooting this sequence at the start of principal photography. "Because it's the only thing I know for sure I'm keeping," replied McTiernan.

Wisher arranged to meet McTiernan later at a place the director was renting in Greenwich Village. He also had a separate meeting in Willis's trailer, where he discovered that the star wasn't happy with the script either. "I didn't get the warmest reception in the world, initially," recalls Wisher. "They hadn't asked for me. I wasn't John's guy and I wasn't Bruce's guy." After a few chilly days in the summer heat, Wisher had taken all he could stand. "You know, I just got married," he recalls telling both the director and the star. "There's this woman that I like to have sex with, and she's not here. So if you guys don't want me here, I'm perfectly happy to go home to my bride." Somehow, that broke the ice. Wisher began collaborating closely with both McTiernan and Willis on the rewrites, promising not to leave until the script was perfect. "Basically, I rewrote everything," says Wisher.

He settled into a junior suite at a posh Midtown hotel, ready to work. McTiernan asked that Wisher write pages for the next day's shooting and fax them to him each night. When Wisher asked the hotel to install a fax line in his room, management declined, saying in-room

ELEPHANT
AS BRONZE

NEW YORK STATE OF MIND

While Hollywood studios frequently use other cities as stand-ins for New York, McTiernan was clear from the start that *Die Hard with a Vengeance* needed to be shot in the Big Apple. "All the movies that I'd ever seen where they shoot Toronto and pretend it's New York, it doesn't work, because all the people seem wrong," the director says. "They don't move like New Yorkers do on the street. They don't talk with the speed that New Yorkers do. There's no sense of New York, and I really wanted a sense of New York. I'd lived there for all the time I went to Juilliard and for a couple of years after, and I wanted the real sense of the city."

The film's opening sequence—Simon's attention-grabbing bomb that destroys a Bonwit Teller department store—was one of the first things shot. Bonwit Teller had just gone out of business, so the production cut a deal to use the company's name. An almost empty building on lower Sixth Avenue stood in for Bonwit's; the only tenant was a shopkeeper who owned a crystal store that somehow remained undamaged by the explosion (created with sand bombs and smoke bombs by special effects coordinator Phil Cory and his team). Twenty-five windows were rigged to explode, with seven cameras positioned around the setup for the Sunday morning shoot.

LEFT AND BELOW *The Bonwit Teller department store explosion rocks the streets of New York.*

OPPOSITE TOP LEFT AND OPPOSITE CENTER RIGHT *Bruce Willis wears the sandwich board. Two versions were created, one with a less offensive message and another with reference marks for the visual effects team so that they could add the real message in postproduction.*

OPPOSITE BOTTOM RIGHT *Filming exteriors for the fictional Chester A. Arthur Elementary School at the Alexander Humboldt School in Washington Heights, Manhattan.*

McTiernan knew exactly how to create the illusion of mass devastation. "I looked at a couple of pictures of buildings actually having explosions, and I discovered you don't see fire and stuff, you see a whole pile of dust," he says. "That's what you see, a pile of dust! You don't see the building flying to pieces. Once we discovered that, I realized it was very easy to rig. . . . You don't need fire." A car was engineered to flip over when the bomb went off, and so was the truck bearing an Atlantic Courier logo—Jackson De Govia's nod to the vehicle used by Hans's crew in *Die Hard*. The scene went off without a hitch, says McTiernan. "It happened in one take."

While the production had the support of the City of New York and the NYPD, the shoot caused more disruptions than most Manhattanites cared to endure. The explosion scene in particular, remembers Willis, created a major jam. Out shopping on the morning that the sequence was shot, he tried to get back to the set across town only to encounter police

barricades keeping him out. "I was fuming," Willis says, "stuck in the car, thinking, 'What is this, some parade? What the hell is going on here?' And then I realized, 'Oops! It's *Die Hard*!'"[13]

People gathered wherever the production went. The scene in Harlem, when McClane first meets Zeus, as he carries the sandwich board with its racist slur, was tough, recalls Vajna. "We had a lot of difficulties controlling the crowd. I think it was a combination of [people] wanting to see Sam Jackson and wanting to see Bruce. Just

watching a movie being made. It was just a bit of a battle." The sequence was actually shot in Washington Heights, just past Harlem. "We didn't want to provoke anything," says Tadross. "We didn't want to cause any problems."

Unsurprisingly, there were concerns that the sign's slur might, in fact, spark some violence in the neighborhood. "It was probably wise to be cautious about it," says John Sullivan, the film's visual effects supervisor, who had joined the production after working with McTiernan on *Last Action Hero*. To solve the issue, two solutions were found. For certain shots in which the lettering wasn't visible on camera, Willis wore a board with I HATE EVERYBODY marked on it. A blank reference board was also used, complete with x's that would help the visual effects (VFX) team add the lettering seamlessly during postproduction. "That showed where we had come at that point in terms of [digital] technology because it's flawless," adds Sullivan.

The production's biggest crowd-control challenge came when they closed off Ninth Avenue between 57th and 42nd streets to film the scene where McClane and Zeus race across town in their taxicab, following in the slipstream of an ambulance. A camera helicopter flew overhead, with the ambulance, taxicab, and other background cars driving in real traffic. "It was all real," says McTiernan. "It was prior to computer shots. Every bit of it was real." The trick was to insulate the hero vehicles from any real drivers. "We were always in a cocoon of other stunt cars," says Menzies. "We were always protected."

Willis, of course, did not drive the cab in these scenes, despite being behind the wheel. The vehicle had been augmented to withstand all of the required stunt work, with a seat, accelerator, brakes, and steering wheel all fitted to its trunk, allowing a stunt driver to take full control from behind.

With the driver hidden from view, Menzies and his camera team were able to squeeze into the cab and shoot Willis and Jackson in the front seats. "We could play those scenes with Bruce and Sam screaming at each other in real traffic, and look out all the windows," says McTiernan. "The car wasn't on one of those goofy [low-loader] trailers that make it all look phony. It really was a car careering between other cars down an avenue. There was a safe and sane, well-trained driver who was on the [back] of the car. Bruce could do whatever he wanted, concentrate on his lines, and be certain that he wasn't going to hit a car."

McTiernan told Menzies that he wanted the camera to be a participant in the action sequences, not just an observer. "[The idea was] to really make the audience be part of that journey, not to be standing on the street and watching the cars go by," says Menzies. "They should actually be in the car, going down the street, with Sam and Bruce." With McTiernan often using just one camera to shoot dialogue scenes, the visceral camerawork reminded Willis of their previous collaboration. "McTiernan uses the camera to tell the story more than any guy I've worked with," Willis says. "His camera gives you information without dialogue being spoken. And it creates suspense."[14]

With the taxi then cutting through Central Park, the stunt crew—led by stunt coordinator and second-unit director Terry Leonard—portrayed the joggers, cyclists, and inline skaters who dodge the vehicle as it ploughs its way along the bridal paths and hilly mounds. "Central Park was tough," says Vajna, particularly the moment when the taxi jumps over the wall and back out onto the street via a ramp built by Leonard and his crew. "We couldn't shut off the whole block, so we could only deal with one-half of the street. That was quite interesting to see where the taxi would land!" Thankfully, the production had a guardian angel, NYPD's Lt. Milton Maldonado, a huge fan of the Die Hard series. "All he wanted to do was help us," says Tadross. "He closed Central Park West, he closed Columbus Circle on a Saturday and Sunday." With Maldonado's much-needed help, it took six weekends to complete the sequence.

The other major car chase happens as McClane and Zeus head to Long Island Sound, picking up the trail of Simon and his team after they've stolen the gold bullion. With assailants

OPPOSITE RIGHT *Storyboards by Warren Drummond depict John McClane's taxi ride through New York.*

OPPOSITE BOTTOM LEFT *The yellow taxi, rebuilt to allow a stunt driver to control it from the rear.*

ABOVE *The cab makes its way through New York's streets and Central Park.*

TOP RIGHT *The early study of Georges Seurat's painting A Sunday Afternoon on the Island of La Grande Jatte, painted on a wall by Jackson De Govia's team.*

in pursuit, Zeus weaves through traffic in the pouring rain, a factor built into the script that made the sequence difficult to shoot on the Taconic State Parkway. "There's a lot of stuff that has been done in the rain, but not a sustained high-speed car chase," says Leonard. "We were at the mercy of the weather and the amount of money they wanted to spend to put rain towers on the road. It was a really demanding and frustrating exercise."[15]

For the crucial scenes at the Federal Reserve Bank, Jackson De Govia and his team were allowed to tour the real building in Lower Manhattan, including the vaults where gold bullion was kept. Fortunately, the institution's officials had no security qualms regarding the film. "Their reaction to the script was that our scenario would never work," says De Govia.[16] Still, Hensleigh, who'd been on that tour, was later questioned by two FBI agents, concerned by the script's detailed knowledge of the bank and its proximity to water tunnels—tunnels which Simon and his team use to ship out the stolen gold in fourteen dump trucks.

Naturally, the production was not allowed to shoot at the Federal Reserve Bank, so the interior set was built in an abandoned bank on Wall Street. A vault was also constructed, complete with hundreds of Styrofoam gold bricks, in an abandoned industrial plant in New Jersey. The aftermath of the collapse of the Wall Street subway station was also shot in the Garden State. A construction site in Queens, meanwhile, was used to create an aqueduct

where McClane chases and kills some of Simon's goons. De Govia took inspiration from the New York City Water Tunnel No. 3, which was under construction at the time.

Just across from the Federal Reserve, De Govia commandeered a vacant lot to create a small public park where Simon impersonates a city engineer (in a neat echo of Hans's American Bill Clay) as he ships in his heavy-duty machinery to break into the bank. The only thing that spoiled it was the unsightly four-story brick wall nearby. At great expense, scenic painters spent weeks decorating it with a "small, nonpointillist version," as De Govia puts it, of Georges Seurat's famous painting *A Sunday Afternoon on the Island of La Grande Jatte*. While it's half-obscured in the film, the much-praised mural lingered for years afterward at the site.

Scenes were also filmed in the New York subway system, including the sequence in which McClane searches the subway train for Simon's bomb. Filmed handheld by Menzies, the Sunday shoot utilized a real train that ran south from 42nd Street. Yet that would only be the first half of the elaborate subway segment; the second part would take the crew all the way to South Carolina.

OH CAROLINA

After two and a half months shooting in New York, the cast and crew moved to Charleston, South Carolina, for several sequences. The production had scoured New York for a sound-stage large enough to house a subway station set, but with no success. In Goose Creek, South Carolina, however, a former General Dynamics nuclear submarine plant stood empty. Then the largest building in the state, it boasted the requisite height and length to house the ambitious set. Constructed during the New York leg of the shoot, the subway set's verisimilitude was remarkable; the tile walls weren't merely painted, but made of the same tiles used in real New York subway stations. A quarter mile of train track was laid and populated with real-life subway trains purchased from the New York City Transit Authority and transported all the way from Brooklyn on flatbed trucks.

The stunt would be the most ambitious of the series, capturing the moment when Simon's bomb detonates and the final train carriage derails, scattering commuters (or, rather, forty or so of Terry Leonard's stunt crew). While the trains were real, the track could not be electrified for safety reasons, so Chevrolet motors were fitted in the vehicles to power them.

OPPOSITE TOP *Simon Gruber (Jeremy Irons) and his team enter the Federal Reserve.*

OPPOSITE BOTTOM *Gruber's trucks arrive on Wall Street.*

BELOW *The subway train skids across the platform after Gruber's bomb is triggered.*

McTiernan had five cameras rolling as the train came along the tracks at fifteen miles per hour, its speed controlled via computer.

In the film, the blast from the bomb causes the final carriage to skid along the platform, swinging almost 180 degrees before flipping on its side as it hits a staircase. Fifteen feet had to be cut off the end of the stunt carriage in order to avoid hitting real pillars holding up the General Dynamics building during filming of the crash. Hydraulic pistons were also attached to the chassis to help swing it onto the platform. The biggest problem was getting the carriage to sail past the ones ahead of it at the right velocity. "We had [air] cannons set in the last [carriage], and when the thing crashed, those cannons blew and shot the last car of the train forward," says Vajna.

It was a one-time-only shot. "You could feel everybody's heart beating," says Bill Schirmer, the film's special effects supervisor. "It was a heartbeater." They got it in a single take.

Although the subway scene was hugely challenging, the shoot's "biggest logistical problem," as Vajna puts it, was the tunnel sequence. McClane is driving a dump truck through New York City Water Tunnel No. 3 when Simon floods it with water. "We had to figure out how to build a mile-and-a-half-long tunnel that looks like a tunnel but didn't cost a billion dollars," says Vajna. Various locations were scouted, including coal mines in Tennessee, but eventually Peter Menzies Jr. hatched a plan to fake the tunnel sequence with an optical illusion. A series of smaller tunnels, spaced apart, were built in nearby woods outside the General Dynamics plant in South Carolina. "Shooting at night, it just looks like this massive tunnel," says Menzies. "It's just a series of smaller tubes."

OPPOSITE *McClane nearly drowns as Simon Gruber floods the tunnel.*

TOP *Jackson De Govia's concept artwork depicts the dump truck that John McClane commandeers in the water tunnel.*

ABOVE *Concept artwork by De Govia shows the cofferdam that is blown up to release the water that engulfs McClane.*

INSERT *De Govia's concept sketch of the aqueduct tunnel.*

To create the moment where cascades of water enter the tunnel, the visual effects team shot the sequence in miniature. A water tower was built, its raised height helping generate the speed and volume of water. The water was then dropped into a twelve-foot tunnel made of reinforced glass, creating a huge swell that could be composited into the shot later. On set, meanwhile, Willis was sprayed with water so he would look suitably drenched. "We did a lot that way," says John Sullivan, "at least trying to get the look of Bruce interacting with the water."

Another reason for choosing Charleston as a shooting location was that it had a bridge and harbor that would be suitable for a sequence in the film's third act in which McClane and Zeus head to Long Island Sound and manage to get aboard Simon's bomb-carrying container ship. The Grace Memorial Bridge was utilized for the moment when McClane hooks a cable from their pickup truck on the bridge to Gruber's ship below, using the cable as a means to climb onto the ship. Eventually, the ship pulls the vehicle off the bridge and into the water.

As he had been years ago during the helicopter scenes on *Die Hard*, McTiernan was extremely cautious with the stunt, which used a crane to swing the car. "My father was an engineer, and I started doing a little bit of geometry," he says, recalling that he scrawled his mathematical equation in the dirt on the body of the car. "I asked the stunt coordinator and the effects people, 'How much cable exactly have you got let out?' And I discovered it was going to hit the tail of the freighter. So we had to put thirty-five feet more cable on the line, something like that. Those things are terrifying. You'll make a mistake and you'll get somebody hurt. You have nightmares about it." With these new calculations, the car missed the boat by six feet. "If it wasn't for McT," says Tadross, "it would have been a disaster."

A real merchant vessel was used for shooting deck and interior scenes. For the sequence in which McClane and Zeus jump off the ship just before it explodes, stunt doubles performed the jump with a controlled explosion set behind them. "We shot that right on the river in Charleston, South Carolina," says Schirmer. "It's a river that's controlled by the tide. And we only had a fifteen-minute window to shoot that sequence because otherwise the water's too fast and you can't even be in it."

As for the dramatic long shot of the container ship exploding, John Sullivan's team took a real freighter off the coast and used huge quantities of magnesium flash powder to create a large burst of light, amplified by the reflection from the surface of the water. The public in the surrounding area was warned in advance, says Sullivan, but it was still a mighty flash of light: "I think a few fishermen lost their fish because the fish spit the hooks out."

TOP *Filming the stunt in which McClane and Zeus board Simon Gruber's container ship.*

ABOVE *Willis and Jackson with the bomb prop aboard Gruber's ship.*

OPPOSITE TOP *John McTiernan, Willis, and Jackson atop the Grace Memorial Bridge.*

OPPOSITE CENTER (left to right) *McTiernan and Jeremy Irons; Willis gets a kick out of the bomb scene; McTiernan and Willis discuss the Gruber ship scenes.*

OPPOSITE BOTTOM *Gruber's ship passes beneath the Grace Memorial Bridge.*

INSERT *Rough notes on the ship stunt.*

DENOUEMENT DILEMMA

The main shoot wrapped on December 21, 1994, just in time for Christmas. The working title, *Die Hard 3*, was dispensed with when the first trailer was cut. "We didn't want to call it *Die Hard 3*," says Vajna. "That was kinda boring. We wanted to give it some kind of juice, so *Die Hard with a Vengeance* sounded OK. I was looking at the teasers and the artwork, [and] it just came into my head." McTiernan remembers Vajna calling him into his office and asking what he thought: "I said, boy that's fucking fantastic. Let's go with it."

With the US release date set for May 19, 1995, just a little over five months away, the postproduction period was "pretty fucked," says McTiernan. John Wright, who cut McTiernan's *The Hunt for Red October* and *Last Action Hero*, not to mention *Speed*, was recruited for the task. When they first met for lunch, McTiernan requested that Wright be on set every day, "which is kind of an unusual request," says Wright. Still, the editor agreed. "I got to know the crew, which was helpful," he says. Better still, he got a sense of the film as it came together.

Michael Kamen returned to score the film, although McTiernan also made notable use of existing music. The film opens to shots of a summery New York, immediately distinguishing it from its Christmastime predecessors. Emphasizing the point, the Lovin' Spoonful's "Summer in the City" plays over the shot until—*boom*—the department store explosion interrupts it. "There was a big debate about that," says Wright. "That was a song that John always wanted in." Others disagreed, with suggestions of rap music coming from some quarters. "I didn't agree," says Wright.

The film also made good use of "When Johnny Comes Marching Home," written by Irish American bandleader Patrick Gilmore during the American Civil War. Throbbing through the second half of the film, providing a rhythm to Simon's military-like operation, it echoes McTiernan's musical references in *Die Hard*. While the first film used music from Stanley Kubrick's *A Clockwork Orange*, this was a nod to Kubrick's 1965 nuclear arms satire, *Dr. Strangelove*. "That's how the [B-52] bomber flies," notes McTiernan, "to the music of 'When Johnny Comes Marching Home.'" Once again, Kamen was reluctant to integrate established pieces into his score. "I had great difficulty getting him to embrace [it]," says McTiernan. "He recorded it, but it wasn't built into his score."

The biggest issue the team faced in post was the film's finale. "We never had an ending that we really liked," says Vajna. The original ending saw Simon escaping with the gold. "That was something that was a bad idea, period," says McTiernan. Nevertheless, the scene was shot. In the sequence, McClane tracks Simon down to a bar in Europe. On the table, McClane places a rocket launcher with the directional arrow removed, so there's no way to tell which direction it will fire (in the original script, it was a daisy cutter grenade). After Simon fails to answer McClane's riddle, McClane presses him to choose a direction and fire the rocket launcher. Simon guesses wrong, self-inflicting a fatal wound. Vajna calls it an "ad hoc ending," shot to prevent any negative publicity swirl around the film and buy them some time as they figured out an alternative.

McTiernan says he conjured his own ending, involving the bomb from the water fountain in Tompkins Square Park that was last seen when Zeus gave it to Simon's henchmen, who were masquerading as cops. As McTiernan conceived it, the explosive would inadvertently end up on a private plane that Simon and his troops use to escape. With every man carrying an aluminum case with a gold bar or two, Simon suddenly realizes he has an extra case by his side.

"He opens it up and finds that it is the water bomb, and he has just triggered it, and he has three minutes to come up with [the solution]. And the last line is: 'Does anybody have a four-gallon jug?' So they are hung on their own petard." Again, it was rejected. "Someone convinced Bruce that wasn't appropriate; we needed a more tough-guy ending," says McTiernan. "So ultimately, we came up with the shoot-out with the helicopter."

It was a troublesome finale. Wisher had returned to Los Angeles after concluding his script duties on the film and recalls taking a call from McTiernan, asking him to rewrite the ending. At the time, he was hosting a Christmas party. "I went to my wife and my guests and said, 'I gotta go work for an hour—I'll be back!' I remember doing that thinking, Jesus, will this thing ever end?"

Shot in Baltimore, Maryland, the revised Wisher ending sees McClane track down Simon to Quebec, Canada, for a shoot-out that leaves our hero under fire and almost out of ammo. Aiming true, his bullet severs a power line (to the immortal words "say hello to your brother"), and the cable swings toward Simon and Katya's chopper, causing them to crash to the ground. McTiernan was never satisfied, though. "I wasn't thrilled with the end," he admits. "It was kind of formulaic and a disappointment, and I had planned something that was a bit more graceful, a bit more comic."

ABOVE *Bruce Willis arrives with a gift for Simon Gruber in the original ending for* Die Hard with a Vengeance.

OPPOSITE TOP *A one-sheet for* Die Hard with a Vengeance.

OPPOSITE BOTTOM *Gruber (Jeremy Irons) surveys his morning newspaper before facing John McClane in the film's original ending.*

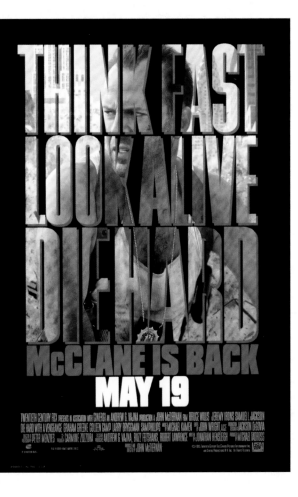

As the release date neared, real-world events put the film under additional pressure. On April 19, 1995, domestic terrorist Timothy McVeigh carried out a bomb attack on the Alfred P. Murrah Federal Building in Oklahoma City, claiming 168 lives. Suddenly, the premise of *Die Hard with a Vengeance* seemed ill-conceived. "If Oklahoma had happened [before we shot], I would not have gone near it in a movie," reflects McTiernan. At the time, the decision was made to plow ahead with the film. "This will not impact the release date," remarked Fox spokeswoman, Meredith Nevins.[17]

With just a week to go before the film was due in theaters all over the country, further panic descended over the production. "They had done the press junket and had shown the film, and they discovered that the line 'yippee-ki-yay, motherfucker' wasn't in the film anymore," says visual effects supervisor John Sullivan. "It had gone away with the ending change." As nobody could get hold of either Peter Menzies Jr. or Tom Priestley Jr., the second-unit director of photography, McTiernan asked Sullivan to shoot the insert shot: Willis in close-up, Band-Aid on his head, with the glow of the burning helicopter reflecting on his face. Sullivan brought Willis to the Lantana Center in Los Angeles, where the film was being cut. "I photographed Bruce, lying with a flame bar lighting his face," says Sullivan. "After shooting that shot, I couldn't sleep until we got a report from the lab the following day that all was good." Remarkably, it was processed and added into the final reel before the release prints were struck the next day. "I remember," says Wright, "one of the executives said, 'Jesus, I've never been so close to missing a date in my life.'"

When the reviews began to surface, the Oklahoma City bombing was referenced by many critics, although *Die Hard with a Vengeance* escaped censure. "The film is off the hook as exploitation," noted Peter Travers in *Rolling Stone*, going on to praise McTiernan's work. "What No. 3 regains, thanks to McTiernan's return, is the human touch. Character counted for little in Harlin's soulless sequel. It does now." *Variety*, meanwhile, suggested the film's "built-in audience will make it a major summer attraction, if perhaps one lacking quite the stamina of the first two movies."

In fact, it far outstripped its predecessors at the box office. It raked in $22.2 million in its first weekend, more than the original. It ended its theatrical run with just over $100 million gross in the US and a very solid $266 million in the rest of the world. Ultimately, it became the second biggest movie of the year; only Pixar's *Toy Story* made more money. "It was the most successful one in the series up until that point," says Vajna, pointing out that the film almost eclipsed the $380 million collective earnings of its two predecessors. Love for John McClane was as strong as ever. But fans would have to be patient before they saw him on-screen again.

PART 4 LIVE FREE OR DIE HARD

"John, you're a Timex watch in a digital age."—THOMAS GABRIEL

Die Hard and John McClane took a pause after *With a Vengeance*, although not for long. Bruce Willis and Twentieth Century Fox discussed a fourth installment as early as 1996, with plans to turn an original script titled *Tears of the Sun* into "*Die Hard* in the Amazon Jungle." The idea was nixed, although Willis would forge ahead with a non-McClane version of *Tears of the Sun* directed by Antoine Fuqua and eventually released in 2003.

While Willis was enjoying critical acclaim for his work in lower budget hits like *12 Monkeys* (1995) and *The Sixth Sense* (1999), the prospect of returning to John McClane still appealed to him: "To have a film, now on its fourth episode in the Die Hard franchise, [that] still lives up to the promise of the first film . . . that was our goal," he says. Achieving that goal would hardly be simple. The action-hero landscape had changed dramatically since McClane defeated Simon Gruber. Doug Liman's *The Bourne Identity* (2002) had reinvented the action genre, so much so that 007 producers Eon Productions recognized the need to reboot James Bond with 2006's *Casino Royale*, making Ian Fleming's spy grittier and more hard-edged. Where would John McClane fit in this new action-movie landscape?

ABOVE *Bruce Willis and Justin Long costar in* Live Free or Die Hard.

OPPOSITE *John McClane shows his authority on the streets of Washington, DC.*

MCCLANE 4.0

Like its predecessors, the fourth Die Hard installment began life as something entirely different. This time, the source material was a script called *WW3.com*, written by David Marconi, who had penned the high-tech thriller *Enemy of the State* (1998). Marconi based *WW3.com* on a "A Farewell to Arms," a 1997 *Wired* magazine article by John Carlin about the possibility of a cyber attack on US soil. Luc Besson was originally attached to produce, but the project was shelved after the terror attacks of September 11, 2001.

Keen to retool the script for Die Hard purposes, Hutch Parker, the president of Twentieth Century Fox, and Tom Rothman, chairman and CEO of Fox Filmed Entertainment, brought in producer Michael Fottrell (*Volcano*, 1997) to steer the project. For the first time in the history of the Die Hard franchise, Willis would also take a key production role.

Back in 2000, the actor had joined production company Cheyenne Enterprises, formed by his former agent Arnold Rifkin. In the years that followed, Willis kept his eye on potential projects he could produce, and his interest was piqued by the possibility of resurrecting Marconi's script. He enlisted up-and-coming screenwriter Mark Bomback, who had previously worked on rewrites for *Me Again*, an unproduced comedy that Willis was attached to at the time.

The idea was to take the central premise of Marconi's script and rework it into the Die Hard realm. "[Fox] liked the villain's agenda, a sort of cyber shutdown of America," says Bomback. "In a sense, America itself becomes the building McClane is trapped in." Even with Willis's backing, Bomback knew he'd have just one shot at impressing the studio. He decided to embrace the fact that the Die Hard franchise and its wisecracking hero seemed a little old-fashioned in the era of films like 1999's *The Matrix*. His pitch: McClane is an analog guy in a digital world.

"To me, the fun of it is that oil and water, seeing what happens when you mash up the tone of a Die Hard film and a character like McClane with contemporary problems like cyberterrorism," he says. The concept excited both Fox and Willis, and in the fall of 2003, Bomback was officially brought on board the project, with Cheyenne Enterprises producing.

The plot pits McClane against a very different type of terrorist: Thomas Gabriel. A former Department of Defense programmer, Gabriel once tried to warn his employers that America was vulnerable to cyberattacks, only to be scorned and humiliated. Now he's out for revenge, using a team of hackers to create a "fire sale": hacker lingo for a systematic shutdown of America's computerized infrastructure—transport, finances, and utilities.

Putting Gabriel in opposition to McClane, a tech dinosaur, was an interesting matchup for the screenwriter. "It's not about brawn over brains; it's about sort of a brawn-brains combination," Bomback explains. He wrote set pieces where, from moment to moment, McClane improvised realistic solutions to incoming threats—"within the sort of craziness of their concepts." McClane, he says, "has reserves of cleverness that even he doesn't know he has at any given moment."

Aside from the McClane-Gabriel dynamic, early script ideas were fluid. Early on, Bomback penned a draft in which McClane teamed up with his son, who went by the name Jack G, the *G* for Gennero. He found it problematic. "I felt like I was just writing McClane Junior and McClane Senior," he says. "Or I was trying to make him the polar opposite and not have any of his dad's attitude, and then you had a character who had no sense of humor and was really dour."

In early 2004, Bomback briefly took a hiatus to work on another project while Willis was shooting the action-thriller *Hostage*, scripted by *Die Hard 2*'s Doug Richardson. In the interim, Willis recruited Richardson to take a crack at the script. "It was on me to deliver a *Die Hard 4* Bruce Willis was willing to get behind," says Richardson. Like Bomback, he toyed with the father-son relationship at the core of the story. "I think [Richardson's draft] was driven a lot by Bruce's notes," adds Bomback, who returned to the project—and his own draft—without taking on any of Richardson's ideas. "I don't think it was a script that I wound up being faithful to in any way."

OPPOSITE *Concept art for a sinister-looking hacking terminal by Robert McKinnon.*

ABOVE *Concept sketch for Thomas Gabriel's mobile control room by Ed Natividad.*

BOYHOOD FAN

In 2005, director Len Wiseman was in postproduction on *Underworld: Evolution*, the sequel to his 2003 vampire vs. werewolves hit *Underworld*, when he received Bomback's script in the mail. After opening the envelope, he was shocked to read the title: *Die Hard 4.0*. "I found out later it was sent to me at the request of Bruce," he remembers. Willis's daughters were fans of *Underworld* and had talked him into watching the film. What Willis didn't know was that Wiseman was a huge fan of Die Hard, so much so that as a teenager he'd made his own Die Hard movie in his backyard, with himself as McClane. "*Die Hard* was such an important movie to me," the director says.

Willis liked *Underworld*, but he liked Wiseman even more. "When I heard Len's vision of the film, a light went off," he notes. "I told him my secret goal, wanting to do a film that was as good as the first film. Hearing his point of view and the technology side of it, bringing the film in[to] the twenty-first century, but still doing an old-school, real stunts, smashmouth hard-core film seemed to be the right thing to do."

Coincidentally, at the time, Wiseman was developing a script for an unrelated project with William Wisher Jr., the uncredited script doctor on *Die Hard with a Vengeance*. Wiseman called Wisher and said he was nervous because he was under consideration for the next *Die Hard*. Wisher told him, "Really? You should do it, man!" But Wiseman worried that the script wasn't ready. "That's a good sign because that's always how they start," Wisher replied. "Don't let that scare you." Ultimately, Wiseman put his fears aside and signed on for the film.

His first task was to help get the script in shape. When he met Bomback, he found the writer exhausted by endless rounds of rewrites. What's more, Wiseman felt there was a major tonal error in the script: McClane was not a reluctant hero. "I had him too eager to join the fight, too soon," Bomback admits. "Len was quick to point out that we need to keep him reluctant until the very end, like this is all just one massive inconvenience that he didn't want to have to participate in."

Wiseman and Bomback also grappled with the question of just how much of a Luddite to make McClane. He had to seem intelligent and capable of doing his job, while still being uncomfortable with modern tech. Wiseman says, "That was a bit of a struggle, especially since the plot was so driven by technology." The director was also careful to keep McClane vulnerable. "There were two characters that I really was drawn to when I was a kid, John McClane and Indiana Jones," he says. "You see them getting beat up, they're unsure. They're making things up as they go, and that's something that doesn't show itself as much in a lot of action films now."

Bomback also credits Wiseman for compressing the three-day doomsday scenario into what felt like a twenty-four-hour movie, echoing the franchise's three predecessors. Both collaborators were also adamant that McClane shouldn't be exactly the same as the character from the earlier films and that his age and experience needed to be factored in. (Willis had turned fifty in 2005.) There was never any plan to make the character seem younger than the actor who played him. "It seemed like the right thing to do, to play it at my age and how I look now," said Willis at the time.

Yet there were changes afoot that didn't sit so comfortably. Fox was adamant that this fourth installment needed to be a PG-13 movie to ensure younger audiences would be able to see it. "When I found out, I almost left the movie, I had no idea," Wiseman says. "Bruce didn't have any idea either. . . . I just assumed it was rated R." When the issue first came up in a script meeting, Wiseman was taken aback. "It's *Die Hard* and I just kept seeing [in my head] 'Die Soft, Die Soft.'"

Ultimately, Wiseman decided to stay on the project and a solution was found: The director would shoot the full-blooded script but also gather everything he needed to create a PG-13 version. "They said as long as you shoot the version that's on the page, and you have time, shoot whatever you want as long as you stay on schedule," says Wiseman.

TOP *Len Wiseman and Bruce Willis on the set of* Live Free or Die Hard.

RIGHT *Wiseman realizes his childhood dream directing a Die Hard movie.*

HACK ATTACK

This time around, the "analog" McClane would be paired with the "digital" Matt Farrell, a young hacker employed by Gabriel to unwittingly help create a malicious algorithm that will unleash the fire sale on America. He proves to be a vital character, helping McClane navigate his way through a cyber world he barely comprehends.

When the FBI suffers a cyber breach, McClane is instructed by his NYPD boss to go to Farrell's apartment in New Jersey and bring him to the FBI Cyber-Security Division. He and Farrell are then attacked by Gabriel's hit men, who are covering their tracks by wiping out the hackers hired to create the fire sale code. The geeky Farrell emerges as a relatable presence whose wide-eyed reaction to the unfolding mayhem would be shared by the audience. "It was a character I really loved to write most," says Bomback, "after McClane himself."

He isn't the only tech-savvy character brought into the story. Farrell's fellow hacker Frederick "Warlock" Kaludis provides McClane with valuable insight into Gabriel when our hero and his techy sidekick visit Warlock in Baltimore. For Bomback, Warlock was a way to give the audience "an information dump" on Gabriel: "That's what those hackers do. They love spouting off fifty different pieces of information." Exposition aside, Warlock also provided some much-needed comic relief. His "command center" is actually his mother's basement, stuffed with his *Star Wars* collectibles—a setting Wiseman could relate to. "It was like what I turned my parents' garage into," he says.

It was Wiseman's idea to introduce a college-age Lucy McClane, twenty years after she was first seen as a toddler in *Die Hard*. The idea was initially met with little enthusiasm from Fox's Hutch Parker and Tom Rothman, among others, but Wiseman felt strongly that Lucy's presence would give the story the emotional dimension that powered the earlier Die Hard films. "I think the resistance came more from an anxiety about making a big change late in the process [rather than], 'Should he have a daughter or not?'" says Bomback. Eventually, Fox agreed to let Wiseman add Lucy McClane, but only if he could avoid disrupting the fabric of the script. "It was about two months before we started shooting that they agreed to the daughter role," says the director.

Lucy and her father's strained relationship became a key element of the final script. (In an echo of the original *Die Hard*, Lucy first uses her mother's name, Gennero, but comes around to calling herself Lucy McClane.) When Gabriel kidnaps Lucy, McClane gains a personal motivation to bring the villain down. "Throughout the story," says Wiseman, "the one person that really, really has to come through for her is her father, who's never really come through for her in her life."

"She has McClane's attitude, but she's clearly her own person," adds Bomback. "She also has resentments toward her father, and what's great is that she's able to voice those resentments in McClane's voice. In some ways she is his better self, sort of his Jiminy Cricket."

Wiseman also redesigned the action sequences, bringing his own ideas to the table at script stage. An early draft featured a car chase through a sports stadium, an idea the director quickly nixed. It was replaced with a sequence set at a super-substation in West Virginia,

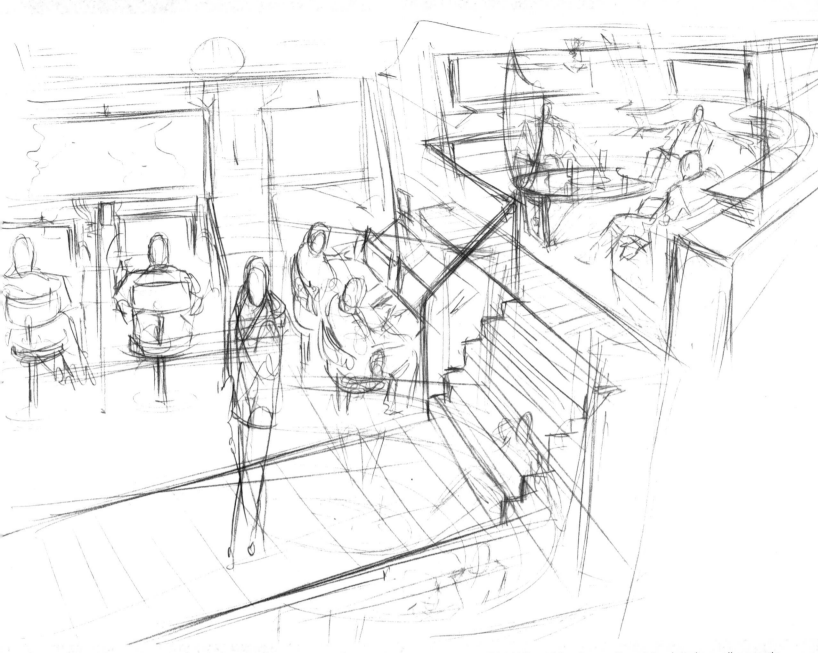

where Gabriel's deadly enforcer Mai Linh and her team attempt to shut down all power in the eastern United States as part of the fire sale attack. Driving a Ford Explorer SUV into the building, McClane rams the vehicle into Mai Linh—and into an elevator shaft. Wiseman initially plotted the sequence out on napkins while on a family vacation in Mexico. "I wanted to have an elevator sequence because it's a Die Hard movie," he says, "and I think it's such a staple of the Die Hard franchise."

By the time Bomback finished his multiple drafts—twelve official, thirty unofficial—a number of other writers had been ushered into the process. Skip Woods, who had scripted the John Travolta film *Swordfish* (2001), came on to polish some of Willis's dialogue scenes. Also recruited was William Wisher, whom Wiseman invited on board. The writer had maintained strong links with Willis since *Die Hard with a Vengeance*, and the two had worked together on *Mercury Rising* (1998). "He and I were good friends," recalls Wisher, "and we'd say, 'We're the only two guys who understand John McClane.' He knows him best, and I know John McClane second best, having written for the guy."

Wisher joined just a month before the shoot began and focused on sharpening McClane's character with the input of Willis and Wiseman. "John McClane is a guy who's good at his job and bad at his life," says Wisher. "I think that's kind of the secret to him. He's really good at being a cop, and he's not so good at being a husband or a father. And there's a certain sadness in the character. But deeper than that, there's an inherent goodness and humility in John McClane because he doesn't think he's a hero."

OPPOSITE *Further concept designs for hacking equipment.*

ABOVE *A rough sketch of the mobile control room by Patrick Tatopoulos.*

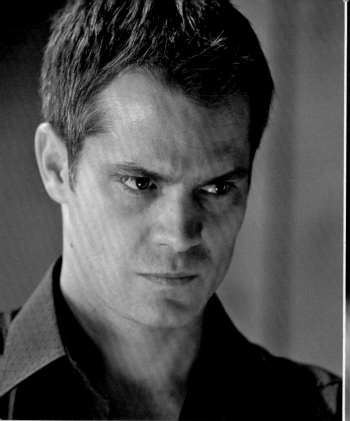

CASTING AND CREWING UP

Casting began while the script was still being fine-tuned. Finding the right actor to play Thomas Gabriel was crucial. Originally, Wiseman pictured Gary Oldman as the cyber mastermind, but it was decided the villain should be younger than McClane, something the franchise hadn't tried before.

He went to *Deadwood* star Timothy Olyphant, who had auditioned for the *Underworld* lead werewolf role that ultimately went to Scott Speedman. In Wiseman's eyes, Olyphant was ideal to embody this puppet master with lethal computer skills; an actor who could do a "great job of creating that danger without having to be like a big, bad physical presence."

Olyphant signed on, conscious of having to live up to Alan Rickman's benchmark for Die Hard villains. "When I first got the call that said they were looking for the new villain for the next *Die Hard*, my first response was: 'Cool, they're making another *Die Hard*!' And my second response was: 'And I could be in it!' So I really was like a kid in a candy store. And then every now and then, a buddy of mine from high school would email me and say, 'I heard you're going to be the villain in *Die Hard*? Don't fuck it up!'"[1]

The role of Matt Farrell went to Justin Long, the Connecticut-born actor who had gained notice for the horror hit *Jeepers Creepers* (2001) and the Ben Stiller comedy *Dodgeball: A True Underdog Story* (2004). Curiously, it was Long's turn as the hip Mac guy in a series of Apple commercials, paired with uncool PC guy John Hodgman, that got Wiseman's attention. "I do know I got *Die Hard* because of those commercials," he reflects. "That was the motivation to bring me in."

Bomback wasn't writing with Long in mind; he was barely aware of the actor as he wrote, he says. "Len was the one who said, 'I think that this guy's voice would be perfect.'" Wiseman's instincts were spot-on. "He's very, very quick-witted," the director says, "really sharp, fast mind. . . . It was very helpful."

During casting, Long was actually torn between taking on Matt Farrell and choosing an indie movie, *My Sassy Girl*, costarring Elisha Cuthbert. He spoke to *Die Hard 4.0*'s casting director, Deborah Aquila, who set him straight and encouraged him to take the role.

The Lucy McClane role went to Mary Elizabeth Winstead, a fast-rising actress who'd appeared in *Final Destination 3* and *Factory Girl*. "She was just like a breath of fresh air," says producer Michael Fottrell. Adds Wiseman, "I thought she had this kind of quiet confidence that felt like McClane's daughter." Winstead astutely noted she felt like she was stepping "into Bonnie Bedelia's role. . . . I'm there to make his [McClane's] mission more personal."[2]

TOP LEFT *Timothy Olyphant as the villainous Thomas Gabriel.*

TOP RIGHT *Mary Elizabeth Winstead as Lucy McClane.*

OPPOSITE *Justin Long as the hacker Matt Farrell.*

Maggie Q was cast as the martial arts–adept Mai Linh. Born in Hawaii, she made her name in Hong Kong cinema under the tutelage of Jackie Chan. By the time *Die Hard 4.0* came around, she was starring opposite Tom Cruise. "*Mission: Impossible III* had come out, and she was all over the place," remembers Wiseman. "[She] was excited. . . . 'I get to kick Bruce Willis's ass!'"

For the actress, there was no drawn-out series of auditions: "I met Bruce and the director. . . . It was very simple, the whole process. Bruce was basically [saying] . . . 'Look, you're it. I mean, I see you, this is you, this role.' I had no idea what to say in response to that."[3]

Another stroke of genius came in the casting of geek icon Kevin Smith as Warlock, Matt Farrell's cyber ally. Like so many before him, the actor-writer-director was a die-hard Die Hard fan. "I've seen every one of them theatrically, owned them on every video format—VHS, laser disc, DVD." But he admits he was worried. "If you're the one that makes the franchise jump the shark, where everyone was like, 'Die Hard was awesome until the *Clerks* guy showed up' . . . you could never live that down."[4]

New Zealand actor Cliff Curtis, famed for his appearances in *The Piano* (1993) and *Whale Rider* (2002), was cast as Miguel Bowman, the deputy director of the FBI's Cyber-Security Division—and one of the more competent authority figures that McClane works alongside.

Suggested by the film's stunt coordinator Brad Martin, French martial artist Cyril Raffaelli won the role of Gabriel's henchman Rand. A regular stunt performer with Luc Besson's company EuropaCorp (on films like *The Transporter* [2002] and *Taxi 2* [2000]), Raffaelli was an expert in parkour, the acrobatic stunt discipline also known as freerunning. Raffaelli's skills are put to good use in a scene following a shootout at Farrell's apartment in which Rand makes his escape by leaping from one building to another.

Alongside Brad Martin, Wiseman recruited some of the crew from his just-completed *Underworld: Evolution*, including cinematographer Simon Duggan, production designer Patrick Tatopoulos, and composer Marco Beltrami. Beltrami would be filling the considerable void left by acclaimed Die Hard composer Michael Kamen, who had died in 2003, aged just fifty-five. New to Wiseman's team was second-unit director Brian Smrz, who'd started as a stunt performer and became a regular on Fox blockbusters, including the X-Men films. Other crewmembers included costume designer Denise Wingate, who had previously worked on *Wedding Crashers* (2005) and *Cruel Intentions* (1999), and visual effects supervisor Patrick McClung, back for his first *Die Hard* since the 1988 original.

OPPOSITE *Maggie Q as the deadly Mai Linh.*
ABOVE *Cliff Curtis as the FBI's Miguel Bowman.*
BELOW *Kevin Smith gets comfortable as Warlock.*

TAKING DIE HARD DIGITAL

Since his days as a model maker on *Die Hard*, McClung had graduated to visual effects supervisor on films like *The Day After Tomorrow* (2004) and the Willis-starring *Armageddon* (1998). During that time, digital effects had overtaken practical effects as the industry standard, used for everything from erasing safety cables on stunt performers to replacing backgrounds with computer-generated vistas.

McClung began his preproduction work on the film by doing a breakdown of the script, outlining what visual effects, special effects, stunts, and effects makeup were needed. He also recruited a number of VFX houses, including the Orphanage and Digital Dimension, to take on the film's extensive workload. As cutting-edge as the production was, McClung still planned to use some old-school techniques, with Wiseman's hearty approval. "He was just a big fan of miniatures," says McClung. Miniatures created for the production included a model of DC's Capitol Building, blown to smithereens in a fake video Gabriel broadcasts across the nation's television channels.

When it came to the film's design scheme, Wiseman chose a palette that eschewed bright colors for darker tones, with some of that effect achieved through set and costume design, some through shooting, and the rest in postproduction color correction.

Production designer Patrick Tatopoulos set out to build an overall palette around sepia-bronze and metal-blue colors, feeling gritty verisimilitude was key: "How can you be visually interesting while never forgetting to be real?" he says. "A truck crashes through a column; if it looks like a set, if it doesn't blend in the way it should, all those things are going to make the movie feel less real."

Even more important, he says, the design had to create "a playground for the stunts." That meant designing sets that served the action and the needs of the stunt team first,

rather than creating something that just looked cool. "It was foremost, 'Oh, that's the shot you want to create?'" says Tatopoulos.

Costume designer Denise Wingate also had to plan her work around the film's extensive physical action. "My costumes sometimes morph around what the stunt is, because [stunt] guys work so hard," she says. For example, the costumes for the Mai Linh character required flexibility to accommodate the movements Maggie Q and her doubles would perform: "She can't be in high heels, but she needs a little bit of a heel," says Wingate. "She has to be wearing pants, so they have to stretch. I felt like she was going to be hanging upside down. How are they going to be wired? Do they need layers? You just have to take all that into consideration."

Wingate reveals that Wiseman asked for a "muted, sort of gritty palette," and that aesthetic certainly helped her evolve yet maintain McClane's iconic look. "Bruce knows the character, and he's pretty specific," she says. "We knew it was going to be jeans, and we knew it was going to be some sort of shirt that looked good on him, that he could move in, and some sort of leather jacket." Her first meeting with Willis was to be a meet-and-greet, but they hit it off well enough that it turned into a fitting, with Willis going through her rack of leather jackets to find one that suited. "He knows what looks good on him, he knows what works, and what works for the character," she says.

When it came to fitting out Thomas Gabriel, Wingate dressed him in a black shirt and suit pants, "to be a little sinister but really slick and look like he had money." Like Hans Gruber, he clearly doesn't do his clothes shopping at a department store. Lucy McClane spends the second half of the film in jeans and a vest top after Gabriel kidnaps her. But in an early scene, when her father finds her on campus making out with a fellow student, "we had her in a jean jacket, a little dress, and cowboy boots," says Wingate. It's a revealing outfit, liable to irritate a protective father like John McClane.

As on previous Die Hard films, continuity was always a problem for the costume department, as the film's scenes would be shot out of order, and Wingate was in charge of making sure the wear and tear on McClane's costume was consistent with the plot. Wingate remembered noticing continuity problems in McClane's white A-shirt when watching the original *Die Hard* film. "White is really, really unforgiving," she says. To sidestep the issue, she opted to put McClane in olive green: "You could sort of get away with more, even with the blood; it's not as glaring as if you did white."

With Willis's look set, Farrell was styled to be complementary. When, on the day before shooting started, the studio asked that he wear a graphic T-shirt, Wingate had to react swiftly. "I remember being in total panic mode and scrambling to find thirteen of the shirt that I could age before we started shooting." She eventually found a suitable design by a company called Dragonfly. "We called and had them FedEx me a ton of them."

OPPOSITE TOP *Bruce Willis and Justin Long film the shoot-out in Matt Farrell's apartment.*

OPPOSITE BOTTOM *Timothy Olyphant models Thomas Gabriel's sleek and stylish wardrobe.*

TOP RIGHT *Costume design concept for the Mai Linh character by Robert McKinnon.*

LEFT *Willis was outfitted in an olive green long-sleeved shirt that would show less grime than John McClane's traditional white A-shirts.*

DOUBLING DC

On September 23, 2006, shooting got underway on *Live Free or Die Hard*, a title inspired by the New Hampshire state motto, Live Free or Die. In most international markets, where the US-centric reference might be lost, the film would be known as *Die Hard 4.0*.

Although the script was largely set in Washington, DC, filming in the nation's capital was always going to be problematic because of post-9/11 heightened security. "You can't fly over Washington, obviously, and you can't really section off any areas," says Wiseman. "There was talk of going to Canada," adds Michael Fottrell, although that idea was soon rejected. After visiting DC to scout key locations, the filmmakers chose nearby Baltimore instead, as it could convincingly pass for the nation's capital. Fottrell recruited Jack Gerbes, Maryland Film Office director, to help location scout. "[We] just hit the ground running. We didn't have a lot of time to prepare," says Fottrell.

The team shot for three weeks in the Maryland city. A home on Madison Street was used to shoot exteriors of Warlock's den, while Calvert Street served for the scene where Gabriel causes traffic chaos in central DC (Baltimore's Battle Monument is even clearly viewable on-screen). Parts of the key sequence in which Rand shoots at McClane and Farrell from a helicopter were shot in Baltimore's central business district. For two weekends in September, helicopters buzzed around the area, although scheduling proved problematic: For safety reasons, no aerial shots could be captured while a baseball match took place at Oriole Park.

The production then moved to Los Angeles for the rest of the shoot. Either sets were built from scratch on soundstages at Universal Studios or preexisting locations were sought and built on. Among the key builds: the inside of Gabriel's truck, which housed his command team and equipment ("The set was built separately from the truck," says Tatopoulos, "but was built with exactly the same measurements the truck was."); the FBI building interior with its hundreds of monitors and work stations; and Farrell's apartment, which gets shot to pieces when Gabriel's men attempt to assassinate him. Like Warlock's pad, the apartment is filled with "dolls," as McClane puts it, including a model stormtrooper and a Terminator robot. "Everything you see on the table, on the shelf, were all things we felt were creating the character," says Tatopoulos.

Built on Stage 12 at Universal, the power plant elevator shaft set proved to be one of the most challenging for the production team. The set was required for the scene in which McClane drives an SUV through the doors of the facility and into the shaft, before engaging in

OPPOSITE TOP *John McClane surveys the vehicular carnage caused by Thomas Gabriel.*

OPPOSITE BOTTOM *The set for Warlock's Baltimore basement hideout interior.*

TOP *Len Wiseman blocks out an action scene on the sidewalk with chalk lines and toy cars.*

ABOVE *Wiseman directs Bruce Willis and Justin Long.*

BELOW *Bruce Willis gets his injury makeup adjusted on set as Wiseman (left) looks on.*

TOP *Concept art by Robert McKinnon shows John McClane hanging on for dear life in the elevator shaft.*

CENTER LEFT *Maggie Q and Bruce Willis film the fight scene that resulted in twenty-four stitches for the leading man.*

ABOVE *Maggie Q attempts to disarm Willis's stunt double.*

OPPOSITE *Willis hangs around during the shooting of the elevator shaft fight.*

a complex and exhilarating fight scene with Mai Linh in and around the vehicle, which hangs vertically by a tangle of steel cables. A five-story section of the ten-story shaft was built, and a real SUV was hung on wires. Cramped and claustrophobic, this four-walled environment "was a bitch of a set to be in," says Wiseman. "It was a nightmare." Access doors and panels were cut into the sides of the shaft set to allow cameras to film, while Willis and Maggie Q both had to be hung on wires and lowered in from the top of the structure.

Enthusiastic to take on as much stunt work as he could, Willis had arrived on set in prime shape. "I wanted McClane to look like he could still take whatever's thrown at him," he says.[5] To prepare, he went to the gym five days a week. "[It was] just to get my muscles big enough so I wouldn't break my bones diving around the concrete with these young stunt guys," he says. Determined to prove he still had what it takes, Willis did more than his share of stunts. "At one point I had a bruise from my hip to my ankle," he reveals. "All completely black and blue. And that's with pads on. I just wasn't going to let anyone know I was hurt."

Even so, he was left reeling during the elevator fight, when Maggie Q's stunt double accidentally clipped Willis in the head with a stiletto heel. "Had I lifted my head up a second later, she'd have kicked me right in the eye with a pair of high-heeled boots," says Willis. "I'd have lost an eye." Wiseman remembers inspecting the injury, as blood started pouring down Willis's face: "When he [pulled] on the eyebrow, the skin opens up and I can see the bone in his forehead." The star required twenty-four stitches. "You can see the stitches in the scene with me and Cliff Curtis in the FBI trailer," Willis grins.

The subsequent sequence sees Gabriel try to take out McClane with natural gas explosions, blowing up the power plant. The smokestack explosion sequence was created using miniature models of the structures, fitted with black powder bombs on a timer, plus one special twist. Miniature effects supervisor Michael Joyce got hold of a stash of old flashbulbs and incorporated them into the explosions. "Flashbulbs are not like an electronic strobe, which is very short duration," says McClung. "Flashbulbs are burning whatever the hell the metal is in there, so the flash lasts a relatively long time. [Joyce] laced these bulbs inside of the model and it looked great." The moment when McClane and Farrell look out to see a series of huge gas explosions coming toward them, taking out several giant high-tension power line towers, was also created with miniatures. "We were running out of money at that point," says McClung, "so I said [to the miniatures team], 'We'll do the towers in forced perspective.' So the first one is six feet tall, the second one is five feet tall, and so on." Propane mortars provided the blasts, and the scene was filmed at 125 frames per second, the super-slow shot creating a more realistic-looking fireball.

TUNNEL VISION

One of the most memorable scenes in *Live Free or Die Hard* comes after Gabriel instigates the first phase of the fire sale by hacking and controlling the city's transportation systems. In a police car, McClane and Farrell evade the stream of bullets from Rand's helicopter and head into a tunnel—but Gabriel manipulates streetlight systems to allow traffic to stream in from both sides, causing carnage. When a car flips into the air and rolls towards them, McClane and Farrell are saved when it lands on the hoods of two oncoming vehicles.

It's a brilliant stunt that almost never was. Wiseman and his stunt maestro Brad Martin had plotted the scene out with Matchbox toy cars, but it took much more than that to convince Fox's Tom Rothman. "I had to pitch the hell out of that one shot," says Wiseman, who ordered a computer-animated previsualization of the sequence to help sell it to Rothman. "That didn't work. . . . It just looked like a cartoon," he sighs. But Wiseman persisted, next time demonstrating the sequence using actual model cars, animated "almost like old school stop-motion." Rothman finally acquiesced. "He said, 'OK, I think it's kind of cool.'" He told the director to shoot half the scene, and if it looked like it had potential, the studio would fund the remainder. "It was a weird way to do a sequence," says Wiseman. "Rothman wasn't responding to it early on, but he definitely responds to a director's passion, so he let me stick with it, and in the end it became one of our favorite moments in the film."

The scene was shot on location in Los Angeles, near the Walt Disney Concert Hall on Grand Avenue. "It was not really a tunnel," says visual effects producer Joe Conmy. "It was more like a service center for trucks to load into the building." The car twisting through the air was shot by special effects director Michael Meinardus and his team. "They launched this car like a yo-yo," says McClung. "Mike rolled this cable around the car. He had this whole rig that would unspool this car and launch it in the air, landing it toward the camera." Landing the vehicle on the hoods of two cars required precision timing, and the shot needed an additional take after it failed to connect first time. "The second time, it hit right on the hoods," says Conmy.

Although the stunt was filmed live-action, Digital Dimension added some computer-generated background cars to the shot, necessary because there weren't enough stunt drivers available for the number of vehicles Wiseman wanted in the scene. Also, because of safety concerns, it was not possible to shoot Willis and Long in front of the flying and spinning car, but McClung successfully lobbied for them to be shot on location rather than in front of a green screen. The live-action footage of the two actors was then rotoscoped (cut out from the background) and composited into an impressively photo-realistic effects shot.

OPPOSITE *A stunt double performs a scene in which John McClane bounces off the hood of a police car.*

RIGHT *Concept art by Robert McKinnon depicts the showstopping car flip sequence.*

BELOW *Filming the tunnel scene on location in Los Angeles.*

The tunnel scene is followed by one of the Die Hard franchise's most outrageous moments. McClane drives a cop car at full speed, bailing from it just before it hits a tollbooth and goes airborne, spectacularly smashing into Rand's helicopter. Filmed at the entrance to the underpass on Grand Avenue in downtown Los Angeles, the shot required a scale helicopter model to be dangled from a one-hundred-foot crane at the location.

"The biggest challenge was determining the angle and speed to launch the police car since the ramp was built inside a breakaway toll booth," explains Wiseman. "The car needed enough force to realistically tear through the toll booth while not throwing its trajectory off course." Propelled by a hydraulic actuator (a cylinder that exerts a large, powerful force), the car hit the stunt team's ramp and went airborne at seventy miles per hour—hitting the helicopter on the first try. "We did it one time and it came out great," says McClung. "That was a good example of mixing and melding the second unit. We had stunts in there. We had visual effects. We had special effects. And then we went to lunch!"

To capture the moment when McClane dives from the car, the team mounted the vehicle on a trailer fitted with a platform that Willis would land on when exiting. While the stunt went off without a hitch, disaster struck when McClung realized that during filming the camera had pulled out wider than expected. "I saw the shot," says McClung, "and I went, 'Holy crap!' You could see the tires were sitting on the trailer, not moving. You could see the bottom of the trailer, you could see Bruce's arm as he lands on this platform." The visual effects team added spin to the tires and created a digital road surface below Willis. "I told Len it's only going to work until his elbow touches the moving tarmac," says McClung. But with a cut to a rolling stuntman, it worked perfectly. "It looks like he's really jumping out of a moving car."

THESE PAGES *The stuntmen and special effects team execute the remarkable set piece in which John McClane launches a cop car into a helicopter using a toll booth as a ramp (stunt ramp can be seen opposite top left).*

A FIERY FINALE

During the script-writing process, Wiseman had struggled with the third act of the film. The director didn't like the finale from Bomback's early drafts, in which McClane and Farrell, riding a motorbike and sidecar, chased a pipeline explosion that's heading toward the city. As written, McClane climbed from the bike onto a truck, steering it into the onrushing explosion before it reached the city. "Ultimately, it was hard to dramatize and it didn't feel particularly compelling," admits Bomback. "It felt a little preposterous and anticlimactic."

The finale was rewritten to feature McClane in a semitruck, dueling with an F-35 Lightning II fighter plane, after Gabriel acquired "go-codes" and duped the jet's pilot into eliminating McClane's "terrorist vehicle." In the initial version, McClane drove his vehicle into a building, the pursuing jet fired a missile, and McClane's truck emerged on fire. By driving into the water, McClane escaped and used air from the truck's tire to breathe underwater. The jet dropped a bomb, and McClane used a dislodged door from the truck as a shield, then rode the blast upward. Finally, he climbed out of the water and onto a dock, heading to a warehouse where he faced off with Gabriel.

TOP *The jet pursues John McClane as he escapes in a boat in this concept design by Robert McKinnon, created for a sequence not used in the final film.*

BELOW *A concept design by Jason Sweers for the truck commandeered by McClane.*

OPPOSITE TOP *Concept art by Robert McKinnon details the overpass location seen in the finale.*

OPPOSITE BOTTOM LEFT *A scale model of the F-35 that would be blended with digital effects to create the perfect marriage of old school and new school effects.*

OPPOSITE BOTTOM RIGHT *The stunt team prepares shots for the F-35 vs. truck duel.*

INSERT *Concept art depicting the freeway collapse by Robert McKinnon.*

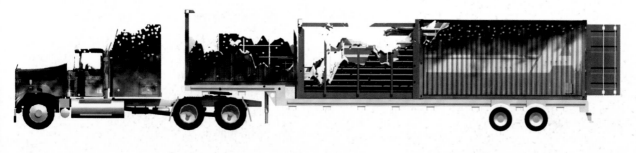

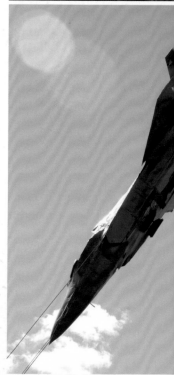

LIVE FREE
OR DIE HARD
IMAGE_05_22

LIVE FREE
OR DIE HARD
IMAGE_05_22

FREEWAY CONCEPT PAINTING

Wisher and Wiseman both liked the scene, but Fox chief Rothman wasn't convinced. It was close to Christmas 2006, around four months into the shoot, when Wisher and second-unit director Brian Smrz were summoned from the set to Rothman's office. "Tom pushes across the desk this little inch-and-a-half-square thing that he's clearly cut out of a magazine, of this wild freeway interchange overpass," says Wisher. "He says, 'I think this is kind of cool. What can you do with that?'"

Wisher took the night to imagine a new truck vs. jump jet sequence, set on a crazy interchange like the one in Rothman's photo. The next morning, he and Smrz went to a toy store to buy vehicles and plastic ramps. Playthings in hand, they returned to Fox to act out the sequence for Rothman and his team. Given the go-ahead by Rothman, Wisher wrote twenty pages of new script over the weekend, and work commenced almost immediately.

Because a large chunk of the freeway interchange would have to be physically con-structed, McClung estimated the sequence would cost an additional $6 million. "I said I don't want to have a truck on a green screen with nothing else there," he recalls. A 180-degree semi-circle of the ramp was built in the vast dirt parking lot at the Los Angeles County Fairgrounds in Pomona. Only a portion of the interchange needed to be built physically; the rest could be added digitally during post-production. "Production built an enormous blue screen out of shipping containers. It was five hundred feet long," adds McClung.

A full-scale model fighter jet was mounted on a hydraulic motion base with 360-degree movement. A nine-foot miniature was also built for some shots over at the visual effects company New Deal Studios. Wiseman came in with the first unit whenever Willis was to be

INSERT *It's truck vs. jet in this concept art by Robert McKinnon.*

filmed where McClane threw a reinforced steel bar, javelin-like, at the pilot, spearing his neck as he ejected from the plane, but ultimately that moment was never used.

FAREWELL TO THE "F" WORD

Principal photography wrapped on February 14, 2007, leaving a pressurized sixteen-week postproduction period before the global release in June. Wiseman was reunited with editor Nicolas De Toth, who had just finished working with the director on *Underworld: Evolution*. Racing to meet the release date, De Toth had to work at lightning speed. The first assembly was created less than five weeks after the shoot concluded. "The first cut was only about fifteen minutes longer than the final cut," says De Toth. "We delivered a very compact first cut."

Arriving so late in the schedule, the changes to the film's finale sent the visual effects teams into meltdown. The Orphanage had started on the CG model of the F-35 back in November 2006, but ongoing design changes to the full-size prop kept the modeling team busy until February 2007. "We even found ourselves in the situation where we had to deliver trailer shots with the F-35 while they were still finalizing the full-size model," says Matthew Hendershot, the VFX supervisor at the Orphanage.[6]

Tensions were mounting at this point. "Bruce was very nervous about certain things," says Wiseman. The six-month shoot had been grueling for the actor-producer, especially with all the last-minute changes to the third act. Yet after Wiseman screened half the film to him, Willis relaxed. "He got really excited, and he said, 'You know what, man, I know I've been giving you a hard time on stuff. This is a big deal for me. It can't go wrong, and I didn't have much faith in parts of the script that we've been nervous about and in certain decisions, but you've always been there.'"

Although Willis's fears were allayed, there was another big concern looming: the film's certificate. The Die Hard franchise had always been associated with the R rating in America. Never mind the violence, John McClane's signature "yippee-ki-yay, motherfucker" line automatically put each preceding film in the R-rated bracket. Willis even told *Vanity Fair*: "Saying *fuck* every other sentence is part of the vernacular of Die Hard."[7]

After Wiseman had shot "soft" and "hard" versions of certain scenes, a compromise was ultimately reached during postproduction to assure the PG-13 rating. Wiseman shoehorned in as much violence as possible, but when it came to the yippee-ki-yay line, the director had to come up with a clever way to get it by the ratings board. In the film, the immortal rejoinder is delivered when McClane, about to be killed by Gabriel, shoots a bullet through his own shoulder and into the villain. Wiseman's solution? Willis says "motherfu—" before the sound of the gun's hammer obscures the "cker." "I remember there being a lot of excitement about it—you can have your cake and eat it too," says Bomback. "We felt it was earned by the moment and wouldn't feel [phony] to the fans."

While the filmmakers were nervous about fan reaction to the abbreviated yippee-ki-yay line, Willis's look received almost as much attention. His face was still the focus of the poster, rendered in the film's sepia-bronze tint, and this would be the first time that John McClane didn't have a single hair on his head. "When the first images were released that John McClane was bald, people flipped out," Wiseman recalls. "They hated me for it." Yet, as Willis had been rocking the hairless cranium since the days of *12 Monkeys*, the complaints seemed pointless. The poster offered a glimpse of one money shot—the flying car hitting the helicopter—while the trailer featured a slew of them, including the F-35 jet and Farrell and McClane barely escaping the rotating flying car in the tunnel. The trailer's electronic version of Beethoven's "Ode to Joy" and the amped-up action signaled this would be a fresh take on the franchise.

Live Free or Die Hard was never test-screened, "which was very odd for a movie like this," says Wiseman. The first time the director saw it with an audience was at the premiere on June 22, 2007, at New York's Radio City Music Hall, amid six thousand fans, including five hundred off-duty police. "The event was part fan convention, part revival meeting, and part old-school Friday night film spectacle," reported *Variety*. "Beer flowed at the concession stands; applause came early and often."[8]

Critics were happy to welcome McClane back, even if there were apparent changes. "Older if apparently no wiser, the blue-collar super-cop from the 'Die Hard' franchise has lost his hair, his foul mouth and apparently his nicotine itch, but he still has the same knack for trouble," wrote Manohla Dargis for the *New York Times*. Aptly enough given the film's cyber subject matter, it was the first time a Die Hard movie would run the gauntlet of online reviews; it garnered a score of 69 on Metacritic and 82 percent critic approval on Rotten Tomatoes.

Live Free or Die Hard earned an estimated $9.1 million on the day it opened, outperforming its predecessors. According to exit polls, the film was drawing younger men and women, not just the audience that had fallen in love with McClane almost twenty years before. It finished with $135 million in the US and almost twice that overseas, ending up with a very solid $384 million worldwide, the twelfth-best total of any film released that year. It was also Fox's top-grossing live-action film of 2007.

That most analog of heroes, John McClane had unceremoniously crashed into the digital age.

PART 5 A GOOD DAY TO DIE HARD

"I'm up for the father of the year award." —JOHN MCCLANE

After four outings, Bruce Willis's love for John McClane and the Die Hard franchise was unshakable: "I remember every film, and I remember everything that we did and where we were. It is a life in itself. . . . I have a warm place in my heart for Die Hard."[1]

Given Willis's affection for the character, not to mention the financial success of the series (the first four movies collectively grossed $1.13 billion), a fifth outing felt right. The timing was perfect, too, with audiences thirsting for retro action movies, such as Sylvester Stallone's *The Expendables*, a 2010 box office smash that reunited 1980s stars like Eric Roberts and Dolph Lundgren and featured Willis in a small role. With studios also increasingly leaning toward established franchises, bringing back McClane was a no-brainer.

In the spring of 2010, screenwriter Skip Woods was hired to write the fifth film. After working on Willis's dialogue for *Live Free or Die Hard*, he and the actor had become friends. "He actually called me up and said, 'I have this idea about his son,'" says Woods.[2] It would mean resurrecting a familial dynamic that was previously toyed with during the scripting of *Live Free or Die Hard*. In the earliest iteration of Woods's script, set in both Russia and Afghanistan, John McClane headed overseas after discovering his son, Jack, had died. "That made it a little too dark for us, and we wanted to keep him alive," says Woods.[3]

As the story evolved, Woods narrowed down the setting to Russia and imagined Jack as a CIA operative working under deep cover in Moscow to engineer the defection of a political prisoner, Yuri Komarov. Years earlier, Komarov and his partner, Viktor Chagarin, had stolen millions of dollars worth of weapons-grade uranium from the Chernobyl nuclear plant prior to its catastrophic meltdown. Now a high-ranking politician, Chagarin is plotting to become the next Russian Defense Minister. But Komarov is willing to reveal all to the CIA about his former ally's shady past. When Chagarin imprisons Komarov on trumped-up charges, Jack intentionally gets himself arrested and agrees to testify against Komarov to keep a close eye on the prized asset. Believing his son is in trouble, John McClane boards a plane to Moscow, arriving just as Chagarin's men raid the courtroom. After fleeing the scene, the McClanes and Komarov hook up with the latter's daughter, Irina, to locate a file of evidence that the CIA intends to use against Chagarin. But a bigger scheme is in play: Irina and her father are plotting to steal weapons-grade uranium from a Chernobyl vault and take a more brutal revenge on Chagarin.

McClane was always a fish out of water in the Die Hard films, but in this fifth outing, that trend was set to expand on a global scale. He was certainly not going to learn Russian and seamlessly blend in. "I think it would be a big mistake to start monkeying with the character and start changing things around now," says Willis. "I think everybody thinks they have it figured out in their thirties or forties. They go, 'This is how I'm gonna be, this is what I'm gonna be.' I think John McClane is that same guy. He always thinks he knows more than he really knows. He certainly thinks he's smarter than his son, and his son is actually far smarter than he is."

As the script came together, several directors were considered for *Die Hard 5*. Len Wiseman was one possibility for the job, the director discussing the project with Willis early on in the process. "The temptation to go back in was pretty high," he admits. But, already committed to developing a pilot for the TV show *Hawaii Five-0*, Wiseman passed. Likewise, commercial director Noam Murro was considered, but he opted to make *300: Rise of an Empire*, the sequel to Zack Snyder's 2006 swords-and-sandals epic. Other potential names included *Fast Five*'s Justin Lin, edgy indie auteur Nicolas Winding Refn (best known for *Drive*), and Joe Cornish, director of *Attack the Block*. In the end, the job went to Irish director John Moore, who had enjoyed a long relationship with Fox that began with 2001's well-received Bosnia-set action drama *Behind Enemy Lines*.

To: PK/SW/AY

See page Notes. Didn't it do Third Act Action
<3 its too overwritten to even read —
went to see pre-viz instead. Pre-viz
A Good Day to Die Hard
will show all action sequences need
to be cut by ½.
Skip Woods
Good job bringing in a more
emotional feel to it.

Draft Comparison
to 1.23.12 draft.

ABOVE *An annotated cover page for Skip Woods's* A Good Day to Die Hard *script.*

OPPOSITE *Bruce Willis returns as John McClane in* A Good Day to Die Hard.

Moore, like Wiseman before him, was a Die Hard fan. "I still have my original ticket stub from when the original movie opened," he says. "I was a kid in Dublin. I know it sounds a little overly romantic, but I do remember queuing in the rain [to see it]." When *Live Free or Die Hard* was in the offing, he'd had his "nose at the trough," but the job went to Wiseman. He wasn't going to miss out a second time around. When the studio messengered him Woods's script in August 2011, he devoured it. A meeting with Willis was set up, and they hit it off. Moore signed on for what became *A Good Day to Die Hard*. He jokingly remembers the one instruction from the studio: "Don't fuck it up!"

More seriously, he says, "We were all diligently aware of what a national treasure this character is, and nobody wanted to screw around with it." The "we" included several of Moore's regular collaborators, including cinematographer Jonathan Sela, editor Dan Zimmerman, and production designer Daniel T. Dorrance, who had all worked on the director's 2008 video game adaptation *Max Payne*.

As was typical for a Die Hard movie, the story was still evolving when preproduction began. Moore wanted to bring his good friend William Wisher Jr., veteran of the third and fourth Die Hard movies, to polish the script. "I was looking forward to finding other sides of John McClane," says Wisher. In the end, Wisher's involvement never materialized. "Maybe people thought [Wisher] was too dark, too gritty, and they wanted to keep it a little more poppy, a little more Die Hard," suggests Moore. Jason Keller, who penned the 2011 Gerard Butler film *Machine Gun Preacher*, came in to do an uncredited rewrite, taking an executive producer credit.

Moore was excited by the idea of dropping McClane into a new world. "John McClane has probably never taken a foreign vacation in his life," he says. "I'm not even sure McClane has a passport, to be honest." The idea of putting this all-American hero in the former Soviet bloc was intriguing. "I can't imagine a bigger ocean of noncommunication than Eastern Europe and Russia," says Willis.[4] In many ways, this was to be Moore's homage to James Bond movies of yore; John McClane even refers to his son as the "007 of Plainfield, New Jersey," in the script.

TOP *John McClane packs a sawn-off shotgun in this concept by Chris Rosewarne.*

CENTER RIGHT *Viktor Chagarin's men raid the courtroom. Concept art by Chris Rosewarne.*

ABOVE *The aftermath of the courtroom attack. Concept art by Chris Rosewarne.*

OPPOSITE TOP RIGHT *All hell breaks loose on the streets of Moscow. Concept art by Chris Rosewarne.*

OPPOSITE BOTTOM *Concept art of the Moscow courtroom by Daniel Dorrance.*

Despite taking McClane to new frontiers, Moore was determined to give the film an old-school feel across the board and opted to use 35mm negative rather than digital cameras. "Certain characters deserve and require the texture that film will give them, and I think John McClane and Die Hard movies are of that ilk," he says. Moore also wanted the audience to feel right there with McClane, so he planned to shoot handheld, eschewing artful framing, elaborate shots, and precise compositions, much like McTiernan had on *Die Hard with a Vengeance*. "The wonderful thing about the Die Hard movies is that they practically happen in real time," he says. "We took that as our lead: Don't let it slow down. Keep our foot on the gas, keep it moving, keep it going, keep it handheld, keep it disorganized, and keep a sense of mayhem going. . . . The film can never be bigger than John McClane's sense of energy or danger."

Although the movie was fully storyboarded, with concept art fleshing out key moments, once shooting began, Moore planned to discard these resources in search of that mayhem he craved. A camera assistant on the opening sequence of *Saving Private Ryan* (1998), Moore remembers director Steven Spielberg telling his camera operators, "I want you to miss it, but don't miss it," meaning they should react to the action, not anticipate it. "We certainly took a leaf out of that book in approaching *Die Hard 5*," says Moore. "Our approach was shoot it as if it's happening for real, so it'll be a bit messy." The art of it, he says, "is in making it look a little artless."

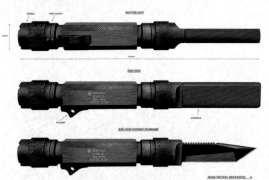

TOP LEFT *Concept art for Jack McClane's knife by Chris Rosewarne.*

TOP RIGHT *German star Sebastian Koch as Yuri Komarov.*

ABOVE *Yuliya Snigir as the duplicitous Irina Komarov.*

OPPOSITE *Jai Courtney plays Jack McClane.*

CASTING ON A GOOD DAY

Jai Courtney, a rising Australian actor best known to American audiences for his role in the TV series *Spartacus: Blood and Sand*, landed the key role of John McClane's son, Jack. In true Hollywood fashion, it almost never happened. Courtney had just finished shooting the Tom Cruise action film *Jack Reacher* in Pittsburgh and was heading home to Sydney when he got a call from his agent. "Literally, I was walking down the Jetway to my connecting flight at LAX when my agent called and said, 'Don't leave—they want you to read with Bruce!'" Turning on his heels, he tested with Willis a week later.

"Jai got the character, and he just seemed like family—like a McClane," says Willis.[5] Channeling the same earthy appeal as Willis, Courtney concurs: "We just complemented each other. The dynamic was right, and I understood where Jack was at."[6] Much of the film's wry humor comes from John and Jack's bickering, which provides insight into the McClane clan's emotional issues. As Jack wryly puts it, "We're not really a hugging family."

Mary Elizabeth Winstead was also set to return for a brief appearance as Lucy McClane, driving her father to the airport at the start of the film and picking him and her brother up at the end.

German actor Sebastian Koch, famed for the Oscar-winning 2006 drama *The Lives of Others*, received an offer to play the McClanes' dubious ally, Yuri Komarov. "I liked the tension in it and the part and said okay, let's go for it," Koch remembers. "I was working in indie art house films, so for me it was amazing, and interesting, to be a part of this big machine. I wanted to experience that." Koch spoke several languages but no Russian, so he learned Komarov's lines phonetically.

Cole Hauser, who'd previously starred with Willis in the 2002 drama *Hart's War*, was brought on to play Mike Collins, a CIA operative and Jack's partner. Model and actress Yuliya Snigir was cast as Irina. After a career largely confined to her native Russia, she says landing the role "was unexpected for me."[7]

Veteran Russian theater and television actor Sergei Kolesnikov, who'd appeared alongside Paul Giamatti in *Cold Souls* (2009), won the part of Viktor Chagarin. Moore had no qualms about depicting an amoral politician, a first for the Die Hard franchise: "If you're going to talk about Russia in the twenty-first century, [it's] oligarchs, corruption, and these big colorful figures, whether its Roman Abramovich or [Boris] Berezovsky. That's really what Russia is in people's minds."

Playing Alik, the Russian mobster hired by Chagarin to take out Komarov, was Rasha Bukvic, a Serbian actor who had previously appeared alongside Liam Neeson in *Taken* (2008). With his cultured interests and lines like, "Do you know what I hate about Americans? Everything. Especially cowboys," Alik evokes the original film's German villain. "It was all definitely a nod to that elegant thuggery of Alan Rickman's Hans Gruber," says Moore.

MISSION TO MOSCOW

During preproduction, Moore and his core team took a twenty-day scouting trip to Moscow, Prague, Budapest, and Belgrade. With so much of the film set in Moscow, the Russian capital was given serious consideration as a base for the production. But ultimately, Moscow was rejected as the main location, although some brief pickup shots would be captured there later in the shoot. The bottom line was "shooting in Moscow was just too much of a wild card," says Daniel Dorrance. Budapest was chosen instead, with good tax incentives, a cooperative government, and excellent studio and production facilities.

Further trips to Moscow for research purposes were nevertheless essential in preproduction. Visual effects supervisor—and another *Max Payne* alumnus—Everett Burrell scouted the city with his team for weeks to work out how it could be re-created in Budapest. "[In Moscow,] we got a really good vibe of the brutalism of the buildings and how vast and abandoned the military bases were," says Burrell. "It was definitely a contrast in worlds, a fish-out-of-water kind of thing for John McClane. That's definitely a theme."

ABOVE *Artwork by Kamen Anev for the LaGuardia set opening, eventually cut from the film.*

OPPOSITE BOTTOM *John McClane arrives in Russia to find his son.*

One of Moore's priorities was to shoot using practical elements wherever possible, rather than relying on visual effects being added in postproduction. "Not to criticize [*Live Free or Die Hard*]," he says, "but it did come in for a little bit of heat for one or two sequences that people thought . . . were a little CG-heavy and didn't feel like Die Hard." For Moore, a Die Hard movie should feel "bloody and salty." He wanted to take it back to the feel of the original.

Even as filming approached, Moore was still finessing elements of the screenplay, including what became one of the film's biggest action sequences. In the original script, after the McClanes and Komarov flee the courtroom, there was "a very limited getaway" scene, says Moore. But that changed when, on the first day of scouting in Moscow, the team got stuck in gridlocked traffic. "Our local fixer said, 'This is the notorious Garden Ring, it's the worst traffic in the world.'" A circular avenue in Moscow's city center, consisting of seventeen streets and fifteen squares, the Garden Ring was the ideal setting for an expanded car chase. "It made perfect sense," adds Moore. "If John McClane was gridlocked, John McClane would drive over the traffic."

GANGSTER CHIC

Moore wanted a costume designer who was used to working in Eastern Europe and who could bring authenticity to the look of the film's Russian gangsters. He found her in Bojana Nikitovic. The Bosnian costume designer wasn't an expert on Moscow and Russia, she says, "but I am familiar with the kind of criminals in the movie, the way they dress and the way they look." Nikitovic was also an expert in uniforms, having created them for several previous films, including Ralph Fiennes's 2011 Serbian-set take on Shakespeare's *Coriolanus*. This proved to be a necessary skill for *A Good Day to Die Hard*, given that McClane would be tangling with Russian paramilitary soldiers. "John [Moore] knew how important it is for the uniforms to be very precise with insignia, with the details, with things that make the whole look real," she says.

Nikitovic found Willis easy to design for and was happy to defer to his ideas for McClane's outfits. "He knows better than all of us what he should wear," she says. They settled on practical traveling clothes, comfortable for Willis to move in. As on previous Die Hard productions, the devil was in the multiples. "You always have to take care to be able to produce twenty, thirty, fifty copies [of McClane's costume]," she says, "because it's going everywhere: doubles, stunt doubles, blood, and all kinds of injuries and things." So while McClane's look might be simple, every garment had to be capable of being made or bought in bulk, which always proved a challenge.

For much of the film, Jack McClane's style echoes his father's look in the previous films: jeans, T-shirt, and Red Wing work shoes. But Nikitovic got to dress him differently for his early appearance in a Moscow nightclub, where he assassinates Chagarin's associate Anton to get himself jailed. "That was one of my favorite scenes," she says, "because we could play there." Courtney was attired in white jeans with a black shirt to look like one of the nouveau riche gangsters, and he played his scenes surrounded by dozens of nightclub extras in glamorous designer outfits.

Dressing her leading lady, Yuliya, was also a pleasure, says Nikitovic. "She was really stunning." First seen pulling up on a motorbike wearing a leather jumpsuit—which she promptly unzips to slip into a little black dress—Yuliya makes quite an entrance. The jumpsuit was a last-minute addition, suggested by Moore, that sent Nikitovic and her crew scrambling to find multiples of the garment for both the actress and the stunt double. "Of course, it's never [just] one jumpsuit," Nikitovic says. "But it was fun. Each time John [Moore] came up with a new idea, I really embraced it."

Irina's father, Komarov, is indifferent to his clothing, says Nikitovic. "[He] doesn't care a lot about what he's wearing." Even so, his clothes were chosen carefully: dark pants and a light-colored shirt to show blood and dust, the inevitable fallout of any adventure with John McClane. Meanwhile, henchman Alik was outfitted with a dark shirt and tailored suit. "[Moore] insisted that he should look really good . . . good-looking, dangerous, sexy." Once again in *Die Hard*, the villains snag all the best clothes.

TOP LEFT AND TOP RIGHT *Irina Komarov (Yuliya Snigir) makes a rapid change.*

OPPOSITE *Rasha Bukvic as the mobster Alik.*

HOT TIMES IN BUDAPEST

The shoot began on April 23, 2012, with Budapest enduring sweltering temperatures. The Hungarian capital provided thirty-two practical locations, mainly doubling for Moscow except for a couple of scenes set in New York. Budapest's Franz Liszt Airport was chosen to stand in for LaGuardia for the airport scenes featuring Mary Elizabeth Winstead as Lucy McClane.

Daniel Dorrance and supervising locations manager Terry Blyther worked closely together, uncovering hidden gems like the interior used for the opening sequence, where Chagarin visits Komarov in his prison cell. "I found this old Roman ruin in Budapest, a cathedral, and we put his cell in there," says Dorrance. "So he's in this little cage in the middle, like a rat."[8]

Other locations were better known, like the Museum of Fine Arts in Heroes' Square, which doubled as the exterior of the courtroom where hundreds of protestors barrack the arriving Komarov. Overall, Moore wanted to express how Moscow is "sick with corruption," according to cinematographer Jonathan Sela, who deliberately played with colors—blues, greens, oranges, yellows—when lighting the pristine architecture of the city. "We needed to figure out, how do you take that and not make it look so perfect?" says Sela.[9]

For the Chernobyl set, where Komarov, Alik, and Irina face off with the McClanes in the finale, Dorrance's crew converted a former Soviet military base in the village of Kiskunlacháza, an hour from Budapest, to create a convincing facsimile of the real facility. "We had to clear out a square mile of trees and brush," he says. Cement was laid to create a helicopter landing pad, and Soviet-era sculptures and decorative pools were also installed.

Several sets were also created at Budapest's Raleigh Studios (later renamed Origo Studios), including the courtroom where Komarov is on trial and the interior of the abandoned bank, visited by McClane and company in the Chernobyl sequence. Covering two full soundstages, the evocative set comprised an exterior facade, a safe-deposit room, a secret vault, and a large circular steel door. There was also the large lobby, which set decorator Jille Azis decked out with Soviet-era props, including typewriters and filing cabinets. She even bought old-fashioned safety-deposit boxes from eBay that were originally used in an Oklahoma bank.

Yet the most impressive set by far was the Hotel Ukraina ballroom, where the McClanes and Komarov meet up with Irina. Designed in what Dorrance calls "garish, rococo-style architecture," the set took eight weeks to build, with squib-loaded panels installed into walls for the moment when Chagarin's armed men lay siege to the ballroom. "It was a very complex setup," says Moore. "We had 1,200 separate bullet hits built into the set." Breakaway chandeliers,

chairs, and pianos were constructed, and the windows were fitted with tempered glass, designed to shatter into small pieces.

Moore's "money shot," as he calls it, comes when the McClanes run the length of the ballroom, dodging bullets from an attack helicopter outside before jumping through a plateglass window. "It took two and a half weeks to set that, so we were praying to the gods of filming that we'd only have to do that once," says the director. "And of course we had to do it twice." Nevertheless, the shot is seamless. "Just as the camera pans around, we switch to the stuntmen," reveals Moore. "Even if you frame-by-frame it, it's very good work. You can't see the handover, and then the stuntmen really do an old-school jump about twenty meters through plate glass onto pads below."

The scene concludes as the McClanes land on scaffolding underneath the window, then escape down a plastic chute used for debris on construction sites. "We built a forty-foot-high section," explains Dorrance, "with the tubes at an angle so we could put a cameraman with the actors in the tubes and not go too fast."

OPPOSITE TOP LEFT *Storyboards by Jim Magdaleno show the McClanes under attack at the Ukraina.*

OPPOSITE BOTTOM *John Moore directs Bruce Willis. Jai Courtney can be seen in the background.*

TOP AND ABOVE *Concept art by Chris Rosewarne depicts the McClanes' escape from Hotel Ukraina.*

Willis was well into his fifties by the time shooting started, and the stunt work he undertook would have been a challenge for a man half his age. Moore says that didn't affect shooting because "Bruce wouldn't let it." When it came to the physical aspects, "He had to grimace through a few stunts," the director adds, "and limp off into the corner now and again, but the last thing he wants to do is ask you to accommodate him."

For exterior shots, the production was able to use one of the Hungarian government's own Russian-made Mi-24 helicopters just weeks before it was due to be decommissioned. Permission was granted to fly it into Budapest airspace to film the copter whirring over the city. Dorrance also created the Ukraina's rooftop helipad at a nearby airfield runway.

Inside the helicopter are Alik, Komarov, and Irina, who has seemingly betrayed her father, turning a gun on him. For the shot of the chopper looping around before it starts firing on the Hotel Ukraina, Snigir had to be perched on the edge of the vehicle, with its doors open—a tough ask for someone with a "severe phobia" of heights. "I was petrified," she admits. But after summoning up the requisite courage, it was an amazing experience. "I could see the entire gorgeous cityscape of Budapest from several hundred feet in the air."[10]

OPPOSITE TOP LEFT *The Mi-24 helicopter open fires on the Ukraina. Concept art by Chris Rosewarne.*

ABOVE *The real Mi-24 during filming.*

BELOW *The McClanes try to escape the Mi-24 on foot. Concept art by Kamen Anev.*

A BEAST BREATHES A FIRE

The Mi-24 wasn't the only helicopter on set. The climactic Chernobyl action sequence features the world's largest helicopter, a Russian Mi-26 Halo. Weighing a staggering 28 tons and measuring nearly 42 yards long, its top speed is 250 knots. "To my knowledge it's never been in a movie before, so we were very keen to put it in," says Moore. To get their hands on the Mi-26, the team went to the Republic of Belarus and its Ministry of Emergency Situations, which owned the rare aircraft and was willing to rent it to the production. "It's a beast," says Moore. "There are only a handful in the world, and only two or three of them are available for rent." It took six months of negotiating to procure the permits to bring it across the Belarusian, Ukrainian, and Hungarian borders, then a week to physically transport it to the set with the help of a police escort. It cost $360,000 to rent and required a crew of six to fly it during the exterior aerial shots.

For interior shots, an additional, nonfunctioning Mi-26 was purchased, after four months of negotiations. "It was actually one of the original helicopters that was used for the Chernobyl cleanup," explains Moore. "I presume it was safe to buy!" The chopper was cut into two separate pieces for use on a soundstage: The cockpit was attached to a gimbal for scenes requiring the illusion of aerial motion and the loading bay was placed on a raised platform for shooting a scene where McClane hangs from a truck lodged into the back end of the chopper.

The finale is spectacular and even manages to work in a reference to the original *Die Hard*: As Jack throws Komarov from the rooftop, he falls backward, Hans Gruber–style, into the Mi-26's deadly rotor blades. "We tried to pepper the film with tiny references, like the Hans Gruber fall," says Moore. "At one point, I was desperately trying to figure out how I could get a Rolex watch in there."

As the Mi-26, piloted by Irina, comes crashing into the building, it burns up into a giant fireball. The production team explored the idea of shooting the scene with a miniature in "homage to the first film," says Burrell. But in the end, a different approach was required and so the team obtained the hull of an Mi-17 helicopter and filmed at the former Soviet military base where the Chernobyl exteriors were built. "We just hooked it up to a massive construction crane and loaded it full of C-4 and gasoline, told everyone to stand back, put twelve cameras on it, and dropped it," explains Moore, matter-of-factly. For the aftermath, Dorrance dressed the area with scrap metal from an aircraft salvage yard.

MI-26 CHERNOBYL APPROACH. | ROSEWARNE 2012

The fully functional Mi-26, meanwhile, proved difficult and expensive to rehearse with. One shot called for the helicopter to be filmed on the ground before taking off, while the set burned behind it. A controlled burn was started in the background, and the helicopter rotors began to spin. Before cameras could roll, though, the helicopter's downdraft proved so powerful it fanned the fire into a real, out-of-control blaze that ripped through portions of the set and sent crew scrambling for safety. No one was hurt, "but it was quite a sickening feeling," says Moore. "It took its three weeks to repair what was damaged," adds Dorrance. "We had to wait for insurance to clear, so that was the biggest deal. We couldn't touch it."

The giant Mi-26 was scanned using lasers so that it could be digitally duplicated by the visual effects team. "One of the hardest things to do is to mimic real life," says Burrell. "You're cutting from a real helicopter to a CG helicopter and back again. That's pretty complicated stuff. Whenever John felt like [the visual effects artists] weren't pushing the limits, he'd bring up the real footage and say, 'You've got to match this, this is our benchmark.'" The digital choppers had to be correct down to the way the light hit the rivets. "It was a bit of a struggle," he admits. "We'd do what I called the Pepsi Challenge. We'd have the CG helicopter on a screen next to the real helicopter and see if John could pick which one was real. That was fun because sometimes John couldn't tell, which was good."

The script had originally featured a cold opening involving the Mi-26 helicopter and an elaborate heist of the antiradiation chemical that is later seen in the third act of the film. (In the finale, the chemical is helicoptered into Chernobyl by the villains who intend to use the substance to neutralize the area.) "It set the tone for what John was looking for," says Burrell. "He wanted this to be sort of his homage to Bond films, in terms of the scope and the spectacle and the elaborate stunts, and Bond always has an amazing cold opening."

The sequence got as far as previsualization, and Moore laments that they ran out of time and money before they could shoot it. "It was a multimillion-dollar sequence," says Moore. "We had a release date for this movie that was set in stone, and the sequence just kept being pushed further down the schedule. And then we cut and previewed the movie, and the sense was the movie could survive without it. But it was a shame. It was a great piece of action."

ABOVE *The Mi-26 Halo, a "beast" of a helicopter.*

OPPOSITE *Concept art shows the Mi-26 arriving at Chernobyl. Concept art by Chris Rosewarne.*

RIGHT AND CENTER RIGHT *Artwork by Kamen Anev shows the fallout from the Mi-26 explosion.*

INSERT *Chernobyl sequence art by Chris Rosewarne / Kamen Anev.*

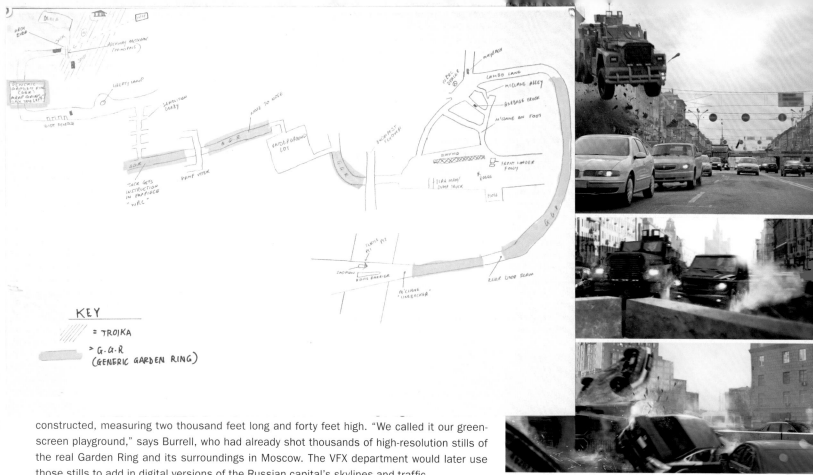

KEY

////// = TROJKA

▬▬▬ = G.a.R
(GENERIC GARDEN RING)

constructed, measuring two thousand feet long and forty feet high. "We called it our green-screen playground," says Burrell, who had already shot thousands of high-resolution stills of the real Garden Ring and its surroundings in Moscow. The VFX department would later use those stills to add in digital versions of the Russian capital's skylines and traffic.

"They had endless work to shoot that chase day after day," says Moore of the effects crew. "They would sometimes go days setting up a shot, and not shooting until the second or third day. It took that level of planning." In one of the most stunning moments, John McClane crashes his vehicle over the guardrail of a bridge, driving over the tops of other cars. Stuntman Larry Rippenkroeger performed the daring drive, which the crew dubbed the "gridlock stepladder." Later, the production moved to Moscow to capture the Garden Ring pickup shots. They also filmed the opening credit sequence in which Irina speeds through the streets on her motorbike.

Moore remains fiercely proud of what he and his team achieved in the Garden Ring scene (the director's cut, released on DVD, contains another seven minutes of the chase). For him, it felt like old-school Die Hard: "The car wreck sequence was quite something . . . because it has John McClane at the heart of it."

TOP *John McClane beats the rush-hour traffic in the film's stunning car chase.*

CENTER RIGHT, ABOVE, AND BELOW *Artwork by Kamen Anev depicts key moments from the Garden Ring chase.*

OPPOSITE TOP *Budapest's Hungaroring is converted into a giant "green-screen playground."*

OPPOSITE CENTER AND BOTTOM *Models are used to meticulously plan out the car chase.*

INSERT *A map of the streets for the car chase used for reference by the production.*

MOVING TO POST

A Good Day to Die Hard wrapped filming on September 1, 2012, moving straight into postproduction for another breakneck race to make the scheduled February 2013 release. Editor Dan Zimmerman, who began his career cutting Moore's 2006 remake *The Omen*, was the perfect choice to assemble the movie; a friend of his who worked on the original *Die Hard* had gotten him on set—when he was just thirteen years old—to witness the moment when helicopters roared down the Avenue of the Stars. "I was there that night when they did it," he says.

After being on set throughout the shoot of *A Good Day to Die Hard*, Zimmerman then spent six weeks in Ireland with Moore cutting the film, before returning to the States with a rough assembly. "It was pretty daunting," he admits. "You're talking about almost thirty years of a character that everybody knows." Gradually, the film took shape, though it was not without its causalities, including Lucy McClane.

Lucy's scenes driving her father to the airport and picking him and Jack up at the end had already been shot—actress Mary Elizabeth Winstead is even shown in the first trailer for the film, pleading with her father to "try not to make an even bigger mess of things." But Moore became concerned that both McClane offspring might be overkill, and the scenes were removed: "I was terribly worried this was going to turn into the fucking *Brady Bunch* of Die Hard. The pet dog and the goldfish were going to get involved."

It wasn't the only issue. Some plot holes necessitated late-2012 reshoots that included a new scene in which the McClanes pick up a bag of guns at a train station locker (explaining how they obtain the bag when they enter the Hotel Ukraina). A skeletal crew decamped to London's Pinewood Studios where Willis was filming *Red 2*. "Lorenzo [di Bonaventura, the producer of *Red 2*] would literally text me and say, 'OK, you can have him for an hour!'" remembers Moore. "He'd pop over from one stage, change costume, be John McClane, and then go back." To complicate matters further, Courtney's reshoots had to be captured in Los Angeles on December 21, less than two months before the film's February 14 release date. "It was really down to the wire," says Moore.

Composer Marco Beltrami returned after crafting the score for *Live Free or Die Hard*; in the interim, he'd also worked with Moore on *Max Payne*. The composition for *A Good Day to Die Hard*—recorded in December 2012 at Fox Studios in Los Angeles—referenced Michael Kamen's original score and even hinted at Beethoven's "Ode to Joy" in the opening track, "Yuri Says." Moore was happy with these winks to the original film. "By the time you're doing the fifth movie of a franchise, if you're not having fun with it, really what's the point?" he says.

A GOOD DAY TO RELEASE

A Good Day to Die Hard was released in February 2013—a marked change from the previ-ous films' summer openings and an indication of an industry shift, with studios now viewing every month as a potential window for a new blockbuster. After the film opened first in key Asian territories, the US release arrived on February 14—Valentine's Day. The message was clear: As McTiernan always intended, Die Hard films are date movies that everyone can enjoy. The posters were accompanied with the tagline 'Yippee-Ki-Yay Mother Russia' in a spin on McClane's signature phrase (used when McClane wedges the truck in the rear of the Halo helicopter piloted by Irina).

A Good Day to Die Hard ultimately grossed $304 million, making it the third-highest-grossing of the five films. Unsurprisingly, with McClane on foreign soil, the lion's share of the takings came from foreign markets. The film grossed $237 million outside the US, some 77 percent of its total, and finished as Fox's third-best performer for the year.

ABOVE *Concept art by Kamen Anev shows the safe passage of the McClanes.*

OPPOSITE BOTTOM *A Good Day to Die Hard's poster, with its wry tagline.*

Reviews were mixed, with some critics believing the film was designed to set up Courtney's character for a spin-off. "One can only hope the studio doesn't plan to pass the franchise on to him," said *Variety*. But Moore vehemently denies there was ever such a plan. "I think everyone involved understands that this only works if it's John McClane, and if his time is over, it's over," he says. "When we were making number five, there was no sense that his son, Jack, would go on to star in a standalone movie."

Moore credits Willis for bringing the character back for a fifth adventure without compromising his integrity. "We didn't get to the point where it starts to get silly and we're making jokes about arthritis," says the director. "The John McClane that people will remember [from our film] is pretty similar to the John McClane from the first movie." Despite having embarked on his first overseas adventure, he was still the same old New York cop at heart.

PART 6 BEYOND THE BIG SCREEN

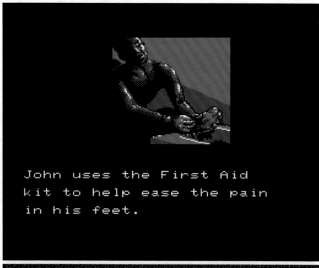

John uses the First Aid kit to help ease the pain in his feet.

Toys, games, soundtracks, action figures, comics, books, video games—the world of Die Hard extends far beyond the movies. While the films have been released on every home-entertainment format imaginable—VHS, DVD, Blu-ray, laser disc, and even UMD for the PlayStation Portable—the movies are just the beginning for the Die Hard fanatic.

The video game market has particularly embraced Die Hard, the franchise's action sequences being ideal material for the format. Mediagenic, the company that owned video games publisher Activision, licensed the first Die Hard game within months of the original film's 1988 theatrical release. At its helm was Tony Van, an associate producer in the division devoted to the Nintendo Entertainment System, the 8-bit home game console commonly known as NES.

A huge fan of the film, Van's vision for the title—simply called *Die Hard*—was unique at the time: The game had a traditional top-down view, but with the twist that players could not see into areas of the map obscured by walls and doors. Van wanted to create the suspense of not knowing who or what was coming and the adrenaline rush of being surprised by an enemy. Sometimes, though, the player could hear footsteps coming from beyond the walls, warning of an approaching foe. To further stoke tension and the feeling of danger, players would only get one life. Die once, and the game was over—a feature practically unheard of in console games at the time.

Released in 1990, the game didn't have the usual fixed tasks and levels. Instead, it was an early example of the sandbox video game genre, allowing players to move freely between floors and avoid or engage with enemies at their discretion, all the while trying to foil Hans's plans. "This meant the player had many choices, which dynamically changed the game," says Van. Tension was ratcheted up further by a variety of game mechanics that kept the player

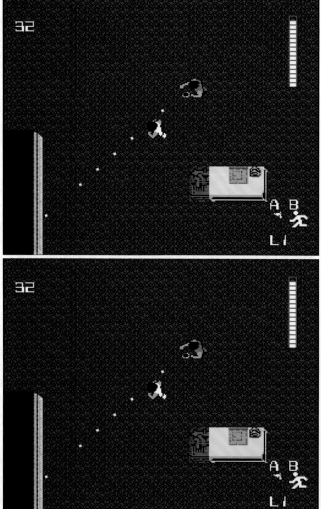

"Our unwelcome guest won't be bothering us any more. Gentlemen, we are now 640 million dollars richer!" YOU LOSE. GAME OVER.

THIS PAGE *Scenes from Activision's* Die Hard *video game.*

OPPOSITE *Laurent Durieux's artwork for Mondo's 2013 screening of* Die Hard.

"NOW I HAVE A MACHINE GUN. HO-HO-HO."

Season's Greetings

MONDO MYSTERY MOVIE XI

DIE HARD™

MONDO PRESENTS A 35 MM SCREENING OF "DIE HARD"

SHOW STARTS AT 7PM ON DECEMBER 14, 2013 AT THE HISTORIC CREST THEATRE

1262 WESTWOOD BLVD IN LOS ANGELES, CA

in constant peril: McClane was able to crawl through ventilation ducts, but, as in the film, bullets could still pierce his hiding spot; he had limited ammunition, forcing players to carefully monitor their bullet supply (there was no on-screen ammo counter); there was even a bare-feet element to the game where, if McClane walked on shattered glass, his movements would be slowed, making it harder to avoid fire. First-aid kits scattered around the game gave the player a chance to heal McClane's feet.

In 1996, Fox Interactive released *Die Hard Trilogy* across a variety of platforms including PlayStation and Microsoft Windows. Developed by UK-based Probe Entertainment, this hugely popular title allowed gamers to play through the storylines of the first three movies in three different gameplay styles. The original film was rendered as a third-person shooter that mixed action and strategy, as players face down Gruber's gang in the Nakatomi building. The second game, a first-person, on-rails shooter, featured bad guy–blasting action in Dulles Airport, plus a snowmobile chase. In the vehicle-based *Die Hard with a Vengeance* game, players got to drive around New York diffusing bombs. Intriguingly, in one element of this third segment, players were able to launch a car at a helicopter, a scenario later echoed in the film *Live Free or Die Hard*. In Germany, *Die Hard Trilogy* was banned due to its violent content following complaints that players could plow through innocent pedestrians in the *Die Hard with a Vengeance* segment. A less successful sequel, *Die Hard Trilogy 2: Viva Las Vegas*, was released in 2000.

Bits Studios' *Die Hard: Vendetta* launched on the GameCube in 2002. A first-person shooter, taking place across eleven levels, it was based on the first three movies, with McClane older and gray-haired. The plot sees McClane's daughter, Lucy—now a member of the LAPD—kidnapped by Piet Gruber, one of Hans Gruber's sons. Despite some endearingly grisly game mechanics—McClane could grab enemies from behind and use them as human shields—reviews were mixed.

ABOVE *John McClane relives his first three adventures in Fox Interactive's* Die Hard Trilogy *video game.*

OPPOSITE LEFT *Toys from the Palisades series* Die Hard Palz: *Al Powell, complete with Twinkies, and Karl with a chain accessory.*

OPPOSITE RIGHT *La-La Land's CD edition of Michael Kamen's* Die Hard *score.*

Away from the digital world, Die Hard has spawned an array of collectibles. In 2005, Palisades produced the lovably cute Die Hard Palz series, featuring fourteen articulated plastic figures. The set included Argyle (complete with teddy bear), Tony (available in an action pose or dead on a chair wearing the ho-ho-ho T-shirt), and Sgt. Al Powell (Twinkies in hand).

As part of its Cult Classics series, the National Entertainment Collectibles Association (NECA) released a detailed seven-inch-tall John McClane action figure, dressed in a blood-stained, sweat-drenched white vest and packaged with a rooftop base stand and an MP5 submachine gun. Curiously, no other character from the franchise was granted a similar figure, although collectors were able to grab themselves a scale-model skyscraper as part of the Nakatomi Plaza: Die Hard Collection, a package of all five movies on Blu-ray plus a bonus disc released in 2015.

Artwork for the franchise also abounds. In 2017, the Los Angeles–based Hero Complex Gallery held a John McTiernan art show with invited artists contributing various limited edition posters inspired by the director's work. Among the gems on display was Rhys Cooper's print of Nakatomi Plaza, drawn with a red outline on a black backdrop with three bloody footprints splattered across the building.

Pop culture company Mondo has also created Die Hard artwork, including an evocative piece by artist Laurent Durieux that depicts Nakatomi Plaza inside a broken snow globe. The poster was created to promote Mondo Mystery Movie XI, a unique 2013 screening of Die Hard at the Crest Theatre in Westwood, Los Angeles, that featured prop detonators planted through-

out the theater, two hundred pounds of fake broken glass strewn across the floor, and counterfeit bearer bonds distributed to the audience. The event was even attended by Reginald VelJohnson.

The Die Hard scores by Michael Kamen and Marco Beltrami have also been made available in a variety of formats, although Kamen's work in particular endured a torturous history. "When [the original] Die Hard came out, there was no score album," explains film historian and author Eric Lichtenfeld. "And that score is one collectors wanted for a long time. For fans of Michael Kamen and fans of film music in general, it was one of those holy grails."

In 2002, record label Varèse Sarabande released a limited edition of the soundtrack for the first film, although, as is the case with many initial soundtrack releases, it included an incomplete version of the score. In 2011, La-La Land Records produced a more definitive two-CD set with many of the previously missing cues restored. Coproduced by Lichtenfeld, it sold out "in a matter of days."

In 2012, Varèse Sarabande released an expanded edition of the Die Hard 2 score—the label had previously released a truncated version in the summer of 1990. La-La Land put out a deluxe double CD of the Die Hard with a Vengeance score in the same year, although assembling it took much detective work. "An epic amount of the material was missing," says Lichtenfeld. It was eventually found in the Disney archives.

When it comes to literary spin-offs, Die Hard has generated some imaginative offerings. Published by HarperCollins, Doogie Horner's Die Hard: The Authorized Coloring and Activity Book allows fans to relive—and shade in—some of their favorite scenes. A huge Die Hard fan, Horner notes the film has "just kind of always been a part of my life, especially around the holidays." He went on to pen A Die Hard Christmas: The Illustrated Holiday Classic an irreverent mash-up of the original film with the classic poem "The Night Before Christmas"—or "A Visit

from St. Nicholas," as its officially known—which *Die Hard*'s hacker Theo briefly recites during the vault robbery.

The book, published by Insight Editions, plays on the perennial debate that *Die Hard* is a classic Christmas movie. "Clearly, this is something that people talk about every year and feel very passionately about, so it seemed like a perfect fit," says the book's editor, Kelly Reed. "I just visualized this book filled with violence and language of the film, but with these adorable, whimsical illustrations. It cracked me up thinking about it."

During his prep for the book, Horner studied *Die Hard* in obsessive detail, taking some six thousand screenshots as he began to make parallels between the film and the poem. He

soon found a number of correlations: Both the poem and the film hinge on surprise visits from a stranger, plus McClane and St. Nick both end up covered in ash and soot. "The stockings being 'hung from the chimney with care' to me paralleled the explosives being hung from the ceiling with care," he adds. He also sought out linguistic connections between the poem and the *Die Hard* story. Imbuing lines from the original poem with a *Die Hard* twist, he came up with a number of hilarious hybrids, including, "They shot the SWAT tank with the surface-to-air missile and blew it away like the down of a thistle.'"

The illustrations were provided by JJ Harrison, who had worked on Cartoon Network's *Adventure Time* and *Clarence*. He was keen to try something a little different with the artwork. "I think they probably assumed I was going to just do something that was straight out of the movie, like, the elevator doors are open, there's Tony and the sweatshirt," he says. "But for me, that was a more fun opportunity to fill in a blank and actually show John drawing on the sweatshirt, which you don't see in the movie. That was kind of like what hooked me: being able to add something new to *Die Hard*." Another detail he added: Twinkies flying out of the car during Sgt. Al Powell's frantic backward drive.

When *A Die Hard Christmas* was published in October 2017, the response was huge, particularly on social media. On Twitter, screenwriter Steven de Souza wrote that the book settled the argument once and for all: *Die Hard* really *was* a Christmas movie. "That made me feel so good," says Reed, "because I wanted the creators to know this was a loving homage to the movie."

OPPOSITE *The cover for Insight Editions' Yuletide-themed book* A Die Hard Christmas.

THIS PAGE *JJ Harrison's unique illustrations for* A Die Hard Christmas.

John McClane has also appeared in comic book form. Publisher BOOM! Studios released *Die Hard: Year One*, an eight-issue, two-volume series written by Howard Chaykin and published between September 2009 and April 2010. Volumes one and two followed separate story arcs, though both—like the films—are set across one day. In Vol. 1, McClane is a rookie cop working the crime-ridden streets of a festering 1976 New York. At the height of the city's celebrations for America's bicentennial, McClane faces off with a terrorist who hijacks a yacht. Vol. 2 is set a year later, during the blackouts that rocked the Big Apple. John meets Holly during the story. "I came up with a criminal underpinning for both events [the bicentennial celebrations and the blackout] and had a great time doing it," says Chaykin. "The narrative is all about my feeling about being in New York in the '70s."[1]

It hasn't stopped there. In 2018, marking the thirtieth anniversary of the first movie, Insight Comics published *A Million Ways to Die Hard,* written by Frank Tieri. A regular writer for Marvel (*Deadpool, Wolverine*) and DC Comics (*Gotham Underground*), Tieri combined forces with illustrator Mark Texeira, whose credits include Marvel's *Black Panther*, *The Punisher*, and *Ghost Rider*. "It's [set] thirty years after events of the first movie," says Tieri. "It's very much a companion piece to the movies. It exists in that same world."

A Million Ways to Die Hard focuses on a conspiracy tale that draws an aging McClane back to the scene of the first film. "We do some flashbacks to John's early career as a detective. So it's a sequel and it's a prequel," adds Tieri. "It begins with a ceremony commemorating three decades of the Nakatomi Plaza, which John, of course, being John, doesn't show up for. . . . He's in a bar, watching it on television." Familiar characters also reappear. "His ex-wife obviously plays a big role," says Tieri. The plot unfolds when those at the event are kidnapped by a character from McClane's past, a serial killer who uses movie-related paraphernalia to kill his victims. "He's the one that got away," teases Tieri. "This was McClane's Zodiac Killer."

Tieri's book is a fascinating next chapter in the life of one of cinema's most iconic characters and evidence that, even after three decades, John McClane's story is far from over.

OPPOSITE *Illustrator Mark Texeira's cover for Frank Tieri's* A Million Ways to Die Hard.

ABOVE *A page from* A Million Ways to Die Hard.

TOP *Covers for* Die Hard: Year One *illustrated by Jock.*

CON**CLUSION**

"I promise, I will never even think about going up in a tall building again." —JOHN MCCLANE

If you drive today along Olympic Boulevard in Century City, Los Angeles, Fox Plaza still towers above its surroundings, a reminder of one of modern cinema's most seminal moments. Back in 1988, John McTiernan immediately saw the value of the building when he was preparing *Die Hard*. "It didn't just blend into the landscape," he reflects. "The architects had it stand out. I just appreciated that, and I wanted to make use of it."

Thirty years on, the Die Hard building, as it's become known, now stands like a monument to one of Hollywood's great achievements. McTiernan didn't know it at the time, but his film *Die Hard* would, like its setting, continue to dominate the Hollywood landscape as it changed the way we thought about action movies. "Certainly enough people have said it," he says, modestly.

Die Hard became a film that would launch careers and copycats in equal measure. "If I was going to make an action movie today and I hadn't done *Die Hard*, I would totally rip it off," says star Bruce Willis. "The claustrophobic building, the good guys, the bad guys, the hostages, everybody's trapped in this building, you put John McClane in all of these tight little spaces, you have him kill or beat the shit out of everybody else, and save his wife—it's really hard to compete with that first film."[1]

It was a lightning-in-a-bottle moment—an all too rare occurrence in moviemaking when everyone was working at the very top of their game. "It was a mission to make that film," says Jackson De Govia. "Everybody who was on that picture, from the bottom to the top, they were just cranking all the time, on all cylinders. We were at a peak together. They just caught us all at the right age, the right experience level, the right hunger to succeed, everything. It was amazing."

There were other contributors to the film's success, from the emotional dynamic generated by Bonnie Bedelia's portrayal of McClane's wife, Holly, to Alan Rickman's glorious performance as Hans Gruber. (Sadly, Rickman passed away in 2016 at age sixty-nine.) Gruber is now considered one of the greatest villains of modern cinema. "He was the best bad guy I have ever seen in my life," says Willis.[2] Although the character's climactic demise precluded him from returning to the franchise, evoking his memory via his brother, Simon, in *Die Hard with a Vengeance* proved to be a stroke of genius.

Die Hard inspired a generation of filmmakers, including those who would take the franchise into the twenty-first century. When they were still teenagers, John Moore was lining up in the Dublin rain to watch *Die Hard*, while Len Wiseman was making his own mini version of the movie in his backyard. By the 2000s, they were living out their *Die Hard* fantasies on the biggest canvas possible, bringing John McClane to new audiences.

Crucially, the stories moved with the times, whether it was the cyberterrorism of *Live Free or Die Hard* or the rise of the Russian oligarch in *A Good Day to Die Hard*. And yet these later entries to the franchise always harked back to the original movie with a distinctly old-school approach to filmmaking. Through all five movies, physical stunts and practical effects have been central, adding a layer of realism that CGI has yet to achieve.

So much of the franchise's success comes down to Willis. To think, the likes of Richard Gere, Paul Newman, and Al Pacino were all considered for his signature role. "All of those guys probably would have been great John McClanes. As it turns out, if you think about John McClane now, you can't imagine anybody doing it but me, right?" says Willis. "Most of what went into making John McClane from a character standpoint was the South Jersey Bruce Willis—that attitude and disrespect for authority, that gallows sense of humor, the reluctant hero."[3]

Willis's portrayal of McClane has been remarkably long-lived, the actor having an innate understanding of what makes this working-class everyman tick. "Unlike any other franchise, John McClane has never been replaced by any other actor," says Moore. "James Bond has been replaced. Superman, Spiderman, Batman—all the mans! They've all been replaced. But John McClane has always been Bruce."

Most of all, *Die Hard*—and its sequels—worked because of one character. "John McClane is very much an iconic pop-culture figure of American cinema," says director Renny Harlin. "I've been on tour with these movies to places like Taiwan and Norway, and it's the same thing. People might look different and talk different, but they can relate to this kind of character. [He's] very universal."

After five movies spanning three decades, McClane's place in cinema history is secure. He's as indelible a hero as the movies have ever produced and one of the great action icons of our time.

Yippee-ki-yay, John McClane.

OPPOSITE *Holly McClane (Bonnie Bedelia) and John McClane (Bruce Willis) reunited at the end of* Die Hard.

NO**TES**

INTRODUCTION

1. Edward Gross, "Die Hardest," *Cinescape*, April 1995, 18–24.

PART 1: DIE HARD

1. Tom Matthews, "*Die Hard* Lasts Forever," *Creative Screenwriting*, November/December 2006, 31.
2. Joel Silver, interview, New York Film Academy, July 5, 2012.
3. Aljean Harmetz, "Bruce Willis Will 'Die Hard' For $5 Million," *Chicago Trubune* (Chicago, IL), February 18, 1988, 22.
4. Alan Rickman: A Life in Pictures, BAFTA, April 15, 2015, http://guru.bafta.org/alan-rickman-a-life-in-pictures.
5. Bonnie Bedelia, "Text Commentary," *Die Hard*, Five Star Collection DVD, directed by John McTiernan, Los Angeles, CA: Twentieth Century Fox, 2001.
6. Jackson De Govia, production notes, 1988, *Die Hard* Archives, 1988, Twentieth Century Cinema Archives, Twentieth Century Fox.
7. Simon Banner, "A Wicked Good Time," *The Guardian*, February 2, 1989, 23.
8. Chris Nashawaty, "Bruce Willis: 'If I hadn't done 'Die Hard,' I'd rip it off'," *Entertainment Weekly*, July 14, 2007.
9. John McTiernan, "Audio Commentary," *Die Hard*, 25th Anniversary Blu-Ray Collection, directed by John McTiernan, Los Angeles, CA: Twentieth Century Fox, 2013.
10. Oprah Winfrey Network, "Bruce Willis on Sudden Fame: 'It's a Scary Thing,'" *The Oprah Winfrey Show*, Video, 3:15, March 22, 2016, https://www.youtube.com/watch?v=wDsb8FYZqaU.
11. Joel Silver, interview, New York Film Academy, July 5, 2012.
12. Joel Silver, interview, New York Film Academy, July 5, 2012.
13. Amy Longsdorf, "Bruce Willis Had His Share Of Thrills Doing 'Die Hard 2,'" *The Morning Call*, July 1, 1990.
14. Joel Silver, "Text Commentary," *Die Hard*, Five Star Collection DVD, directed by John McTiernan, Los Angeles, CA: Twentieth Century Fox, 2001.
15. Alexander Godunov, "Text Commentary," *Die Hard*, Five Star Collection DVD, directed by John McTiernan, Los Angeles, CA: Twentieth Century Fox, 2001.
16. Al Di Sarro, "Text Commentary," *Die Hard*, Five Star Collection DVD, directed by John McTiernan, Los Angeles, CA: Twentieth Century Fox, 2001.
17. Joel Silver, interview, New York Film Academy, July 5, 2012.
18. Bruce Willis, production notes, *Die Hard* Archives, 1988, Twentieth Century Cinema Archives, Twentieth Century Fox.
19. Di Sarro, "Text Commentary," *Die Hard*, Five Star Collection DVD.
20. Nashawaty, "Bruce Willis: 'If I hadn't done 'Die Hard,' I'd rip it off'.'"
21. Banner, "A Wicked Good Time," 23.
22. Adam Eisenberg, "Exaggerated Reality," *Cinefex*, November 1988, 20–31.
23. Joel Silver, interview, New York Film Academy, July 5, 2012.
24. Eisenberg, "Exaggerated Reality," 20–31.
25. Eisenberg, "Exaggerated Reality," 20–31.
26. Di Sarro, "Text Commentary," *Die Hard*, Five Star Collection DVD.
27. Stephen Hunter Flick, "Text Commentary," *Die Hard*, Five Star Collection DVD, directed by John McTiernan, Los Angeles, CA: Twentieth Century Fox, 2001.
28. Flick, "Text Commentary," *Die Hard*, Five Star Collection DVD.
29. Vanessa Theme Ament, *The Foley Grail: The Art of Performing Sound For Film, Games and Animation* (Waltham: Focal Press, 2009), 37.
30. Flick, "Text Commentary," *Die Hard*, Five Star Collection DVD.
31. Eric Lichtenfeld, "Die Hard from the Ground Up," *Die Hard Original Motion Picture Soundtrack*, La La Land Records, 2011.
32. Bryan Alexander, "Bruce Willis talks 'Die Hard,' McClane and film No. 5," *USA Today*, February 13, 2013.
33. Martin Grove, "Hollywood Report," *The Hollywood Reporter*, July 6, 1990, 10.

PART 2: DIE HARDER

1. Robert Seidenberg, "'Die Hard 2' Fights an Uphill Battle," *New York Times*, April 29, 1990.
2. Seidenberg, "'Die Hard 2' Fights an Uphill Battle," *New York Times*.
3. Renny Harlin, "Audio Commentary," *Die Hard*, 25th Anniversary Blu-Ray Collection, directed by John McTiernan, Los Angeles, CA: Twentieth Century Fox, 2013.
4. Harlin, "Audio Commentary," *Die Hard*, 25th Anniversary Blu-Ray Collection.
5. John Leguizamo, *Pimps, Hos, Playa Hatas, and All the Rest of My Hollywood Friends: My Life* (New York: HarperCollins, 2006), 70–71.
6. Amy Longsdorf, "Bruce Willis Had His Share of Thrills Doing 'Die Hard 2,'" *The Morning Call*, July 1, 1990.
7. John Vallone, production notes, *Die Hard 2* Archives, Twentieth Century Cinema Archives, Twentieth Century Fox.
8. David Heuring, "Die Harder: Another Cat & Mouse Sequel," *American Cinematographer*, August 1990.
9. Army Archerd, "Just for Variety," *Daily Variety*, February 5, 1990, 2.
10. Mark Cotta Vaz, "Maximum Impact," *Cinefex*, February 1991, 46–63.
11. Al Di Sarro, production notes, *Die Hard 2* Archives, Twentieth Century Cinema Archives, Twentieth Century Fox.
12. Bruce Willis, production notes, *Die Hard 2* Archives, Twentieth Century Cinema Archives, Twentieth Century Fox.
13. Heuring, "Die Harder: Another Cat & Mouse Sequel."
14. Willis, production notes, *Die Hard 2* Archives.
15. Vaz, "Maximum Impact," 46–63.
16. Vaz, "Maximum Impact," 46–63.
17. Longsdorf, "Bruce Willis Had His Share of Thrills Doing 'Die Hard 2.'"
18. Vaz, "Maximum Impact," 46–63.
19. Heuring, "Die Harder: Another Cat & Mouse Sequel."
20. Vaz, "Maximum Impact," 46–63.
21. Vaz, "Maximum Impact," 46–63.
22. Vaz, "Maximum Impact," 46–63.
23. Vaz, "Maximum Impact," 46–63.
24. Vaz, "Maximum Impact," 46–63.
25. Robert Osborne, *The Hollywood Reporter*, April 6, 1990.

26. Michael Fleming, "Variety Buzz," *Variety*, May 2, 1990.

27. Jesse Kornbluth, "*Die Hard* Blowhard," *Vanity Fair*, August 1990.

28. Longsdorf, "Bruce Willis Had His Share of Thrills Doing 'Die Hard 2.'"

PART 3: DIE HARD WITH A VENGEANCE

1. Jeffrey Wells, "Off-Centerpiece: 'Die Hard 3' blown out of the water by 'Siege,'" *Los Angeles Times*, November 1, 1992.

2. Edward Gross, "Die Hardest," *Cinescape*, April 1995, 18–24.

3. Wells, "Off-Centerpiece: 'Die Hard 3' blown out of the water by 'Siege.'"

4. Wells, "Off-Centerpiece: 'Die Hard 3' blown out of the water by 'Siege.'"

5. Bruce Willis, production notes, *Die Hard with a Vengeance* Archives, 1995, Twentieth Century Cinema Archives, Twentieth Century Fox.

6. Jonathan Hensleigh, "Audio Commentary," *Die Hard*, 25th Anniversary Blu-Ray Collection, directed by John McTiernan, Los Angeles, CA: Twentieth Century Fox, 2013.

7. Fred Topel, "Ten Questions with Jonathan Hensleigh," *Screenwriter's Utopia*, February 15, 2009.

8. Jeff Gordinier, "Nice Cop Nasty Cop," *Empire*, September 1995, 95–101.

9. Edward Gross, "Die Hardest," *Cinescape*, April 1995, 18–24.

10. Michael Fleming, "Buzz," *Weekly Variety*, February 21, 1994, 10.

11. Samuel L. Jackson, production notes, *Die Hard with a Vengeance* Archives, 1995, Twentieth Century Cinema Archives, Twentieth Century Fox.

12. Joseph G. Aulisi, production notes, *Die Hard with a Vengeance* Archives, 1995, Twentieth Century Cinema Archives, Twentieth Century Fox.

13. "No Escape From New York," *People Magazine*, July 11, 1994.

14. Bruce Willis, production notes, *Die Hard with a Vengeance* Archives, 1995, Twentieth Century Cinema Archives, Twentieth Century Fox.

15. Gross, "Die Hardest," 18–24.

16. Jackson De Govia, production notes, *Die Hard with a Vengeance* Archives, 1995, Twentieth Century Cinema Archives, Twentieth Century Fox.

17. "Bombing Won't Delay Third Die Hard Movie," *Boston Globe*, May 4, 1995.

PART 4: LIVE FREE OR DIE HARD

1. Timothy Olyphant, "Die Hard 4.0," interview by Rob Carnavale, http://www.indielondon.co.uk/Film-Review/die-hard-40-timothy-olyphant-interview.

2. "Good Girl," *Empire*, July 2007, 22.

3. Maggie Q, "Interview with Maggie Q," interview by Kristie LuStout, November 19, 2007, http://www.cnn.com/2007/WORLD/asiapcf/11/14/talkasia.maggieq.

4. Lisa Collins, "Live Free or Die Hard N.Y. Premiere," June 22, 2007, Hollywood.com.

5. Bruce Willis, production notes, *Live Free or Die Hard* Archives, 2007, Twentieth Century Cinema Archives, Twentieth Century Fox.

6. Alan Bielik, "Live Free or Die Hard: A VFX Race Against Time," July 2, 2007, https://www.awn.com/vfxworld/live-free-or-die-hard-vfx-race-against-time.

7. Peter Biskind, "Free Willis," *Vanity Fair*, June 2007.

8. Dade Hayes, "Willis's Waiting Game," *Daily Variety*, June 26, 2007, 32.

PART 5: A GOOD DAY TO DIE HARD

1. Sheila Roberts, "A GOOD DAY TO DIE HARD Stars Bruce Willis and Jai Courtney and Director John Moore Talk about the DIE HARD Franchise and the Appeal of John McClane," *Collider*, February 10, 2013, http://collider.com/die-hard-5-bruce-willis-jai-courtney-interview.

2. Fred Topel, "Like Han Solo: Skip Woods on A Good Day to Die Hard," February 20, 2018, http://www.mandatory.com/fun/205293-like-han-solo-skip-woods-on-a-good-day-to-die-hard.

3. Topel, "Like Han Solo: Skip Woods on A Good Day to Die Hard."

4. Roberts, "A GOOD DAY TO DIE HARD Stars Bruce Willis and Jai Courtney and Director John Moore Talk about the DIE HARD Franchise and the Appeal of John McClane."

5. Bruce Willis, production notes, *A Good Day to Die Hard* Archives, 2013, Twentieth Century Cinema Archives, Twentieth Century Fox.

6. Emma Dibdin and Tom Mansell, "Bruce Willis: 'Good Day to Die Hard' is about family conflict," *Digital Spy*, February 13, 2013.

7. "A Good Day to Die Hard: Yuliya Snigir Exclusive Movie Interview," *ScreenSlam*, January 31, 2013, https://www.youtube.com/watch?v=9xaJ1cu5HtU.

8. Bryan Adams, "He Builds It, Audiences Come: A Q&A with *A Good Day to Die Hard* Production Designer Daniel Dorrance," February 12, 2013, https://www.mpaa.org/2013/02/he-builds-it-audiences-come-a-qa-with-a-good-day-to-die-hard-production-designer-daniel-dorrance/.

9. Bryan Abrams, "Q&A With Jonathan Sela," *The Credits*, February 15, 2013.

10. Yuliya Snigir, production notes, *A Good Day to Die Hard* Archives, 2013, Twentieth Century Cinema Archives, Twentieth Century Fox.

PART 6: BEYOND THE BIG SCREEN

1. Brannon Costello, ed., *Howard Chaykin: Conversation* (Jackson, MS: University Press of Mississippi, 2011), 286.

CONCLUSION:

1. Chris Nashawaty, "Bruce Willis: 'If I hadn't done 'Die Hard,' I'd rip it off'," *Entertainment Weekly*, July 14, 2007.

2. Bryan Alexander, "Bruce Willis talks 'Die Hard,' McClane and film No. 5," *USA Today*, February 13, 2013.

3. Nashawaty, "Bruce Willis: 'If I hadn't done 'Die Hard,' I'd rip it off'.'"

TITAN BOOKS

144 Southwark Street
London SE1 0UP
www.titanbooks.com

Find us on Facebook: www.facebook.com/TitanBooks

Follow us on Twitter: @TitanBooks

Published by arrangement with Insight Editions, PO Box 3088, San Rafael, CA 94912, USA. www.insighteditions.com

A CIP catalogue record for this title is available from the British Library.

ISBN: 9781789090512

PUBLISHER: Raoul Goff
ASSOCIATE PUBLISHER: Vanessa Lopez
CREATIVE DIRECTOR: Chrissy Kwasnik
DESIGNER: Jon Glick
EXECUTIVE EDITOR: Chris Prince
EDITORIAL ASSISTANTS: Hilary VandenBroek and Anna Wostenberg
SENIOR PRODUCTION EDITOR: Elaine Ou
PRODUCTION DIRECTOR/SUBSIDIARY RIGHTS: Lina s Palma
PRODUCTION MANAGERS: Greg Steffen and Jacob Frink

ROOTS of PEACE   REPLANTED PAPER
Insight Editions, in association with Roots of Peace, will plant two trees for each tree used in the manufacturing of this book. Roots of Peace is an internationally renowned humanitarian organization dedicated to eradicating land mines worldwide and converting war-torn lands into productive farms and wildlife habitats. Roots of Peace will plant two million fruit and nut trees in Afghanistan and provide farmers there with the skills and support necessary for sustainable land use.

Manufactured in China by Insight Editions

10 9 8 7 6 5 4 3 2 1

ACKNOWLEDGMENTS

We would like to express huge gratitude to the following people, who generously gave their time to speak about their Die Hard experiences or helped facilitate the interviews:

John McTiernan, Gail Sistrunk, Bruce Willis, Jeb Stuart, Steven E. de Souza, Jackson De Govia, Beau Marks, Jan de Bont, Frank Urioste, Marilyn Vance, Richard Edlund, Thaine Morris, William Atherton, Charles Picerni, Jackie Burch, Reginald VelJohnson, Hart Bochner, Grand L. Bush, Dennis Hayden, Brent Boates, Al Leong, Andreas Wisniewski, Andy Lipschultz, Scott Eddo, Ron Bartlett, Mark Stetson, Renny Harlin, Doug Richardson, William Sadler, Franco Nero, Sheila McCarthy, Art Evans, Paul Huston, Greg Grusby, Andrew G. Vajna, Gergely Ábrahám, William Wisher, Peter Menzies Jr., Len Wiseman, Kelly Chapek, Mark Bomback, Denise Wingate, Patrick Tatopoulos, Simon Duggan, John Moore, Sebastian Koch, Daniel T. Dorrance, Heather Griffith, Debbie Haeusler, Connor McNeish, Everett Burrell, Bojana Nikitovic, Dan Zimmerman, Eric Lichtenfeld, Frank Tieri, Tony Van, Kelly Reed, Doogie Horner, and JJ Harrison.

Thanks also to Carol Roeder, Nicole Spiegel, Stephen Eads, Gene Kozicki, Joe Fordham, Greg Shay, Janine Pourroy, Brandon Alinger, Ryan Faja, Warren Drummond, Chris Rosewarne, Kamen Anev, Allison Klein, Jock, Jeric Llanes, Tim Wiesch, Patrick McClung, Robert A. Ferretti, Jonathan Hensleigh, Jeremy Irons, Rima Horton, De'voreaux White, Bill Schirmer, John E. Sullivan, John Wright, Michael Tadross, Jeffrey Lerner, Brad Martin, Joe Conmy, Michael Fottrell, and Nicolas De Toth.

A special thanks to our editor Chris Prince, who scaled heights higher than the Nakatomi to make this book possible.

STILL PHOTOGRAPHERS

Die Hard – Peter Sorel
Die Hard 2 – John R. Shannon
Die Hard with a Vengeance – Barry Wetcher
Live Free or Die Hard/A Good Day to Die Hard – Frank Masi

John McClane wallet image (page 58) courtesy of Adam Bosman.
McClane gun/Christmas tape image (page 88) courtesy of Prop Store.
PAGE 110 Michael Kamen image courtesy of Photofest.
PAGE 112 *Die Hard* theatrical poster courtesy of Photofest.
PAGE 155 *Die Hard 2* theatrical poster courtesy of Photofest.

ABOVE *A view from above of the carnage created by the* Die Hard *team just outside the entrance to Fox Plaza.*